A Cultural History of Dress and Fashion
General Editor: Susan Vincent

Volume 1
A Cultural History of Dress and Fashion in Antiquity
Edited by Mary Harlow

Volume 2
A Cultural History of Dress and Fashion in the Medieval Age
Edited by Sarah-Grace Heller

Volume 3
A Cultural History of Dress and Fashion in the Renaissance
Edited by Elizabeth Currie

Volume 4
A Cultural History of Dress and Fashion in the Age of Enlightenment
Edited by Peter McNeil

Volume 5
A Cultural History of Dress and Fashion in the Age of Empire
Edited by Denise Amy Baxter

Volume 6
A Cultural History of Dress and Fashion in the Modern Age
Edited by Alexandra Palmer

A CULTURAL HISTORY OF DRESS AND FASHION

VOLUME 2

A CULTURAL HISTORY OF DRESS AND FASHION

IN THE MEDIEVAL AGE

Edited by Sarah-Grace Heller

Bloomsbury Academic
An imprint of Bloomsbury Publishing Plc

B L O O M S B U R Y
LONDON · OXFORD · NEW YORK · NEW DELHI · SYDNEY

Bloomsbury Academic

An imprint of Bloomsbury Publishing Plc

50 Bedford Square
London
WC1B 3DP
UK

1385 Broadway
New York
NY 10018
USA

www.bloomsbury.com

BLOOMSBURY and the Diana logo are trademarks of Bloomsbury Publishing Plc

First published 2017

© Bloomsbury Publishing 2017

Sarah-Grace Heller has asserted her right under the Copyright, Designs and Patents Act, 1988, to be identified as Editor of this work.

British Library Cataloguing-in-Publication Data
A catalogue record for this book is available from the British Library.

ISBN: HB: 978-0-8578-5687-6
        HB set: 978-1-4725-5749-0

Library of Congress Cataloging-in-Publication Data
A catalog record for this book is available from the Library of Congress

Cover design: Sharon Mah
Cover image: Gottfried von Strassburg (13th century), King Mark exiles Tristan and Isolde (DEA/Getty Images)

Typeset by RefineCatch Limited, Bungay, Suffolk
Printed and bound in Great Britain

CONTENTS

LIST OF ILLUSTRATIONS

INTRODUCTION

CHAPTER 1

CHAPTER 6

CHAPTER 7

Introduction

SARAH-GRACE HELLER

Fashion in a medieval age, is that even possible? Weren't those centuries the Dark Ages?—the antithesis of the dazzling world of catwalks and designer labels?

These are questions worth debating. "Fashion," "Medieval," and "Dark Ages" are lenses for interpreting human experiences and the traces they leave. As lenses, they are capable of bringing certain things into focus; equally capable of distortion. The medieval sources are always fragmentary. From bones to books to damaged frescoes, they all require significant interpretation to derive information about medieval material culture and how people felt about it. Lenses, in short, are necessary, but also intrinsically limit the field of vision: we must proceed aware of limits and potential slants.

"Fashion" is a universal term for some, signifying simply the human impulse toward adornment, present even for our Neolithic ancestors. As such, it was unquestionably present through the periods we term the European Middle Ages, when all types of records attest desires for jewelry, rich cloth, and color. The noun "fashion" denotes work performed on an object to shape it, pattern it, personalize it. In English, it comes to connote "the manners and customs of a land" around the end of the medieval period, in the late fifteenth century. The French "mode," similarly, can signify the way either an individual or a group does something. Philosophers begin wondering why the French dress "à la mode des Français"—constantly changing their minds about what to wear, as Montaigne observes—around the sixteenth century. From these early modern lexical moments, "fashion" would evolve into its own field of journalism. In the medieval period, however, certain habits of modern fashion systems are already in effect, in certain milieus: there were seasonal cycles of wardrobe renewal, changing styles, efforts to use appearance to attract others, and to increase one's influence.

Some theorists see fashion, or more specifically Modern Western Fashion, as a historical phenomenon with a specific and unique evolutionary trajectory. This view is predicated on the idea that societies operate differently with regard to clothing and ornament. Fashion demands attitudes and industries supporting constant change, continuous new consumption, and outmoding of styles before they are worn out. Cultures in which there are no surpluses, where innovation is hampered, or change discouraged would not be "fashionable" in the manner that the West has become.[1]

Dating the birth of Western Fashion based on visual sources, Paul Post observed what he termed a "revolution" in men's dress in the mid-fourteenth century. After centuries of preferring longer robes, men began wearing short doublets and showing ample expanses of leg[2] (Figure 0.1).

Along with this style change, the steadily more numerous illustrations show more and more variety and exaggeration in cuts and embellishments. The premise that Western Fashion began in the fourteenth century has become a commonplace for many.[3] Some have argued that fashion was born with the invention of the set-in sleeve tailoring technique and the practice of "remodeling the body" through clothing.[4] Others argue for

FIGURE 0.1: A fashionable knight in the new style for shorter robes, a "wasp" waist, and pointed shoes debates with a cleric in long robes as the king, also in long stately robes, adjudicates, from *Le Songe du Vergier*, Paris c. 1378. Royal 19 C IV, f. 154. © British Library.

a late medieval birth of fashion based on the increasing complexity of dress, as more and more garments and items become necessary to the respectable person's wardrobe[5] (Figure 0.2).

There is a long tradition of viewing the empires of antiquity and the "Dark Ages" as the antithesis of fashion. Some archeologists, in contrast, have comfortably used the term "fashion" ("*mode*") to describe the regular changes observable in the jewelry styles of the early Middle Ages.[6] Claims that with the Germanic migrations came a "new fashion" for trousers, tight tunic cut, and bright color have been stridently dismissed in favor of a notion of Roman continuity.[7] Some scholars looking closely at the Carolingian courts and Byzantine Empire, however, observe evidence of the "conspicuous consumption," theatrical use of appearance, and interest in experimenting with personal style and choices that typify a fashion system.[8] Although some might assume the clergy would be immune to fashion as men devoted to higher matters, they composed a powerful economic force in the Middle Ages, and the evidence is clear that they were major consumers of both the richest and humblest varieties of cloth, shoes, and adornment in the land. Some argue that they were in the forefront of medieval fashion.[9] Vernacular poets begin to embroider their stories with hundreds of verses describing dress styles, fabulous fabrics, and shopping experiences, as early as the twelfth and thirteenth centuries.[10] As scholars probe the pre-fourteenth-century evidence with the lenses and tools of fashion, there is much to find worth discussing.

This volume will address "fashion" from both perspectives. The essays ask how people dressed, and how they made and/or purchased the materials necessary and desired for their personal adornment. They will also probe attitudes toward the fashionability of clothing and consumption. They explore centers of creativity and production. In some cases, they also describe the disappearances of these places, as cultures and languages changed, borders were redrawn, and trade routes shifted due to calamity or competition.

FIGURE 0.2: A fashionable variety of cuts, exaggeration of styles, and sumptuous fabrics are clearly visible on the courtiers depicted in this Flemish tapestry c. 1440–50. The Metropolitan Museum of Art, New York.

SOURCES AND DISCIPLINES

It is not particularly easy for medievalists to describe clothing or attitudes about consumption effectively. They cannot consult a continuous run of fashion magazines for the millennium or so associated with this period and observe the annual changes. Written sources are composed in dead languages, preserved in books usually copied decades or centuries after the works were composed, with all of the attendant potential for mistakes, and which have often only survived the ravages of the intervening centuries (the regular cycles of town fires, floods, mobs burning public buildings, bombing campaigns, etc.) by wild chance and the protective zeal of bibliophiles. Some medievalists examining fashion come from university language departments and history units. Such scholars are trained to read, analyze, and compare Latin and early vernacular texts, which requires rather significant philological preparation and capacity for mental acrobatics to interpret the fluctuating spellings, dialectal variations, and evolving grammar systems of these periods. Terms for dress are often *hapax legomena*, words only occurring once in the extant texts, presenting lexical quandaries. Latin is present throughout the millennium, used for legal and official documents, notarial records, saints' lives, poems, sermons, and treatises. Vernacular texts only begin to appear in profusion around the seventh to ninth centuries for Anglo-Saxon and Old High German; in the twelfth century for Old French, Occitan, Catalan, Castilian, Middle High German, and Old Norse laws; the thirteenth for Galician-Portuguese, Scanian (Danish), and Sicilian; the fourteenth for Middle English and Dante's

Tuscan. Certain languages are less studied, partly as a result of the size of teaching faculties (the Old and Middle English specialists are far more numerous than the Old French, Dutch, German, Catalan, Castilian, Italian, and so on, due to the prominence of English departments in the Anglophone world). The current national lines are not necessarily those of the Middle Ages, either. (Universities have no Sicilian or Frisian units these days.) Philologists, lexicographers, and historians of dress often find it difficult to leave their linguistic and national silos.

Examples of actual medieval clothing and jewelry are rare. Naturally enough, who keeps clothing for a thousand years? The Church, surviving as an institution over the centuries, is one answer, but one that imposes a certain ideological filter on the objects preserved. Extant garments are usually relics, preserved by churches, or items found in burials. Sometimes secular garments were remodeled into liturgical garments and cloths, and kept in treasuries. Grave goods speak to a certain moment in life. They particularly reflect the feelings of the mourners who created the assemblages as a last representation of a beloved. Some garments have been found in trash heaps, revealing patterns of use, reuse, and discarding, but distorting what they might have been when new. Finding and interpreting these things is the work of archeologists, whose work has been evolving since nineteenth-century building programs began opening up cemeteries for railroads, subways, and urban construction. Early finds were dispersed and sold by antiquaries. It was only gradually that scholars began to realize the necessity of retaining burial contexts to facilitate dating and interpretation (Figure 0.3).

Recent scientific advances such as the use of high-powered scanning microscopes, chemical dye analysis, and DNA analysis are permitting exciting new insights into these long-buried objects, for instance revealing the presence of bright dyestuffs in fibers that now appear brown, and permitting better interpretation of the age, gender, and health of the deceased. Even when fibers are only preserved as impressions in corroded metal on the backs of brooches and buckles, they are now able to consider questions such as spin direction, and from which they can derive certain cultural information. This is a far cry

FIGURE 0.3: Early medieval belt buckle, identified only as Frankish c. 675–725, typical of collections in many museums from nineteenth-century excavations before there was concern for burial context. Iron with silver inlay and copper alloy rivets. The Metropolitan Museum of Art, New York.

from what the reader will find in volumes five and six of this series! But it is information worth considering in the long history of fashion, and must be slowly and painstakingly accrued to present any kind of valid picture. Archeologists are obliged to piece together ideas of social practices from disparate puzzle pieces. Their training prepares them to observe, describe, categorize, and offer conjecture with great caution. They are constantly limited by funding and excavation time, obliged to work within government grants and builders' schedules. Certain chronological periods have been privileged due to greater national interest, as well. Countries have been more apt to fund excavations of what are seen as "glorious periods" in their history.

A third category of sources is visual images, requiring expertise in the discipline of art history. Some of the earliest publishing in the history of medieval fashion emerges from this domain, for instance the work of architect Eugène-Emmanuel Viollet-le-Duc and archivists Jules Quicherat and Camille Enlart, who sought to date (and thereby assign value) to works of medieval art they sought to preserve after centuries of neglect and damage, particularly from the wars of religion and the French Revolution. Analysis and categorization of datable art images such as sculptures, wall paintings, and book images have provided a chronology for dating buildings and manuscripts, although when dates are reconsidered, or later emendations revealed, this edifice is destabilized. This can be a tricky cycle. Many visual images are undated, presenting another set of problems.

Manuscript images are often stunningly well preserved, presenting clothing in an array of vivid colors; but do pigments for rich patrons necessarily reflect dye practices on actual clothing? While some illuminations are dazzling full-page affairs designed for display on processions or swearing on the gospels, many are tiny. Historiated initials could be compared to the scale of postage stamps. How much about material culture could we derive from philately? Even mid-sized manuscript images often contain detail comparable to that now found in comics: these were not intended as designers' sketches or pattern books. The majority of medieval manuscripts are sacred texts, illustrating ancient Israelites and biblical contexts—at times with contemporary updates, but at times they are deliberately archaizing. The work of scribes and illuminators was often separate, so many images only illustrate their accompanying texts very approximately. Illuminated books are relatively plentiful for the Carolingian Renaissance, more so for the later Middle Ages, but there are other centuries when they are extremely sparse.

Medieval fashion studies are moving in the welcome direction of interdisciplinarity. The initial editing of texts and discovery of extant images have been largely accomplished by past generations. Archeology continues to offer new discoveries, as does the practice of learned reconstruction. The task ahead is to combine information and come to new insights through comparative analysis. The essays here assembled engage in some of that work, as well as suggest some of the many avenues where new inquiry is needed.

MEDIEVAL AGES: DIFFERING CHRONOLOGIES

To speak of fashion is to speak of time. Changing styles present a framework for chronology, the always-challenging attempt to comprehend the passing of time. Arranging styles in a tidy order can be elusive and problematic, however. Different individuals within any culture might treasure heirlooms while others covet novelty. Reuse is a medieval norm, as for some now: part of fashion is the experience of feeling something is new, even if it is only relatively new, purchased used or received as a gift. Caveats aside, time and chronology are intrinsic parts of fashion. The "medieval" millennium is not a monolith, and so a brief discussion of how different groups periodize it may assist the reader through the pages that follow.

Many set the beginnings of the Middle Ages during the Great Migrations, once termed the Barbarian Invasions, that transformed the European population and the Roman Empire from the fourth to eighth centuries. Others treat this period as "Late Antiquity," emphasizing the continuity of Roman social structures and the Latin language.

Among the Germanic peoples migrating were the Franks, who established kingdoms in what are now France and northwestern Germany. In the continental chronology, the early Middle Ages begin with the Merovingian dynasty of Frankish kings, and conversion to Christianity. Clovis I, the first Christian king of the Franks, was crowned in 496. This period gives way to the Carolingian, as this new dynasty comes to power around 750 (see Figure 0.3). The Early Middle Ages end at some point in the tenth century, as the Carolingian Empire weakened and fractured, and Viking incursions spread fear and destruction. The designation of High or Central Middle Ages usually refers to the period from the eleventh or twelfth to thirteenth centuries. For France, this was the Capetian period, which stretched from the modest ascension of Hugh Capet in 987 to the death of the last of Philip the Fair's sons in 1328. This was a period of climatic warming, expanding royal power and centralization, emerging vernaculars, urban growth, increased trade, and professionalization of crafts, notably cloth and garment production. Most European countries consider the fourteenth and fifteenth centuries the Later Middle Ages. While this was a time of splendor in dress and luxury production, this period is also marked by calamity: climate instability, cold, and famine; the Plague c. 1348–50, recurring at intervals thereafter, reduced many populations by half or more, up to 80 percent in some of Italy's banking cities; and the long-disruptive Hundred Years War between France, England, and Burgundy (1337–1453).

England's chronology is often presented in linguistic terms. The Roman cultural retreat from the island was more profound than on the continent. In the fifth century, groups from Saxony, Anglia, Frisia, and Jutland were invited to defend the Britons against the Picts and Scots to the north. An Anglo-Saxon society developed in the sixth century, with conversion to Christianity occurring over the seventh. The Middle Anglo-Saxon period, from the mid-seventh through the ninth century, saw dominance by the kingdom of Mercia, and the spread of monasticism and a learned culture. The Late Anglo-Saxon period ranges up to the Norman Conquest by William the Norman c. 1066. England was shocked by the Normans' new legal systems and French dialect. By 1200, a new language was emerging, termed Middle English, which is the moniker used to describe the period from the eleventh to the fifteenth century.

Iberian Late Antiquity is characterized by Visigothic rule of all Hispania from c. 415 until the defeat by the Arabs in 711. The Umayyad Dynasty ruled all of Iberia except the northern Asturias coast by 720, creating the civilization known as Al-Andalus, later ruled by the Fatimids. The Christian Reconquest period stretches from the eighth to the fifteenth centuries, splitting the peninsula into smaller polities: Christian Castile, Leon, Aragon, Portugal, Galicia, Navarra, and the Catalan counties, all with shifting boundaries (Figure 0.4). The Mozarabic culture and language shared by Muslims, Christians, and Jews prevailed in the south in Andalusia, Cordoba, and Granada from the eighth to the fifteenth centuries

The Italian peninsula was not a unified polity during the Middle Ages. Italy lost its centrality as the imperial center with the fourth-century shift toward Constantinople, as well as the famines and devastations of the Gothic War (535–54) and Byzantine policies

FIGURE 0.4: A pauper, a pious patron, and a pilgrim dine together at the Pia Almoina (Pious Almshouse) of the Seu Vella (Old Cathedral) in Lleida, Catalonia, Spain. Wall painting, later thirteenth century. Photo: S.-G. Heller.

that ravaged its economy. Ravenna was the capital of the Western Roman Empire 402–76, obviously short-lived. The Lombards, a Germanic tribe, took over most of northern Italy from 568 to 774, when Charlemagne conquered the region, and this name was used to refer to Italians through much of the medieval period. Much of central Italy became the Papal States by various donations, notably that of Pepin the Younger in 751, and remained under the direct sovereignty of the Pope into the nineteenth century. Byzantium ruled parts of the east coast and south on and off through the centuries (Figure. 0.5), employing Arab and Norman mercenaries who eventually turned on them to rule Sicily, Naples, Amalfi, Calabria, and Puglia in turn.

Muslim rule in the ninth century brought this kingdom of Sicily (called the "Regno") excellent bureaucracy; the Norman period of the eleventh to twelfth centuries brought Romanesque architecture and new feudal structures. Angevins from France ruled the Regno for a while in the late thirteenth and early fourteenth centuries, before the Aragonese took the ascendant. Between the twelfth and fifteenth centuries, northern Italy was wracked by strife between the Guelphs, loyal to the Holy Roman Empire, and the Ghibellines, loyal to the papacy.

Germany's medieval history is similarly not one of a continuously unified polity or landmass. Its history was continuously intertwined with Italy's. It is treated in terms of the Holy Roman Empire, a multi-ethnic confederation of kingdoms stretching from central Europe to northern Italy, including Bohemia, Bavaria, Burgundy, and many duchies, principalities, and free states. The term "Holy Roman Empire" was not used until the thirteenth century, but Charlemagne's capital was situated at Aachen, effectively

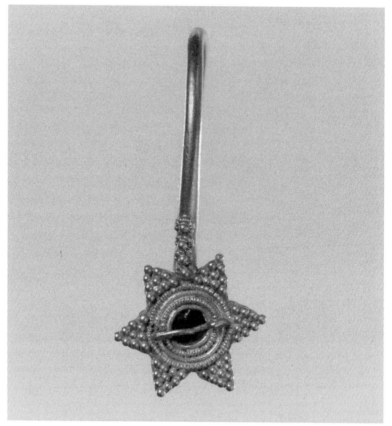

FIGURE 0.5: A Langobardic/Byzantine gold earring, sixth to seventh century. The Metropolitan Museum of Art, New York.

transferring imperial rule into Germanic lands during the Carolingian period. After the Treaty of Verdun in 843, the eastern part of the Carolingian Empire developed into the *Regnum Teutonicorum*, which united Franks, Bavarians, and Swabians under Saxon leadership. Limited elective monarchy was established under the Ottonian dynasty (919–1024), and would continue into the sixteenth century, without the centralized power or organization established in France. The Ottonians brought about a cultural renaissance, but its success was limited by military crises with the Slavs and with Byzantium over the annexation of northern Italy (Figure 0.6). The Investiture Controversy of the eleventh to twelfth centuries pitted secular authorities (notably Emperor Henry IV), appointing their own bishops and abbots to these powerful positions that effectively controlled cities and large regions, against the papacy, which claimed all authority for appointments. This was a critical conflict in determining the separation of Church and state that would characterize the power balance of later centuries. It ultimately strengthened the papacy considerably. The Hohenstaufen dynasty ruled the kingdom of Germany 1138–1254, the duchy of Swabia from the eleventh century, and also the kingdom of Sicily 1194–1268. In the later Middle Ages, there was a shift in power away from the emperor toward individual territories, as well as expansion toward Baltic and Slavic lands. The Hanseatic League (the

FIGURE 0.6: Ivory plaque showing Christ receiving the Magdeburg Cathedral from the Ottonian Emperor, possibly made in Milan c. 962–8. The Metropolitan Museum of Art, New York.

Hansa) was a confederation of trading towns along the North Sea and Baltic littorals with a shared legal system and military defenses. It dates to the rebuilding of Lübeck in 1159, is documented from the thirteenth century, and dominated northern shipping trade through the eighteenth century.

Scandinavian medieval chronology is a bird of a different feather. For the early Middle Ages the term Iron Age is often used, referring to the fifth century BC to eighth century AD (or even beyond, when the archeological record is ambiguous). The Viking Age stretches from about 793 to 1066, subdivided into the Settlement Period of the ninth and tenth centuries, with a Christianization period occurring over the tenth. It is also subdivided into different art style periods. The eleventh to fifteenth centuries are often just termed "Medieval." From 1397 to 1523 is the period known as the Kalmar Union, when Denmark, Sweden (which then included Finland), Norway, and its dependencies (Iceland, Greenland and the Faroe Islands) were confederated, partly to block expansion into the Baltic by the Hanseatic League. Iceland has its own unique chronology, as seen in Chapters 2 and 7.

In short, "medieval fashion" refers to a striking diversity of times and places, and generalizations can get us into trouble. There were times and places where life was isolated, primitive, and rather desperate. These chronological overviews show how cultures developed, often to a degree of dazzling sophistication when it came to the display of rich fabrics, accessories, and clothing, but many saw calamitous setbacks and wars that dispersed their resources. "Medieval fashion" should not be imagined as a continuous story of uninterrupted innovation and consumption. But innovation and consumption were ambitions and concerns, even in the most isolated regions. People invested heavily in looking good. The fabrics were finer than most anything available on today's market. Brilliant color mattered. It demanded careful chemistry and compounds imported from vast distances. Merchants took great risks to bring rich fabrics to markets, and artisans cared ardently about their reputations for quality products.

As I have tried to show here, medieval scholars must specialize in certain methodologies, disciplines, and languages, and this is reflected in the chapters that follow. Some chapters bridge multiple centuries and lands, such as Production and Distribution (2), The Body (3), Visual Representations (8), and Literary Representations (9). Other chapters function as case studies, for instance Ethnicity (7), which takes a diachronic look at how cultural identity could be expressed through cloth, clothing, and adornment on the northern margins of Europe and the colonial outposts of the Atlantic. Belief (4) is a case study of the "original garments of skin" created by God as presented in Genesis 3:21, and how this difficult idea was interpreted and used as a moral directive. Gender and Sexuality (5) proposes a way of thinking through how medieval sexuality is represented and understood through clothing, rather than tracing a history of garments associated with men or women. Status (6) examines how garment ensembles conveyed status, and then how sumptuary laws and dress codes emerged in the later Middle Ages in the face of anxiety over perceived erosions in visual distinction. Readers interested in gender, status, ethnicity, textiles, literature, and images will find discussions of them in every chapter. An English emphasis is found in Textiles (1) and Belief (4); French in Gender and Sexuality (5); and Scandinavian in Ethnicity (7). The broader ideas driving these specific discussions, however, identify commonalities of thought, belief, practice, as well as underlying concerns, rather than resistances and unorthodoxies.

Medieval material culture studies are an active area of inquiry, given new vigor in recent decades by improvements in analytical methods and ongoing discoveries in archeology, greater and better library and archive access thanks to internet technology, and the rise of feminist and post-Marxist scholarship giving legitimacy to study of questions of daily life, once excluded from serious historical investigation. There is much still to learn about this period, in which we can find the roots of our own modern fashion systems.

CHAPTER ONE

Textiles

ELIZABETH COATSWORTH AND GALE R. OWEN-CROCKER

INTRODUCTION

The extremes of wealth and poverty of the Middle Ages, and the many levels between, were exemplified by the textiles that clothed bodies and furnished environments. Textiles were an essential and ubiquitous part of medieval life, from the luxurious and decorative to the utilitarian, from coronation robes and episcopal vestments to sanitary towels. The increasingly elaborate beds that became fashionable in the later Middle Ages required good quality mattresses, sheets, pillowcases, blankets, and bedcovers, as well as decorative, draught-excluding hangings around and above them. Table cloths and towels were used both in secular homes and at the altars in churches, and both environments also required seat covers, cushions, and the curtains which both insulated and provided a little privacy in the essentially public medieval existence. All of these soft furnishings were precious possessions, bequeathed in wills and inventoried among the possessions of their late owners or the churches to which they belonged. When traveling, medieval people made use of tents; cloth covered their waggons and wrapped their bundles of goods, which were tied with string or rope. Flags and sails of ships were made of cloth.

Most of the garments people wore were made of textile, supplemented with leather, fur, and metalwork. Dress was an identifying characteristic of gender, status, and role in life: the fiber that it was made of, the quantity of cloth, the expense of the dye, the elaboration of the finishing, all contributed to an impression of the wearer's rank and calling. Ecclesiastical dress ranged from the undyed, coarse robes of monk and nun to the mass vestments of priests, bishops, archbishops, and popes, which at their most elaborate might be of expensive silk cloth, encrusted with pearls and gemstones, and decorated with embroidery in gold or silver. The rich and royal could command new outfits for every season and special occasions, of the finest native or imported cloth and the most fashionable colors of fur; even their horses were dressed in trappers sometimes decorated with the heraldry of their aristocratic owners. Many of the poorer people, in contrast, probably never owned a garment of new material: their clothes might be made up of pieces of old textile or items passed on from previous owners. In the early Middle Ages, and probably to the end of the medieval period in rural areas, domestically-produced textiles were normal. With the growth of towns, professionally-made garments and furnishings could be readily bought, both new and second-hand.

Textile was not only utilitarian: it could also be both decorative and instructive. Painted, embroidered, or tapestry-woven cloths might depict scenes from the life of Christ or the Virgin Mary, images of saints or inspirational secular stories, or they could carry emblems, such as the cross, the shell of St. James, the heraldic emblem of a family, or a composite of the arms of two families linked by marriage. Such decorative cloths could be found as wall hangings in churches and secular dwellings. Ecclesiastical copes, chasubles, stoles, and maniples were sometimes decorated with an embroidered, instructive, iconography (Figure 1.1). Heraldic imagery might represent the patron on precious textiles presented to the Church or it might make appropriate decoration on secular domestic furnishings.

The medieval textile industry was necessarily productive, keeping up with demand that was not only for purpose of replacement but was also subject to fashion, to competitive dressing and furnishing among the upper classes, and to the requirements of officials who needed to demonstrate their status through their clothes and household furnishings. Armies of merchants and cloth workers were also employed to produce textiles for individual occasions that might take months to prepare: providing wardrobes of clothes and furnishings for royal brides; costumes, hangings, and carpets for coronations. At more short notice, they provided for the funerals of major figures that might demand a pall cover and clothing given as charity to the poor who were hired as formal mourners, as well as clothing for the bereaved family.

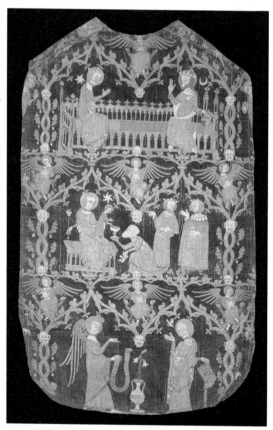

FIGURE 1.1: Chasuble showing the famed English embroidery style called *opus anglicanum*, embroidery and pearls on velvet, c. 1330–50, British. The Metropolitan Museum of Art, New York.

In response to such demands, in the course of the Middle Ages textile production became increasingly commercialized, mechanized, regulated, and international.

RAW MATERIALS AND PRODUCTION

The manufacture of textile, from its start as plant or animal fiber, was one of the major sources of wealth in the medieval period, and at many stages was highly labor intensive, such that few people, whether as landowners, merchants, laborers, or craftsmen and women, would not have been involved in it at some level. The processes involving wool and linen would have taken place across the medieval world, for at least local use, though quality of raw materials or production, especially in weaving or dyeing, dictated which areas benefitted from international trade. Cotton, though grown in the Mediterranean area, was probably not exploited in northern Europe in the early medieval period, and was first used there as cotton wool for stuffing, especially for the padded doublets which became fashionable male dress. It came to be used increasingly as thread for weaving later in the medieval period. The production of silk, both thread and textile, took place for much of the medieval period entirely outside Europe: it was an expensive import for the luxury end of the market.[1]

The main raw materials of textile throughout the medieval period were the wool of domesticated animals (sheep and goats) and linen processed from flax crops and also from hemp, though there is less surviving evidence of the latter (Figure 1.2).

Sheep, smaller and more hairy, less wooly animals than the highly developed breeds of our own time, were an essential part of the medieval economy, providing meat, milk, and cheese for food, horn for various uses from knife handles to translucent panels for lamps and windows, and skin for parchment. Their coats yielded whole fleeces for warmth, as well as the sheared or plucked wool which was spun into thread. Primitive sheep moulted naturally, and it is likely that much of the wool for spinning was acquired by simply plucking and pulling it off a sheep ("rooing"). Such a natural method of harvesting wool would make it less liable to be prickly when woven into cloth than wool which had been

FIGURE 1.2: Sheep and goats depicted in the Old English Hexateuch, compiled at St. Augustine's Abbey in Canterbury, second half of the eleventh century. Cotton Claudius B iv, fol. 22 v. © British Library.

sheared, producing sharp ends. Wool contains lanolin, a natural wax that protects sheep from the weather. Modern treatment of wool involves washing processes which remove the lanolin, but in medieval times the waterproofing qualities of wool would have been a large part of its appeal. Worsted wools were not scoured to remove this lanolin. Woolens *were* scoured but were then artificially greased.[2] Since washing the woven cloth would have diminished this protective element, or the expensively generated surface texture of woolens, wool textiles were generally not immersed in water but were spot-cleaned (as was silk). Different substances were used to clean the cloth according to the nature of the stain. Fifteenth- and sixteenth-century German recipes include cleaning agents for stains from axel-grease, urine, wine, and ink.[3]

Primitive sheep displayed a wide range of natural colors, from white and gray through shades of tan, brown, and blacks. Poor people, or those wishing to display simplicity in their dress for religious reasons, are likely to have used undyed material for their clothes and furnishings, but that does not mean that the textiles used by such people were necessarily monochrome: selection of wool by color at the spinning stage would mean that different hues were available to create striped or checked cloth; or a mixture of tones could have been used in weaving to produce mottled effects. Wool then, from the earliest medieval times was a fiber that would have been readily available to villagers at any time of the year, a versatile, practical material. Long stapled wool was competently spun into hard, glossy threads which are found preserved in the metal oxides of metalwork, chiefly women's dress accessories, in furnished graves of the early Middle Ages (fifth to seventh centuries). Later, the introduction of the spinning wheel and of elaborate finishing techniques (see below pp. 21–22) made it possible to exploit shorter, woolier fibers, and a greater range of wool textiles was developed. While sheep breeds in the modern sense are not recognized before the eighteenth century, selective breeding, crossing-breeding of sheep from different areas, sometimes as a result of human population moves, ensured a considerable variety of types with different colors and wool qualities long before the end of the fifteenth century. Wool fabrics of different weights and textures were commercially produced, and the range of cloth types, together with the added value of different dyeing processes meant that in the late Middle Ages there was wide choice of wool cloths for different purposes and at different prices. Wool was used for garments, furnishings, and the sails of ships. Britain, especially England, was in the forefront of the wool trade, reaching its peak in the thirteenth and fourteenth centuries, exporting vast quantities, especially to Flanders for weaving and also selling to Italian merchants.[4] Trade in soft Spanish merino wool developed from the twelfth century and this was exported in large quantities to England and Flanders for weaving.

Goats, which are biologically similar to sheep, have received less attention in relation to the medieval economy than sheep, and there is less archeological evidence of goat fiber in textile. However, they are known to have been domesticated early and they provided all the foodstuffs and materials that sheep did. Their fine hair may have been a luxury equivalent to wool: the correspondence of Boniface, the eighth-century Anglo-Saxon missionary to Frisia and Saxony, records that he sent goat-hair bedclothes and a cloak of silk and goat-hair to England as gifts;[5] and fragments of well-preserved, gray, twill textiles preserved on prestigious square-headed brooches worn by women at Tittleshall, Norfolk, and Wasperton, Warwickshire, demonstrate that the soft underwool of goats was used to make a fabric similar to the "cashmere" of today. The Tittleshall garment, dated to the mid-sixth century by its accompanying brooch, was especially luxurious as it also had a fur collar or cape[6] (Figure 1.3).

FIGURE 1.3: Tittleshall woman from grave 13 (Walton Rogers, 2013, figure 7.2) with "cashmere"-like cloak. She also wears a linen veil and linen under-gown. Illustration by Anthony Barton. © The Anglo-Saxon Laboratory. The authors are grateful to Penelope Walton Rogers for supplying this illustration.

Flax had been introduced into northwest Europe in prehistoric times and was cultivated for linen by methods that, in some regions, hardly changed until as recently as the early twentieth century.[7] Flax cultivation was arduous and labor-intensive. It began with the preparation of the fields in early spring, planting after the last frost, and constant weeding until the harvesting of the crop three to four months later. The flax plant, *Linum usitatissimum L.*, is fast growing and may reach a height of 100–145 centimeters (over 4 feet). At harvest time, the stems were pulled by hand and the seeds removed by combing or rippling, after which the stems were retted to loosen the fibers from the outer bark. Retting involved leaving the stems in water for about three weeks. This could be achieved by spreading them in dewy fields or by using rivers; alternatively, some flax producers seem to have dug ponds, or exploited existing ones, which avoided the polluting effect of the rotting process on the local river. The stems were then hung up to dry, after which they were beaten with a mallet to loosen the woody part of the stems, then scutched with a heavy knife-like tool to release the inner fibers. These fibers were then heckled (or hackled), passed through a series of combs with metal spikes, to remove the last traces of the woody outer coating. The resulting cleaned fibers could then be wound round a distaff in preparation for spinning. Spinning was carried out in the same way as for wool, with a drop spindle (below), until the introduction of the spinning wheel, and it was woven on the same kinds of loom. It could be dyed, but was most often used undyed, in the creamy-white color it assumed after bleaching. Flax cloth could be washed frequently. Laundering was a predominantly female task, and in towns with public facilities, or at washing places on rivers, it was a social, communal activity. Linens were immersed in water and rubbed with soap, made from animal fat and lye, an alkaline liquid, then rubbed together and beaten.[8] After drying, it could be bleached, and pressed smooth with a hot stone or a ball of glass. Although linen could be used for outer garments, the fact that it could be laundered made it especially suitable for undergarments, so that people could wear fresh, clean clothing next to their skin. Richer people, who owned more shirts, and who could afford to pay for laundry, might appear fresher and cleaner than the poor who could not spare their few clothes to be laundered very often. Its washable nature also made linen suitable for textiles subject to staining, such as table linen, towels, and bedding. Churches were required by statute to keep their altar linen clean, though lazy priests and impoverished parishes might not always maintain standards.[9]

Cotton is also a plant fiber. It is harvested from the fluffy boll, or capsule, found protecting the seeds of shrubs of the genus *Gossypium*. Preparation involves removing the fiber (lint) from the seed and cleaning it before spinning. Cotton was exploited for spun and woven textiles in ancient times in parts of the Americas, Egypt, India, and Pakistan, but its introduction to Europe came relatively late in medieval times, under Islamic influence. It seems to have appeared initially as cotton wool, used as padding in quilted textile armor, for example, as in the still surviving coat armor of the Black Prince.[10] A cotton trade was established in Italy by the twelfth century, using cotton grown and processed in various countries around the Mediterranean;[11] but the penetration of cotton cloth in recognizable form into northern and western Europe has not been fully explained. It was most familiar (and possibly unrecognized as a different fiber) in various forms of mixed cloths—fustian, for example, in this period was made with a cotton weft and linen warp, and there were also half-silks with a silk warp and cotton weft.[12]

The luxury fabric of the Middle Ages was silk. Iridescent, fine, and beautiful, it was also mysterious to early medieval Europeans. The art of sericulture had been discovered in China before 3630 BC, but it remained a Chinese monopoly until a period contemporary with the European Middle Ages. It had reached Central Asia by at least the seventh century AD. Although the Romans and Byzantines produced silk textiles they imported their raw materials. Sericulture only reached Europe with the Islamic conquests of Spain, southern Italy/Sicily, and Cyprus, and production was certainly established in those regions by the tenth century.[13] The cultivation of silk was taking place in Italy by the eleventh century and by the thirteenth had grown into a largely luxury trade in which individual city states specialized in different products. Lucca became a leading exporter of luxury silk cloth.

Silk threads were obtained by unraveling the cocoons of the silk moth *Bombix mori*. To obtain the cocoons, it was necessary to collect the eggs of the moth, which would remain dormant for about ten months, then to incubate them for about twelve days until the larvae ("silkworms") hatched. They had to be fed continuously, preferably on the leaves of the white mulberry (*Morus alba*) and they had to be kept clean, quiet, and at an even temperature and humidity. After twenty-five days and four moults, the larvae would then be ready to spin their cocoons, which were made of silk filaments produced from their salivary glands. A cocoon could contain up to 900 meters of silk filament. After about twenty days, the larvae would begin to emerge from the cocoons, breaking them and producing only inferior silk, so for the best results, the larvae were killed within the cocoons so the silk could be reeled off in a continuous filament. This was achieved by placing the cocoons in hot water, which softened the natural gum that held the cocoon together. After reeling, it was not necessary to spin the silk, though spinning was used on filaments from broken cocoons, on "wild silk" from similar but undomesticated moths, and recycled silk; these products were less lustrous and even than unspun cultivated silk.[14]

Silk first appeared as an item of secular dress north of the Alps in the early sixth century. Very early examples, silk found in two female graves at Unterhaching in Bavaria, Germany, was probably a personal or diplomatic gift from the Mediterranean. The women probably used it as head veils, with gold brocaded bands. They belonged to a wealthy and select group of people, distinct from other inhabitants of the area. At that time, silk was rare and exotic, restricted to the elite by Byzantine law.[15] By the Viking Age, however, silk was evidently being traded. The Scandinavian populations of Dublin, York, and Lincoln made caps from imported silk of similar design to their wool caps, and the Dubliners also used silk hairbands.[16] The medieval Christian Church valued shiny, colorful silks as both soft furnishings and garments, sometimes recycling them in tombs as bedding and wrappings for important and saintly clerics and royalty. For example, the recently opened tomb of Holy Roman Emperor Henry VII in Pisa, Italy, contained a silk cloth, 3 meters long and 120 centimeters wide with alternating bands of red and blue. The blue bands are embroidered in gold and silver with lions confronted and addorsed; a monochrome decoration is still visible but not yet explained, on the red. A crimson strip edged with yellow, at the top of the silk, bears traces of an inscription, not yet deciphered.[17] The recovery of silk textiles from tombs accounts for the survival of many medieval Persian, Byzantine, and Islamic silks in western Europe today.[18]

TECHNIQUES OF MANUFACTURE

Textile techniques proper begin with the preparation of the shorn or harvested fiber into continuous threads and qualities suitable for weaving. Spinning is the first step, the most labor intensive, and was the province of women throughout the period. Experiments have suggested that the length of time required to produce thread of a given quality (spinning before the invention of the spinning wheel) to the time required for the weaving of a given length of cloth, was at least 5:1.[19] Spinning must therefore have been going on continually in medieval households, but the job was interruptible and could be carried out alongside other domestic tasks.

Until the introduction of the spinning wheel in the twelfth century, all spinning was carried out with the drop spindle. The basic techniques were the same for all fibers though flax fibers, longer than wool, required a longer distaff; and linen thread required continual moistening during the spinning process, usually with the spinner's saliva.

The necessary tool was the spindle itself, at its simplest a stick with a notch or hook at one tip to which the new thread could be attached. Turning the stick puts a twist into the fiber which continues into the new lengths of the fiber as they are attached. A whorl, in the form of a large bead with a central hole, was thrust onto the stick and acted as a flywheel: the combination of spindle and whorl is called a drop spindle. A few fibers would be pulled from the distaff by hand and twisted and fixed to the top of the spindle. The spindle was rotated with the fingers, putting a twist in the fibers which the spinner continued to feed from the distaff with her fingers. The whorl kept the stick in rotation until so much thread was spun that the spindle reached the floor, when the spun thread was wound around the spindle, secured so that it would not come off, and the task

FIGURE 1.4: Spinning in the Old English Hexateuch, second half of the eleventh century. This spinner is not using a distaff. Cotton Claudius B iv, fol. 28r. © British Library.

resumed. Medieval spindles rarely survive, being usually made of wood and hence liable to decay, but spindle whorls are common archeological finds. The addition of a distaff, a stick used as a means of carrying the raw material for the thread, made the ensemble extremely portable. Distaffs appear more infrequently in the archeological record for the same reason as spindles, but they are a frequent element in visual representations (Figure 1.4).

Medieval art in all media is full of images of women walking or tending to other tasks while spinning, and this motif is found in illustrations of biblical, historical, romance, and comic stories, and in calendars and Books of Hours. The many examples include St. Margaret spinning while watching sheep (Figure 1.5) or Eve shown spinning after the fall. Spindle whorls are an important indicator of textile processing and are found widely on early medieval archeological sites but in greater concentrations on some urban sites from the tenth century, providing some evidence for the development of commercial activity even before the process began to be mechanized.

The spinning wheel was invented in Asia, and reached Europe about the twelfth century, probably via Muslim cotton industries which were exporting their products to Italy. It had reached Flanders by the late thirteenth century and England by about 1330.[20] While the large fixed wheel replaced the weaver's fingers to rotate the spindle, the spinner still drew out the fibers from the distaff and twisted them by hand, so the process was not

FIGURE 1.5: Detail of a *bas-de-page* scene of Margaret spinning, with sheep feeding beside her, and the prefect Olybrius approaching on horseback, between 1310 and 1320. Royal 2 B VII, fol. 307v. © British Library.

entirely mechanized (Figure 1.6). The spinning wheel speeded up the spinning process, and it could be used for flax, cotton or wool threads; but it did not entirely replace the drop spindle. Warp threads for the finest woolens continued to be produced on the drop spindle throughout the Middle Ages.

Both hand- and wheel-spinning methods could produce thread of different gauges, as required, a heavier whorl producing a thicker thread and a lighter whorl a thin thread;[21] or with a clockwise (Z-spun) or anti-clockwise (S-spun) twist. Both wool and linen were

FIGURE 1.6: Detail of a *bas-de-page* scene of a man and a woman at a spinning wheel, last quarter of the thirteenth century or first quarter of the fourteenth century. Royal 10 E IV, fol. 147v. © British Library.

more commonly spun in the Z direction in northern Europe (despite the fact that S is the more natural direction for flax fiber). Sometimes varied spin direction—usually Z in the warp and S in the weft—was used deliberately to create the illusion of color/pattern effects in a monochrome weave. Silk thread was often left unspun, and was imported into northern and western Europe either in this state or with a twist already added, in the form of thread for embroidery or the making of cords and laces, as well as finished textile. Cotton would also have been imported as thread, textile, or cotton-wool.

The design of looms on which weaving, the interlacing of warp and weft threads to produce a length of textile, was carried out, changed considerably through the medieval period. In the early part of the period in England and Scandinavia especially, there is most evidence for the warp-weighted loom, so-called because warp threads suspended from a horizontal cloth beam at the top of the structure were held in place by attachment to stone or ceramic loom-weights at the bottom. The beam could rotate so that finished cloth could be wound on to it, so that the length of cloth produced was not limited to the height of the loom. Weaving progressed from the top downwards. The weaver would stand in front and inserted the weft, beating it upward with a weaving sword (beater or batten), changing the shed by means of horizontal rods. The presence of this loom type is attested by archeological finds of the loom-weights and occasionally other tools, such as the sword-shaped beater. An advantage of the warp-weighted loom was that it leant against a wall and could be easily be set up or dismantled.

The vertical two-beam loom required fixed uprights, supporting beams at the top and bottom to which the warp threads were attached. Again the weaver stood in front of the loom, this time weaving from the bottom upwards. The quantity of cloth produced was restricted by the height of the loom, although extra length could be obtained with the addition of an extra cord or stick across the front of the loom, around which the warp was also wound—this produced a tubular cloth. As every part of the two-beam loom was wooden it has left few, if any, archeological traces. It was probably used in parts of Britain, especially where there is no evidence of loom weights, and was also widespread on the Continent throughout the early medieval period.

The horizontal treadle loom was a major medieval innovation (Figure 1.7). Appearing in the late eleventh century, this mechanical loom had two cloth beams, disposed horizontally in front of the weaver; the warp thread was attached to the far beam, while finished cloth was wound around the nearer one, thus allowing for longer lengths of cloth than those produced on vertical looms. The weaver was seated, and using both hands and feet, wove considerably faster than a vertical-loom weaver. Sheds were raised by shafts linked by pulleys to foot-operated treadles. The linen ground cloth of the Bayeux Tapestry, made in the 1070s or 1080s, is almost certainly a product of the horizontal loom, created in the first century of that loom's existence. The Bayeux Tapestry is the largest surviving medieval textile. In its present incomplete state, it is 68 meters long. It was made in nine sections, the longest of which measures 13.9 meters. The width of the cloth on the horizontal loom was originally limited by the width of the weaver's arms and the Bayeux Tapestry, 50 centimeters wide, probably consists of half-widths of cloth woven about a meter wide.

A major development of the horizontal treadle loom was the introduction, by the thirteenth century, of the broadloom, at which two weavers sat side by side. This made possible the weaving of textile up to 4 meters wide.[22] The wool cloth produced on this loom was accordingly called "broadcloth," while cloths made by a single weaver were called "straits" ("narrow" cloths).

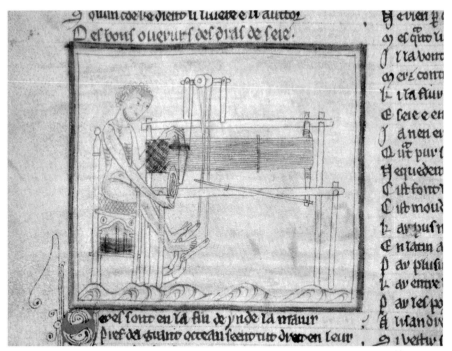

FIGURE 1.7: Man weaving on a horizontal treadle loom. MS Cambridge, Trinity College 0.9.34 fol. 32v (thirteenth century). By kind permission of the Master and Fellows of Trinity College.

Linen, although it could be woven in twill, was characteristically tabby- (plain-) woven. It could be produced in various qualities, from loose, almost transparent cloth, used, for example, for head veils, to denser material. The average thread count of the linen of the Bayeux Tapestry is 22 warp threads by 18 weft threads per centimeter: a firm, fairly fine weave which has proved a durable foundation for thick embroidery in wool. The shirt believed to be a relic of St. Louis, King Louis IX of France, was 28 by 28 threads per centimeter, and is perhaps, Tina Anderlini suggests, an example of the "cloth of Rheims" which was highly prized in the Middle Ages,[23] being frequently mentioned in both poetry and documentary texts such as accounts and wills.[24] The finest known example of medieval linen, at 50 threads per centimeter, is the cloth in which the embalmed heart of Richard the Lionheart (King Richard I of England) was wrapped after his death in April 1199.[25]

Wool can be woven in plain weave or twill. In early medieval times, the most skilled and decorative weaves were twills which had repeated diamond or lozenge patterns on the surface. By the thirteenth century, such cloths, which were made from combed wool, spun with a drop spindle, were called "worsteds," in England, named after the Norfolk village of Worstead which was one of the areas where they were produced. In the thirteenth and fourteenth centuries, changes in technology and development of finishing processes made possible the creation of "woolens." Using wool cards to align the fibers before spinning, rather than the traditional combs, manufacturers were now able to exploit softer, curly, short-fibered fleeces which were then wheel-spun. Densely woven on the horizontal loom with a worsted warp for strength and a carded and wheel-spun weft for fluffiness, woolens were subsequently fulled to make them shrink and felt, tentered (stretched) to make them regular sizes, teaseled to brush up the fluffy surface, and sheared to smooth them. Woolen cloths were heavy and soft. They were more expensive than worsteds, and came in various qualities.

Narrow wares—such as ribbons, tapes, and cords—were made in a variety of ways such as weaving on small box looms, braiding on small, square tablets, and looping on the fingers. Belts, points for securing items of clothing together, and strong, decorative edges for garments, purses, and furnishings were among the many items which were not woven on large looms but made individually in this way.

Textile could be dyed at various stages in its manufacture, from the fleece ("dyed in the wool"), the spun thread, or the woven cloth. Vegetable dyes could be used alone or in various combinations, especially woad, which produced indigo, for blue; madder for red; bedstraws for red, weld, and dyer's greenweed for yellow. Lichens and barks could also be used for coloring. The most expensive dyestuff of the Middle Ages was the red-producing kermes, extracted from the eggs of an insect (the Mediterranean shield-louse), and given the name "grain" from the appearance of the desiccated eggs.[26] It was imported into northern Europe from the Mediterranean. The finest woolens were called "scarlets" and although they were not always red in color, kermes was used in their production. Other expensive colorants imported into Europe included saffron (yellow), and Tyrian purple which was extracted from shellfish.

From about the sixth century, very wealthy people wore garments enhanced with precious metal. At first this consisted of strips of thin gold brocaded into tablet-woven bands and beaten flat. By about the eighth century, embroidery threads made of gold spun round a core of fiber (silk or animal tail hair) became available and by the eleventh century, silver threads were also used. Later still, gilded membrane wrapped around a core of linen or cotton supplied a cheaper alternative. Originally used for ladies' headbands and garment borders, gold threads came to be used in the rich embroidery which was known as *opus anglicanum* (Figure 1.1).[27] It was a speciality of England, though versions of it were produced in other European countries. It reached its peak of production in the twelfth and thirteenth centuries and was used on the most opulent of ecclesiastical vestments and royal garments.

Cloth of gold and cloth of silver were manufactured by inserting brocading wefts of gold or silver thread while the textile, usually silk or half-silk with linen warp and silk weft, was on the loom. Originally imported into Europe from Byzantium, by the thirteenth century cloth of gold was being manufactured in Spain and Italy under exotic names like *baudekin* and *racamaz* which implied Middle Eastern origin, as well as being imported from further east. Such cloths were used for vestments for the highest ranking clerics, or hangings in the great cathedrals; and as garments for royalty. By the late thirteenth century velvet woven with gold had been imported into Europe, and continued to be documented in the fourteenth and fifteenth centuries, again for the very highest ranks: popes and kings.[28]

INDUSTRIAL AND SOCIAL REVOLUTION

While many medieval techniques for textile making remained in use until the development of mechanized tools in the eighteenth century, in the course of the Middle Ages a series of both non-mechanical and mechanical developments were adopted to speed up the process. They were not all adopted in all areas.

Among non-mechanical innovations, the flax break, a series of intersecting wooden blades, set in a frame and operated by mean of a handle, facilitated the process of breaking the woody outer stems of the flax plant after they had been retted. The alternative was to beat the stems with a mallet. They still required scutching with a knife to remove the remains of the woody part, but the flax break made the work lighter.

Various methods of combing had been used to prepare wool for spinning since time immemorial. The spiky dried heads of teasel plants and combs of wood or bone were probably used. Specific tools, wool combs with metal teeth, are known in archeological contexts from about the seventh century. They were used in pairs by the worker, who held a comb in each hand by a wooden handle and combed the wool fibers from one to the other, removing tangles and debris, and leaving the fibers parallel, ready for spinning. In about the fourteenth century, this technique was improved by making the teeth longer, and mounting one comb on a fixed post. Wool combs continued in use for worsted fiber throughout the medieval period.[29]

The alternative practice of "carding" wool developed in the thirteenth century. It was a major innovation which enabled short fluffy wool fibers to be processed, contributing to production of the soft, heavy, silky cloths called "woolens" which became fashionable in the later Middle Ages. Wool cards (which were named for the teasel plant, Latin *carduus*) consisted of wooden paddles covered in leather in which rows of small bent tines were set (Fig. 1.8). As with wool combs, the operator prepared the wool by combing it from one to the other. The result was a small roll of cleaned and intermixed fibers which were ready for spinning. Carding did not replace combing, but existed alongside it for different types of wool fibers.

Among mechanical developments, the most important is the horizontal loom. Before its introduction, textile production appears to have been exclusively women's work. Weaving on a vertical loom, whether the warp-weighted or the two-beam, was heavy, tiring, and slow work. The weaving process involved passing a bobbin or shuttle of weft thread between the upright, fixed warp threads. After each pass it was necessary to change the shed, which had to be done by hand, by means of rods attached to the uprights on each side of the loom. The weft threads had to be compacted by beating, either up or down depending on the type of loom. The horizontal loom, which was from the first associated with men, changed the shed mechanically by means of treadles operated by the feet. The shuttle was tossed from hand to hand and the beating took place by means of a fixed bar, later called a weaver's reed, which compacted the cloth toward the weaver.

The introduction of the horizontal loom resulted in a gender revolution and long-term social change. Although women continued to operate vertical looms for specialist weaving, such as tapestry work, and to provide weavers with spun thread, the horizontal loom brought men into the textile industry. This would result in the commercialization of cloth weaving and other processes, and the organization of the industry into guilds which established and maintained standards, instituted apprenticeships, and carried out charitable work. Though individual manufacturers and sellers might have been rivals for customers, they were allies in that they belonged to a guild and would promote the power of that guild. The increasing urbanization of medieval life went hand in hand with the rise of the middle classes, and the High Middle Ages would see prosperous guildsmen become influential leaders in city life. The rise of a cloth industry made for new rivalries and new alliances. Men dominated most aspects of the medieval cloth industry, at least the public face of it, including embroidery and knitting, tasks which have become much more

FIGURE 1.8: Detail of a miniature, showing different stages of the production of woolen cloth. The woman to the right is combing or hackling, the central figure has a pair of wool cards, the woman on the left is spinning with a spindle, behind is a loom, c. 1440. Royal 16 G V fol. 56, Gaia Caecilia. © British Library.

female-associated in recent centuries as they have been revived as crafts alongside commercial production. Spinning and the making and marketing of silk narrow wares, however, remained female work (Figure 1.9).

The spinning wheel, though it never completely replaced the drop spindle, was also responsible for some social change. While the spinner using a drop spindle could take her work with her, the spinning wheel was a fixed instrument so the spinner became more constrained; and although spinning remained largely a domestic task throughout the Middle Ages, the investment in the equipment would pressure the spinner to maintain output to justify expense. The spinning wheel, which went through various technical improvements in the course of the Middle Ages, was important in the rapid production of wefts for woolens, which were such an important part of the late medieval economy.

Mechanical means of "throwing" or twisting silk were introduced in Italy in the thirteenth century, but remained confined to that area. Like fulling mills (see p. 25), these throwing mills were powered by water. Italy may also have used a mechanical

FIGURE 1.9: Detail of a miniature of Pamphila collecting cocoons of silk worms from mulberry trees and weaving the silk, c. 1440. Royal MS 16 G V, fol. 54v, Pamphila. © British Library.

device to reel together up to four silk filaments. These devices produced stronger silk threads than the unspun filaments, and speeded up the production of silk-woven goods.[30]

Fulling, a process which has existed since ancient times, was essential as one of the finishing processes that produced woolens. Traditionally carried out by men trampling the cloth in a bath of which the ingredients might include urine, fuller's earth and butter, fulling cleaned and felted the woven cloth. A mechanical alternative, the fulling mill, which used water power to drive hammers that pounded the cloth, began to appear in Europe in about the eleventh century. With the increasing popularity of woolens, fulling mills were becoming widespread in the thirteenth century, situated close to fast flowing rivers in areas associated with sheep that had short, fluffy coats. They were erected, for example, on the large estates of the Cistercian order who had become major wool producers in England in the thirteenth century. However, not all fulling mills were commercially successful or enduring.

REGULATION

It is a measure of the importance of textiles that governments made efforts to raise tax from the movement of the goods involved when these crossed national borders. The erection of customs barriers and trade restrictions to protect domestic manufacture may be seen as an economic parallel to the rise of political nationalism in Europe in the thirteenth and fourteenth centuries.

To establish fair and equable standards for trading, it became desirable to regulate for qualities, weights, and measures of cloth. Developments of this kind took place across Europe, but evidence from England is instructive, showing that attempts at standardization started as early as the seventh century, in the Laws of Ethelbert of Kent; and that by the eighth century international, intergovernmental relations could include complaints that standards of textile goods were not being met, as in an exchange between Charlemagne and Offa of Mercia about changes in expected lengths of English cloths. The Parliament Rolls of Medieval England provide a series of examples of standards for lengths, widths, weights, and qualities of various cloth types, stated, confirmed and reconfirmed over a long period.[31] This regulation in England also raised revenue for central and local governments, which clearly involved recognition that markets depended on various kinds of recognized standards, but in this, England was unusual: the only other country in medieval Europe to raise a sales tax on cloth was Catalonia. The taxes were collected locally by alnagers (or ulnagers) but were appointed by the king to collect alnage (ulnage) which means "measurement" (and indeed local authorities sometimes employed alnagers to measure cloth for sale); but it was basically a tax levied on high quality woolen cloths.[32] Customs duties on wool in England began first for the export of raw wool (by denizens or foreigners) and only a little later, in the thirteenth century under Edward I, on cloth imports and exports by foreigners. Taxes on worsteds were added in the fourteenth century. Again, the English example is of wider interest, showing preferential treatment for denizens, and also for allies such as the Hanseatic League. These taxes became a major part of the royal (therefore national) income, subsidising wars as well as the royal household.[33]

TRADE IN TEXTILES AND ECONOMIC DEVELOPMENT

One aspect which illustrates the huge importance of textile trade in medieval life must be the impact of outlets for its purchase on urban life and development. It seems fairly clear that, as far back in the medieval period as we can go, while some textiles may indeed have been "homespun" for local use, trade within and between countries was always important. For the early medieval period, discussion has centered on the development of markets and trading centers, especially in areas that saw a decline in urbanism in the post-Roman period. In Britain for example (but also across northern and western Europe), evidence for temporary "beach markets" has been associated with Viking traders. Everywhere the development of fixed markets (held at short intervals, weekly or even more frequently), and fairs (held annually over several days) are associated both with the Church, and increasingly with the role of local authorities and rulers interested in increased revenues from commercial activity, which also necessitated protection of traders and trading standards[34] (See Chapter 2). The importance of the development of financial instruments, such as advance contracts to the furtherance of the wool trade, has been demonstrated in the dealings of English monastic producers of wool with Flemish and northern French, but

primarily with Italian buyers such as the Riccardi of Lucca and others.[35] Indeed, the social
and cultural importance of the wool trade in European history can hardly be ignored. It
was responsible for the migration of both workers and middlemen, and the establishment
of cosmopolitan communities, especially in London. It was not all racial harmony,
however. There could be hostility toward the migrant workers as in the massacre of the
Flemings (Flemish weavers) during the Peasants' Revolt in London in 1381.

Attempts to set trading standards for this important commodity in England, for
example, can be traced back to Anglo-Saxon times, and numerous statutes from this
period forward were concerned with setting and policing standard weights and measures:
the frequency or repetition of similar and improved laws implies the need for both
national and local vigilance, since both fines for infringements and taxes levied per ell
of cloth were important sources of revenue.[36] Every country had its own production
of wool and woolens (the finest cloth), but some countries were ultimately best known
for production of the raw material (for example, England, for which the trade was a
mainstay of the exchequer to the very end of the medieval period); other areas for the
production of fine cloths. John Munro has written extensively not only on the value of
the trade in fine woolens in medieval and early modern Europe, but also on its social
significance—for example in comparing wages of even comparatively well paid workers
to the (to them) unattainable cost of the finest cloths dyed with kermes, the most expensive
dye—and its cultural significance both as a signifier of status and of fashion, in the change
from the various shades indicated by the term "scarlet" to black, an even more expensively
achieved color.[37]

THE SOCIAL SIGNIFICANCE OF TEXTILE TRADE AND TEXTILES

Medieval sources in various genres provide some account of how the textile trades and
those who worked in them were regarded, and even how much scholarly writers knew
about them and about their development. For example, we have the dictionaries of
English scholar-grammarians of the twelfth to thirteenth centuries, who taught and/or
pursued their own studies in Paris. One of these, Alexander Nequam or Neckham, in his
De nominibus utensilium, is particularly interesting on weaving, since he gives a detailed
description of the male-operated horizontal loom, before the end of the twelfth century.
He describes the weaver as "a horseman on *terra firma* who leans upon two stirrups and
who gives rein constantly to the horse, content with a short journey; but the stirrups
representing the condition of his fortune enjoy mutual vicissitudes, since when one goes
up the other is depressed without any indication of rancor [sic]." The full description
includes the use of shuttles and heddles but as a translator says, needs a picture of the
loom to aid understanding.[38] The full account also makes clear that the work of the
weaver could not begin without the preparation work of the carder, or be turned into
clothing without the intervention of the fuller to wash and finish the cloth. A slightly later
study, c. 1220, the *Dictionarius* of John of Garland, a tool for teaching Latin vocabulary,
shows less understanding of the processes, but is incidentally interesting with snippets of
information on and attitudes to various trades. For example, girdlers, he says, sold not
only leather girdles, but those woven in silk ornamented with silver bars. Drapers are
described as greedy and inclined to fraud, both in the description of qualities of cloth and
in providing short measure. Men selling linens for all purposes—tablecloths, sheets,
towels, shirts, underwear, wimples, and kerchiefs—are scorned for usurping women's

work. Fullers and dyers are described, also weavers—apparently females working on upright looms—and female silk weavers making girdles and headbands. Female wool-combers clearly have a dirty job, sitting dressed in "old pilches and filthy veils" near the sewer/privy and the bum wipers.[39] The French poem the "Dit du Mercier" satirizes traders rather later (c. 1300), showing that at this stage mercers were indistinguishable from haberdashers, carrying girdles, wimples, needles, purses, skins, thimbles, arrowheads, pins, bells, spoons, soap, cosmetics, and spices as well as some cloth.[40] Later still, in England, the late fourteenth-century poet John Gower satirized various "estates" (social categories), among them guilds, including textile guilds, in Anglo-French in *The Mirour de l'Omme*; and in Latin in *Vox Clamantis*.[41] Included among textile guilds were mercers (original exporters and importers of cloths; also makers and sellers of small goods made from these—which became more important as time went on); and drapers (also exporters of wool and English woolen cloth; and importers of luxury woolens): in both cases Gower was critical of the social climbing expressed by such merchants. A mercer, he said, enticed purchasers to see his "Beds, kerchiefs, ostrich feathers, silks, satins, imported cloths" in terms implying that as a group the mercers aspired to rise socially; drapers were satirized for keeping their shops poorly lit "So that one can hardly tell green from blue."[42]

Textiles themselves were important as signifiers of social status—or its lack—and were the subject of legislation and moral commentary. It is often assumed that sumptuary laws and fulminations against impropriety in dress on social or religious grounds were concerned mainly with specific items or styles of dress, or its scantiness. However, it is often the materials themselves that are the subject of legislation, customary disposal, or disapproval. This is clear in the case of furs, which were important as linings and decoration in the garments of all ranks of society, especially in the winter months, save for the poorest. How such restrictions ever worked in view of the enormous economic importance of recycling of used cloth and clothing is probably as much of a dilemma to us—in trying to assess how it worked in relation to this legislation—as it must have been at the time.

Re-use was an essential stage in the life-cycle of textiles, since so much human effort and expense contributed to producing them in the first place. Recycling involved not merely the "handing down" or re-sale to younger or socially dependent users of finished garments, but remaking: turning worn garments into other garments and worn cloth into smaller artifacts (such as sheets into pillow cases and ecclesiastical silks into seal bags). This was, in effect, the returning of dress and furnishings back to their constituent parts as textiles which could be put to a variety of new uses, of gradually lessening dignity, until they were worn out.[43] Even as rags, textile had uses. The rich archeological finds of textile from London derive in large part from the use of domestic rubbish between the twelfth and fifteenth centuries as land-fill, a necessary part of increasing the facilities for shipping on the north bank of the river Thames as trade and travel increased. In many European cities, the public collection of rags was established by the late medieval period. Linen rags were ripped up and pounded to be made into paper; the caulking thrust between the planks of ships to keep them watertight consisted of tarred fragments of what had once been cloth. Thus in a changing world inhabited by an increasingly literate and mobile population, textile completed its life-cycle with a return to fiber for non-textile purposes.

CHAPTER TWO

Production and Distribution

EVA ANDERSSON STRAND AND SARAH-GRACE HELLER

Who made medieval clothing, and where did it come from? During the approximately thousand-year period of the Middle Ages, the production, organization, and distribution of textiles and clothing changed considerably, although it is important to emphasize that these changes did not take place at the same time and in the same manner all over Europe. Whether the settlement was large or small, textile manufacture and garment production took up a great deal of time. Knowledge and ability to produce textiles and clothing were lodged in more than one individual; many different members of each society were involved in the production process.

This chapter examines six observable organizational modes throughout western Europe in the medieval period: basic household production; advanced household production; attached organized production; household industry; putting-out system; and workshop production (see Figure 2.1). One organization mode does not necessarily exclude another, as different modes were often combined. From the isolated rural households to growing urban centers in the tenth to fifteenth centuries, the sources for understanding modes of production vary widely, from archeological remains to guild records, inventories, and tax documents. These production models serve as a baseline for combining different sources, which are always fragmentary for this period, aiding comparative discussion of production structures. The first part of the chapter will examine evidence of earlier production, then look at distribution modes and trade routes. The second part will consider textual evidence of urban craft organization, how practices of "shopping" emerged across Europe, and the expansion of fashionable variety in the market.

Basic household production is the most visible during the earlier periods (400–1050), in settlements and burials where textile tools are frequently excavated. This production mode is invisible in written sources, although individuals probably manufactured textiles to cover their own needs during the entire period. This mode only covered the absolute needs, i.e. textiles for clothing.

Advanced household production catered for not only basic needs, but also more exclusive textiles such as embroidery or tapestry weaving. It is visible in written sources such as poems, sagas, saints' lives, and Latin chronicles, where women are mentioned as actors/producers. This mode is generally not visible in the archeological record. As surpluses and decorative novelties emerge in production, the presence of "fashion" becomes more germane.

Textile production organized in an attached textile production mode is evidenced in written sources and in excavations of some estates in the middle and later Anglo-Saxon period, and possibly in Scandinavia. Written sources show it was an important part of the

Production mode	production scale	skill level	raw materials	time devoted
Household production basic	solely household's own needs	general knowledge and skills	Raw materials commonly accessible	not full-time
Household industry	beyond producers' needs	general knowledge and skills	surplus of raw material	not full-time
Household production advanced	household's own needs or gifts	special knowledge and skills	Raw material of better/higher quality, e.g. imported silk	not full-time
Putting-out system	beyond producers' needs	general knowledge and skills	buyer supplied raw material, perhaps also tools	not necessarily full-time
Attached specialist production	high-quality products, e.g. desirable gifts	craft specialists, skills enhanced by full time occupation	raw materials were of a better and/or higher quality	full-time
Workshops	for direct market; stand-ardized items; great demand for products	professional	varying quality, according to supply/demand	full-time

FIGURE 2.1: Model of different levels of production (Andersson, 2003 and Andersson Strand, 2011), revised by Eva Andersson Strand, 2016.

gift economy around Merovingian and Carolingian courts on the Continent. The products of this mode could be kept for household use, exchanged, or given as political gifts.

Household industry required access to surplus raw material, and it is hardly possible to separate it archeologically from household production. The putting-out mode of organization, where merchants accrue large quantities of raw materials to distribute to artisans, exchanging payment for finished products, and then assuring distribution, is also difficult to trace in the archeological record. Written sources clearly show that both organizational modes were used at least from c. 1000. The presence of this system is important evidence of fashion: it required significant demand for commodities, and long-distance trade networks.

Workshop production requires larger population centers as well as well-organized trade structures, which permit greater specialization among crafts. Such workshops existed in Byzantium and cities around the Mediterranean up through about the seventh century, longer in some areas. As the European population recovered from the demographic depressions of the early Middle Ages, the wealth of emerging cities both in the Mediterranean and northern Europe was built on cloth production. Córdoba and later Almería in Andalusia were known for their patterned silks and fine leathers in the tenth to twelfth centuries. Artisans in Lucca began processing imported silk in the eight to tenth centuries, and developed their own sericulture by the twelfth as Sicilian production declined. Northern French and later Flemish towns gained renown for luxury woolens, exchanged wholesale at fairs such as those organized in Champagne, beginning in the tenth century, flourishing in the twelfth, and no longer needed by the fifteenth as trade and finance had become more systematized. Merchants from Italy, Provence (principally from Cahors and Montpellier), and later the Hanse got rich moving oriental silks, Mediterranean dyestuffs, northern woolens, and Baltic furs, as well as creating banking systems. By the thirteenth century, Paris was a center for fashionable luxury items such as bags, belts, arms, and head ornaments, as well as various fine textiles. One could buy some ready-made clothing, accessories, and fur linings in towns, as well as used clothing. For new sets of robes, servants and bourgeois coordinated with networks of drapers, mercers, cutters, stitchers, and embroiderers to have garments made.

TEXTILE AND CLOTHING PRODUCTION IN THE EARLY MIDDLE AGES

The Migration Period of the fourth to eighth centuries profoundly altered both Europe's ethnic composition and trade routes, and thereby its dress and consumption practices. The Mediterranean connected the distribution of fashionable products up to around the seventh century. Merchants brought goods on ships from the Levant and Constantinople into Marseille, Narbonne, Toulon, and Fos in Gaul, the Catalonian and Asturian coasts in Visigothic Spain, Carthage in North Africa, and Ostia and Ravenna in Italy as well as the nascent towns of Venice and Comacchio. Frequenting the ports were independent merchants, many of them Jewish and Syrian, as well as agents of the great ecclesiastical institutions, who moved goods inland by mules and carts. Trade was facilitated by Byzantine gold coinage (as well as western copies of these coins), almost the only monetary unit in circulation in the fourth to seventh centuries. Trade of fabrics and objects of adornment is minimally documented, but evident from archeology.[1]

Around the seventh century, Frisians and Anglo-Saxons began minting silver penny coins. Such coins became the monetary standard through the thirteenth century and rejuvenated the western economy. There was a shift in power and court consumption toward the Holy Roman Empire in the north. Scandinavian, Norman, Frisian, Irish, and Anglo-Saxon sailors connected the ports of London, York, Quentovic in northern Gaul, Ribe in Jutland, Birka in Sweden, and the North Sea and Baltic coasts, as well as the Moselle and Rhine rivers. New Mediterranean trade networks evolved as Arab trade law and practices developed from the seventh century, as well.

In the Merovingian period (c. 450–750) in what is now France, Germany, and Belgium, furnished burials reveal the continuity of Mediterranean trade as well as its gradual breakdown. There was a fashion for embellishing brooches and weapons with garnets from Sri Lanka, until that route was suddenly disrupted c. 600[2] (Figure 2.3).

Multicolored glass and clay beads made their way from the Mediterranean to such places as Normandy, Picardy, England, Alemania, the Italian Marche, and the northern Caucasus via the Danube.[3] The polychrome style is a major cultural manifestation of this period, with a greater love of color appearing on many surfaces: cloisonné brooches and buckles, bright dyes for tunics, trousers, cloaks, veils, and tablet-woven decorative bands, even colored leathers for fine shoes.

As the Roman Empire shifted east from Rome to Constantinople, from the fourth century on, the Basileus established strictly-controlled workshops to produce the priceless textiles and clothing exclusive to the magnificence of the imperial image, reserved for the emperor, given as a kind of wages to his courtiers, and as political gifts to allies across

FIGURE 2.2: Map of Western Europe from *Berg Encyclopedia of World Dress and Fashion Vol. 8: West Europe*, 2011. By Martin Lubikowski, ML Design.

FIGURE 2.3: Frankish garnet bird brooch, sixth century. The Metropolitan Museum of Art, New York.

Europe, Asia, and Africa. There were three state guilds of the later Roman Empire, the *demosia somata*, which existed in remarkable continuity over the subsequent seven centuries, a kind of aristocracy of labor by the ninth and tenth centuries, with hereditary positions: the clothiers and tailors (*gynaecarii, raptai, isourgoi*), the purple dyers (*ozybapheis, purpurarii*), and the gold embroiderers (*chrysoklabaroi, barbarikarioi*). They formed a kind of caste, and could never withdraw from their jobs: there was significant anxiety over keeping their trade secrets exclusive. The early *gynaecarii* workers were men, contrary to what the name suggests. Later the title "procurators of the women" appear in the Justinian and Thedosian codes, suggesting that men had supervisory roles. A law stipulates fines against men who "corrupt" women workers, hinting at the potential problems with this system—was this to protect the women from rape, or to protect trade secrets from women who might disclose them? Women probably executed the primary stages of production while men engaged in the final processes. The head of the *Eidikon*, a branch of the imperial treasury, held supreme authority over the factories. The three workshops were located in wings of the palaces, kept close to the epicenter of power in concentrated spaces for optimal surveillance.[4]

For the broader public and foreign trade, private guilds in Byzantium were allowed to engage in second quality silk and dye work. Again here, the variety of vocabulary is telling, suggesting the importance of silk and clothing in this culture and its relations with the world. Merchants of raw silk were *metazopratai*. Next in the process came spinners, *katartarioi*. Dealers in domestic silk, *bestiopratai*, were distinguished from importers, *pravthriopratai*. Finishers, makers of silk clothing and dyers, were together known as *serikarioi*.[5]

In Frankish lands, the woman buried at Saint-Denis identified by her ring as Aregonde (Queen Arnegonde?) c. 580 wore a long gold and red shot silk veil, a tablet-woven silk head band with a geometric motif, a woolen robe opening down the front with decorative silk cuffs with a ribbon of gold thread, a wide kidskin belt with a large decorative buckle, calfskin cuffs embroidered with silk, pointed embroidered slippers crossed with leather garters with decorative metal buckles and ends, and various pins, brooches, and earrings.[6] The sophistication of this ensemble demonstrates connections to Byzantine or oriental suppliers, as well as a level of garment and accessory production skill on the Continent able to outfit elites to colorful and impressive effect. Her gold earrings, however, are an imperfect match: one is probably Byzantine in manufacture, the other a local copy, one example of the "Byzantine influence" on women's adornment in this period.[7] This is a difficult period to study, with texts scarce and funerary material largely mute to questions of production and attitudes, but the glimpses available suggest that the presence of fashion should not be dismissed.

Rural Production and Distribution

Production modes and distribution networks were more limited in rural and isolated areas. After the Romans left England at the beginning of the fifth century, long-distance trade decreased and it was necessary to be self-sufficient in most raw materials.[8] Initially, the Anglo-Saxons lived in small communities where textile and clothing production was solely at a household level, using commonly available raw material, producing textiles primarily for their own needs: clothes, furnishing, tapestries, tablecloth, bags, sacks. The demand for different types of textiles must have been substantial. Many people were involved in the various textile production processes, and even if they did not work at this full-time, they would have possessed general knowledge and skills for textile and garment production.

Archeology shows that the tools used had changed little from antiquity. A spindle (with a spindle whorl) with a distaff was used to spin yarn (Figure 2.4).

Loom weights found in excavations indicate that the warp-weighted loom was still in use[9] (Figures. 2.5a and b). Triangular and pyramidal loom weights were replaced by ring-shaped weights, but this did not affect the weaving or the fabric produced. Anglo-Saxon loom weights have been found in sunken-floor houses, and the number of weights in rows sometimes indicates large looms, up to 2.44 meters wide. It would be immensely difficult to work alone on such a loom, suggesting that weaving happened in a common house in a village workshop.[10]

Weaving was a task for not merely the individual family itself, but carried on at the village level, and similarly for the cultivation and preparation of fibers. In the early Anglo-Saxon period, women were generally responsible for the production and the organization of the textile work, but it is likely that men and women, young and old were all involved.

At the beginning of the middle Anglo-Saxon period (c. 650) indications of organizational changes in the villages appear. Loom weights are still common finds from archeological excavations, but now from individual buildings within the single farm, suggesting

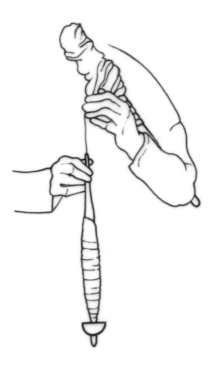

FIGURE 2.4: Spinning with a drop spindle and a short distaff. Drawing by Christina Borstam, © Eva Andersson Strand.

household production. Evidence for common textile weaving workshops and organized textile production at trading centers ceases for the seventh and eighth centuries.[11]

Written sources suggest that textile production was more organized on large estates. Centralized royal control increased from c. 600 in Anglo-Saxon regions. Several more state demesnes and estates were founded, to which tax was paid in wool and flax. Extant wills and deeds indicate it was the mistress of the estate who was in charge of the organization of textile production. Women were similarly charged with hospitality and domestic management throughout the Carolingian world on the Continent.[12]

Large manors developed over the following centuries and raw material was transported to an estate's workshop for the production of textiles. A text dated to the late tenth or early eleventh declares that:

> . . . the estate's reeve is advised to plant madder, sow flax, and woad seed as well and to supply the workshops with many flax-processing tools, flax line [raw fiber], spindle reel. Swift. Loom uprights, heddle rods, press [or cloth beam?], comb sheath, seam-pins, shears, needle, slick stone.[13]

The workshops on the estates were most likely *gynaecea* where women worked on producing textiles. In the workshops, textiles to cover the manor's household needs were manufactured, but sometimes also products for gift or trade, as seen in Brandon, Suffolk and Flixborough, Humberside. The archeological material attests to all textile manufacturing stages from fiber procurement to finished product.[14]

A

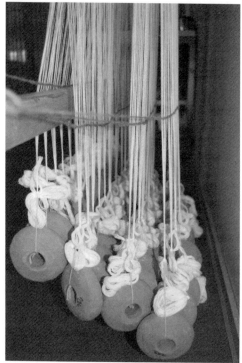

B

FIGURES 2.5A and 2.5B: A warp-weighted loom with a 2/2 twill set-up with four rows of loom weights; close-up of loom weights. Photo by Linda Olofsson. © Ulla Lund Hansen and CTR.

Gynaecea are mentioned on the Continent already from the sixth century. Gregory of Tours writes in 589 that, one should distribute the meal among the women who are working in the spinning and weaving room, and it is plausible that he refers to a *gynaeceum*. As for Byzantium, the status of the *gynaecea* workers is unclear. In some cases, it was freeborn women, in others, female slaves, but both were women who earned a living from textile production.[15]

From c. 800, references to textiles manufactured at manors by women abound in various written sources, such as letters, law texts, and hierology. The Carolingian *Capitulare de Villis* mentions that the women in the "genitia" workshop should have linen, wool, woad, vermillion, madder, combs, teasels, soap, oil, vessels, and other "small things," and that women workers should be protected by good enclosures. A statute dated to 789 describes women's assignments, such as fiber preparation, spinning, weaving, and tailoring.[16]

Production during this period was not exclusively the result of slave labor, on the contrary. High-ranking women were not only expected to direct the work, they were required to be proficient. In the eighth century, Charlemagne wrote in a letter his insistence that his daughters "learn to spin and weave wool, use the distaff and spindle and acquire every womanly accomplishment."[17]

In another letter, dated to 796 from Charlemagne to King Offa of Mercia, he requested cloaks in the same length and quality they used to receive. This confirms that there was a trade or exchange of textiles between England and France, but also that Offa had the resources to produce textiles, possibly in a *gynaeceum*. Moreover, there are law texts stating that men who have a sexual relationship with slave girls who are members of a woman's fabric shop should be punished.[18] These documents signal that clothing production was very much the domain of women.

The adoption of Christianity played a role in the production and distribution of high-quality textiles. Silks from Byzantine and Islamic workshops were given as gifts to churches across Europe. Furthermore, silk and gold embroidery, produced in convents, was considered as highly valuable, both within and outside Britain.[19]

It is likely that the matron, her daughters, and other noble women of large estate families were proud of the textiles they made for their homes and as gifts to the church. Old English poems state that, "a woman's place is at her embroidery."[20] However, it is not certain that the high-ranking women always performed all the work; it is quite plausible that unfree women either assisted or had a greater role to play. Skilled slaves could be inherited, as Christine Fell observed from a tenth-century will bequeathing two female slaves—*ane crencestre* and *ane semester*—to a granddaughter. The former is a term linked to cloth production, the latter denotes a woman with sewing and embroidery skills.[21] It was probably most important that the textiles produced at the estate were of such a high quality as to accord both the women and the family high status, regardless of who produced them.

At the end of the ninth century, textile production changed, as vertical two-beam looms and the pin-beater (a small multifunctional weaving tool) became commonly used on the estates. According to Penelope Walton Rogers, double-ended pin-beaters are known from early Anglo-Saxon settlements onwards, found together with loom weights. The single-ended pin-beaters are generally associated with estates and later, towns. Single-ended pin-beaters increase in number in the tenth century at the same time as 2/1 twill became more common, replacing the production of simpler textiles. These changes indicate not only that new textile types became fashionable, but also that the adoption of a new loom type and the production of more complicated patterns first took place on estates.

In Scandinavia, changes in loom type similarly affected the location where the weaving took place: looms moved from public long houses to sunken-floor huts, a more separate specialist sphere. Textile analysis has also shown that multiple weavers worked at the wide two-beam looms, but warp-weighted looms in sunken-floor huts in Scandinavia are generally narrower and it is plausible that only one weaver at a time worked on these looms. Tools and fiber changes increased the thread density, and clothing design also changed (Figure 2.6).

Instead of being shaped on the loom, clothing was patterned and cut from woven yardage. All these changes took place over a long period of time and differ between regions and type of settlements. Archeological investigations indicate that changes first took place at larger farms.[22]

The eighth to eleventh centuries are difficult to study for many regions of Europe, as furnished burials disappear and extant texts and images are not numerous. Viking raids disrupted supplies and trade for at least a century in many areas. However, Scandinavian and Anglo-Saxon archeology have produced unique insights into this period, with better preservation of remains than elsewhere. Osteological analysis of bone remains as well as analysis of extant textiles attests that wool was the most common raw material used in

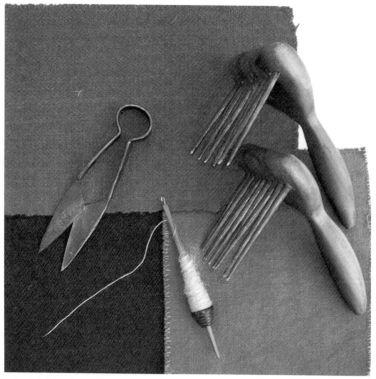

FIGURE 2.6: Tools and textiles reconstructed after Viking Age originals, ordinary Viking Age quality textiles. © Eva Andersson Strand.

Scandinavia in the eighth to eleventh centuries. It is unclear how much linen came from native flax cultivation of flax and how much was imported. Flax was certainly cultivated around the trade ports of Birka and Hedeby, presumably intended for textile manufacture there. There was demand for a wide variety of textiles ranging from everyday dress, furnishing, tapestries, sacks, bags, and sails.

Although at agrarian sites there is only evidence for household textile production,[23] one exception is Löddeköpinge (present-day Sweden) near the Viking Age ring-fort, Borgeby, considered a stronghold of a Danish king.[24] It is possible that textile production in Löddeköpinge increased due to political changes in the late tenth and early eleventh centuries, combined with a growing need for sailcloth. Leif Christian Nielsen has suggested that multiple settlements with sunken-floored huts near the Trelleborg ring-fort in Denmark were used for manufacturing sailcloth and clothing for the king's retinue, as well as to meet local demand for sailcloth and the clothing for the housecarls in nearby Borgeby.[25] The craftspeople of Löddeköpinge would thus have produced textiles beyond their needs, corresponding to the definition of a household industry.

The tools found at the Viking towns and ports of trade Åhus and Birka in Sweden, and Hedeby in present-day Germany, also suggest a more varied manufacture of textiles than on domestic sites. Textile tools were found all over the settlements—including a high proportion of light spindle whorls, probably used for fabrics with a high thread count, or for transparent veil-like cloth[26]—although there is no evidence of textile workshop areas. If specialist products were manufactured at Birka and Hedeby, it is likely that the work was organized on a level above the household production mode by craftspeople with specialist skills working full-time. The raw material was exclusive and could have been imported, suggesting the need for support by patrons. Certainly, textiles of consistently high quality are found in wealthy graves at Birka and Hedeby, such textiles would also have been desirable as gifts for living people.

Icelandic Production and Distribution

In Iceland—settled by Northmen during the ninth century with a rapid colonization process and a degree of centralized control[27]—information about dress and production can be extracted from texts such as the *Grágás*, a law text, the church inventory called *maldagarna*, and the Icelandic sagas. These testify that textile production was one of the main tasks of Icelandic women. Matrons probably organized the work, with family members, slaves, and employed weavers involved.[28] Helgi Þorláksson suggests that high-ranking women did not produce textiles for everyday use, instead they spun and embroidered.[29] In *Egil Skallagrimson's Saga*, a "*dyngja*" is mentioned, a room or house where women manufactured textiles. A *dyngja* could be identified when quantities of textile tools and loom weights are found in the same space, for instance the textile room found on the *Farm Beneath the Sand* on Greenland dated to the thirteen century.[30]

Homespun cloth, termed *vaðmál*, was one of Iceland's most important means of payment and trade in the medieval period (see Chapter 7). In the laws, women who worked at home would receive 25 percent more in salary than if they worked at the employer's farm. According to the *Búalög* price and wage collection, a spinner should produce 5.2 kilograms of spun wool a week, and a weaver 22 ells of fabric.[31] This is a high quantity, however, and it is more likely that weavers produced c. 1.5 ells a day, depending on the type of fabric.[32] Regulations specify that textile workers should have the possibility of focusing on their work undisturbed by other tasks, and further that they should be provided with good light.[33] Were these women professional craft workers? Marta Hoffmann observes that the use of the word *vefkona* (weaving women) rather than *vinnukona* (maid servant) suggests specialization.[34] Jenny Jochens considers the textile workers were professionals, earning their living from their work.[35] They clearly produced textiles for trade, sale and exchange, production beyond a household's needs.

HIGH MEDIEVAL DEVELOPMENTS

Across Europe, textile as well as garment production in towns became more specialized and divided at the end of eleventh century.[36] The question is, who controlled it? One interpretation for England and Scandinavia is that estate owners were still in charge, supplying textile workers with raw material and remunerating them. It may have been organized like a putting-out system with the advantage being the proximity to a market.[37] As towns developed, instead of one workshop where all production stages were performed, the work was divided among specialized crafts, such as weaving, dyeing, fulling, and also cutting and stitching. The larger the town, the greater the variety of specialists. Spinning was still done by women: there are descriptions of both female slaves spinning in workshops and wool and flax fibers being given out to be spun in the countryside, although silk spinning seems to have been reserved for noblewomen. At the end of the eleventh century, men and women are mentioned as weavers, but while men used a new type of loom, the horizontal treadle loom, women continued weaving on the well-known vertical looms. There is a major shift during this long period from self-sufficient, domestic household activity to a more commercially based and compartmentalized industry.

LATER MEDIEVAL DEVELOPMENTS

The Growth of Urban Trade Organization

The Arab conquest of the seventh and eighth centuries brought many changes to European trade. Europe's supply of silk, cotton, some flax, and many other luxury textiles and products was routed through or produced in the Muslim world. Under the Umayyad caliphate, Byzantine *gynaecea* were converted to *tiraz* workshops, particularly in Alexandria and Syria. *Tiraz* probably originally signified "embroidery," but over time the term came to denote bands woven with kufic script displaying the name of the ruling caliph, used as tokens of honor, as well as weaving workshops in general. The Fatimids also created workshops for clothing, tents, rugs, bedding, and other textiles for court use. Both types of workshops were strictly regulated by government officials, as in Byzantium. The raw materials were precious: silk, and gold and silver for weaving insignia with metallic threads.[38] Chrétien de Troyes' vision of hundreds of miserable, ill-clad women working in such a workshop, attached to a palace in his twelfth-century romance *Yvain* has been much discussed.[39] The Norman king Roger II of Palermo was known for his putting concubines and slave girls "to good use," as the *tiraz* production mode was well appreciated in the Sicilian kingdom as well[40] (Figure 2.7).

Consumers came to covet luxurious products from Spain in the tenth to twelfth centuries.[41] Trade routes between western Europe and the Islamic world were limited in these centuries,[42] but obstacles can increase desire. The caliphate of Córdoba ruled Al-Andalus, southern Spain and parts of North Africa, from 929 to 1031. Relatively rural and sparsely populated under the Umayyad emirate through the ninth century, with trade

FIGURE 2.7: An example of *tiraz* weaving given as an ambassadorial gift, Fatimid Egypt, 11th century. Woven silk on linen. The Metropolitan Museum of Art, New York.

regulated by Muslim law and confined largely to domestic production, industry and trade expanded considerably under the caliphate, supplying Europe with coveted silks, decorative *tiraz* bands and brocades, stamped cottons, embossed leathers, and other fashionable products such as rugs and coverlets (Figure 2.8).

A major advantage for trade was the extensive reach of Islamic law through the Mediterranean at this time, where *suks* (markets) were systematically regulated to verify quality and punish fraud. From the ninth century, there were organized craft corporations in Córdoba, grouped by profession in the town's geographic layout. Revenues enriched princes, who invested in commercial architecture. The marketplace for luxury objects, called *al-caicería*, was built to make shopping an esthetic pleasure, with spacious courtyards surrounded by porticos. Córdoba's jewelers rivaled Byzantium's and Baghdad's. The clothing market, the *markatal* (note the more Latinate name), was similar, accessed by a covered passage. The *Muhtasib* also supported industries such as weaving, dyeing, and tanning that required capital expenditures for equipment. Business owners supplied their own materials and employed qualified workers and apprentices, often working in partnership to share a store and costs. Their clerical staff regulated production and maintained consistency. Wholesale trade was monopolized by specialized merchants (*djallas*), intermediaries between artisans producing goods and the courtier-commissaries who ordered them (termed a *dallal*). For foreign merchants there were *funduk,* designated warehouses full of merchandize on the ground floor with storage above. *Suks* had stalls for ready-to-wear merchandize, as well as designated areas for the used trade. Buyers also could deliver yard goods to tailors to have clothes made. Advertising was effectuated by criers (*munadat*) for both new and second-hand goods.[43] There were dealers in fine linen underclothes, makeup artists, hairdressers, perfumers: those of means could embellish themselves with many fashionable options. The caliphate was fractured by civil war in the eleventh century, but similar business models appeared in Muslim and Norman Sicily

FIGURE 2.8: An example of Iberian silk weaving, thirteenth century. The Metropolitan Museum of Art, New York.

through the thirteenth century, in later kingdoms of Christian Spain (where some of these crafts survived or were revived), and later in many European towns.

Until the late twelfth century, there was little demand in eastern markets for western industrial goods. Then there was a dramatic change: high-quality Flemish, northern French, and to some degree English woolen cloths became the preferred export of Genoese, Pisan, and Venetian merchants. In return for these, heavy woolens, silks, alum, dyes (particularly the high-prestige kermes, or grain) as well as spices traveled back on the Italians' ships and pack animals. This new balance of trade marks an important moment in the development of the European fashion industry.[44] Records increase at a steady rate from the twelfth century, allowing scholars to study production and distribution from guild and craft records, notarial records, and some legal and tax documents. Inventories become useful tools from the late thirteenth century onwards, permitting insight into household consumption and distribution of garments and cloth to subordinates (liveries, see Chapter 6). Archeology is less dominant as a source for the twelfth to fifteenth centuries.

Venice was considered part of the Byzantine empire throughout the early Middle Ages. The emperors sent magistrates and directives to this Adriatic naval outpost, and there was a long tradition of political intermarriage. In 1171, there were some 10,000 Venetians at the *fondaco* (colonial outpost) in Constantinople. It was at about this time, in the twelfth century, that Venetians began to act independently from the eastern empire, engaging in international Mediterranean trade for their own gain. Venetian great galleys brought Levantine silks to Antwerp and Bruges in exchange for Flemish woolens and English wool. These convoys, termed *mudas*, were auctioned off annually to the highest bidder in Venice. Systems of credit emerged to deal with the risks involved in this trade, postponing payment until the *muda* returned successfully with its cargo.[45]

Genoa and Venice were fierce rivals, at war during four periods in the thirteenth and fourteenth centuries. Genoa and also Pisa were devastated by Arab raids in the eleventh century, but recovered to take control of many Mediterranean ports. The Pisans dominated the Tunisian trade, while Genoa interacted with Iberia, Sicily, and the Levant. The Genoese were the primary movers of raw silk, which was finished in various cities, notably Lucca, which produced rich brocades and damasks[46] (Figure 2.9).

Montpellier became the southern French and Iberian marketplace for these silks, as well as others coming from Byzantium and even Persia and China on Italian ships.[47] For markets to the north, the wholesale distribution centers were the fairs of Champagne, and also Lendit outside Paris.

FIGURE 2.9: An example of a rich silk lampas woven and finished in Lucca, fourteenth century. The Metropolitan Museum of Art, New York.

Buying, Selling, and Shopping

The Champagne fairs mark an important intermediate stage in the development of western fashionable commerce and banking techniques. Count Thibaut IV of Blois, count of Champagne, established charters promising safe-conduct to merchants beginning in 1137. Merchants were housed in designated temporary quarters, grouped by "nation" and language, making these fairs one of the ethnic meeting grounds of Europe. Fairs required significant capital investment: for Champagne this came from the counts, but in other areas it was financed by the Church (note the exaggerated importance of the prelates in Figure 2.10).

The term "fair" itself is linked to ecclesiastical institutions, signifying feast days ("*feria*"), to which the shopping calendar was tied. The fairs came to be held on a fixed annual cycle, for two weeks in each different town, assuring regular commerce: in January

FIGURE 2.10: A representation of the fair at Lendit, showing the temporary stalls, conversations between a variety of merchants, and how the wholesale woolens (*draps*) appeared, as well as the centrality of ecclesiastical sponsorship. From the Pontifical of Sens, fourteenth century. MS Lat. 962, fol. 264. Bibliothèque nationale de France.

in Lagny-sur-Marne, Bar-sur-Aube during Lent, Sézanne during Passion week, May in Provins, following St. John's Day in Troyes, in late September to October in Provins, and November to December in Troyes again. The initial weeks were devoted to merchandize display, followed by a period for purchase, and another for payment, although notarial records show that extended credit and payment periods came to exist.[48] The fairs closed with festivities, making this wholesale shopping experience pleasurable for merchants. The fairs existed through the fourteenth century, although by the end of the thirteenth Flemish shipping activity, competing with the Italian, was opening up new trade routes, and fairs in the Parisian region also provided competition.

Household records, such as those of countess Mahaut d'Artois in the early fourteenth century, offer some insight into how these woolens and silks in gross became wardrobes.[49] To provide clothing for her person, her children, and the thirty to forty members of her household for the twice-annual distributions of clothing (livrées) at All Saints' and Easter, Mahaut sent her treasurer, her tailor, or one of her "familiers" (the clerics in her circle of counselors) to buy wools, silks, and linen by the yard in large quantities, as well as furs prepared for use as linings. At times they went to the fair at Provins, or the towns of Douai, Ghent, Ypres, Arras, Saint-Omer, Hesdin, or Paris. The choice of colors and weaves was up to this delegate, although sometimes letters give general parameters. Like her father Robert, she kept a tailor in her employ for the construction of outer garments and hats. For underclothes, veils, and wimples, Parisian stitchers were sometimes employed; some of this was the work of the women at the court, as well. Gloves were purchased in town. Pins for hairdressing and attaching garments were also purchased in towns, by the thousands. The men on her staff were given a shoe allowance, so they must have ordered their shoes directly from cobblers. High-ranking men and knights in her employ also received wages, so they would have had spending money to choose some of their own outfits and accessories, and to clothe their retinues in turn. There were multiple models of garment production at work, in short. Interactions with merchants were delegated to lesser nobles attached to courts rather than handled by elites themselves.

Paris became the largest city in the West in the twelfth and thirteenth centuries. As it gradually became a Capetian capital and major university town, it also became a fashion center, ready to entice nobles, prelates, and a steadily growing merchant class with innovative products. It was a market for woolens from the north and silks from the Mediterranean. There was also manufacturing: a wool industry from at least the eleventh century, specializing in mid-level woolens called "biffes" by the thirteenth; a significant linen industry; a blended fabric called tiretaine, two kinds of tapestries for furnishings (using "Saracen" looms and domestic looms, the distinction between which remains uncertain); and small silk luxury items such as decorative purses (aumonières), belts, and head-dressing accessories.[50]

The first evidence of Parisian craft organization appears in the twelfth century, in 1160 when Louis VII conceded revenues to the group of leather artisans: tanners (tanneurs, baudroyeurs), stitchers (sueurs), tawers (mégissiers, who worked white leather such as goatskin), and purse makers (boursiers). King Philip II recognized several crafts, such as the drapers and furriers (pelletiers), with grants of groups of buildings in the 1180s.[51] In 1268, one of the first provosts of Paris, Etienne Boileau, appointed by Louis IX, gathered together the statutes and regulations of some hundred crafts (mestiers) in Paris. This, along with tax records from 1292–1313, forms a rich corpus for understanding medieval urban producers and distributors of fashionable goods (Figure 2.11).

FIGURE 2.11: Parisian textile and garment producers in the *Livre des Metiers*, 1268

Old French	English	ch.	description given	gender	sample regulations
Laceurs de fil et de soie	Linen and silk ribbon makers	34	made lacings (i.e. to adjust garments) and ribbons for various uses, including sealing documents	male/female	limit 1 apprentice, unless wife works too, then 2; no work by candlelight
Fillerresses de soye a grans fuiseaus	Silk spinners, large spindles	35	divide, spin, double and twist thread	female	limit 3 apprentices, unless own children, min. 7 years service
Fileresses de soie a petiz fuiseaux	Silk spinners, small spindles	36	divide, spin, double and twist thread	female	no work on holidays, limit 2 apprentices
Crespiniers de fil et de soie	Linen and silk fringe-makers	37	made ladies' *coiffes* (caps) and cushions and canopies for altars using needles and looms	male/female	1 apprentice; no work after the curfew bell rings at Saint-Merri
Ouvrières de tissuz de soie	Silk fabric workers	38	[decorated silk fabrics]	female	limit 2 apprentices, 6–10 years; fraudulent work mixed with linen must be burnt
Braaliers de fil	Linen underwear makers	39	[made braies, linen undergarments worn primarily by men]	male	must work in good white thread; no work on feasts of Apostles or Virgin
Ouvriers de draps de soie, de veluyaus, et de boursserie en lac	Silk, velvet, and brocade drapers	40	made the most important silks, velvets, and brocades used for purses	male	measures regulated by Châtelet; must work through guild master, not other bourgeois or merchants
Tesserandes de quevrechiers de soie	Silk kerchief weavers	44	[made women's veils]	female	no holiday work; 1 apprentice, 2 if family; no independent work by non-members
Toisserans de lange	Wool weavers	50	[Extensive statutes covered both drapers and dyers up to 1362, when they were divided]	male	only masters allowed to own looms; limit 2 wide and 1 narrow loom; may work with brothers, nephews; apprentices = min. 4 years service

Tapissiers de tapiz sarrasinois	Weavers of Saracen tapestries	51	[made thicker tapestries, cf. oriental rugs]	male	limit 1 outside apprentice, 8–10 years service; must use quality wool; women prohibited because work too arduous
Tapissiers de tapiz nostrez	Weavers of Parisian tapestries	52	[made narrower tapestries, probably smooth rather than piled]	male	unlimited valets, limit 2 apprentices, min 4 years service; must use quality wool, linen or hemp only for edges
Foulons	Fullers	53	[scour and mill/thicken woolens]	male/female	limit 2 outside apprentices; women must relinquish craft if they remarry a non-fuller
Tainturiers	Dyers	54	dye fabric in woad and other colorants	male	must use quality alum and mordants; no woad-dyer may weave
Chauciers	Hosiers	55	[made men's close-fitting leg coverings of linen, silk, or leather]	male/female	unlimited apprentices, no night work, no hawking ready-made garments in streets due to fraud, no Sunday sales
Tailleurs de robes	Clothiers/ tailors	56	cut wool outfits (*robe*= set of outer garments, including cote, surcot, and mantle)	male	unlimited valets and apprentices; masters regulate cases of bad tailoring
Liniers	Flax merchants	57	buy flax wholesale by weight, sell once prepared and ready to spin, dealing with transport	male/female	limit 1 apprentice, but unlimited female workers; no flax from Spain or Noyon
Marchans de chanvre et de file	Linen and hemp merchants	58	buy flax and hemp, once dried	male	unlimited valets and apprentices; servants may not engage in commerce, only wives and children
Chavenaciers	Canvas dealers	59	buy and sell *toile*, utilitarian cloth made in Normandy at market of Champeaux (Les Halles), handle transport	male	must not deal in napkins, tablecloths, or bags

(Continued)

FIGURE 2.11 Continued

Old French	English	ch.	description given	gender	sample regulations
Merciers	Mercers	75	sold and embellished fine fabrics, hats, hair accessories, *aumonières*, pins, laces (not allowed to manufacture)	male/female	two apprentices or workers; must use quality gold and silk thread
Frepiers	Used clothing dealers	76	buy and sell old robes, old wool, linen, and leather goods	male/female	must willingly testify before provost in cases of accusations, must not buy from thieves, no re-fulled wool
Boursiers et braiers	Leather purse and breeches makers	77	made bags and breeches of deerskin, pigskin, horse hide and sheepskin	male/female	leather must be tanned with good alum; limit 1 apprentice; report to master *sueur* (leather stitcher)
Baudroiers	Tanners	83	tanned and prepared leather for belts and shoe soles	male	limit 1 apprentice, except family member; no work after compline rings at Notre Dame
Cordouanniers	Cordwainers	84	made fine shoes and hose of cordovan leather	male/female	No sheepskin soles, no tanned kid; unlimited apprentices; widow could buy business
Çavetonniers de petits solers	Cobblers of slippers	85	made slippers from sheep and kidskin	male/female	Cordovan forbidden and burnt; widow could buy business
Çavetiers	Cobblers	86	made and repaired more modest quality shoes	male	fines for bad thread or leather
Corroiers	Curriers, belt makers	87	finished and fashioned leather tanned by *baudroiers* into belts and other objects	male/female	no female apprentices except daughters of members; only women married into profession may take apprentices; no night or candlelight work
Gantiers	Glovers	88	made gloves of sheepskin, deerskin, calf, *vair* and *gris* (imported squirrel)	male	deer and calfskin must be tanned with alum; used leather forbidden

Chapeliers de fleurs	Floral hatmakers	90	made hats and circlets with floral and herbal materials	female	day and night work allowed, no Sunday work; no watch duty, since work destined for noble clients
Chapeliers de feutre de Paris	Felt hatmakers	91	made felt hats of pure lambswool	male	no early morning or night work; no Sunday sales except by turn
Chapeliers de coton de Paris	Cotton hatmakers	92	made hats of cotton and animal fibers	male	unlimited valets and apprentices, allowed to work nights
Chapeliers de paon de Paris	Plumed hatmakers	93	made hats with peacock plumes and metallic accents	male/female	must use quality bronze
Fesserresse de chappeaux d'or et d'œuvres a un pertuis	Orfrey hatmakers	95	made women's headdresses decorated with gold orfrey bands and beads	female	must work in daylight; work on parchment or muslin considered fraudulent

Certain crafts, however, do not appear in these regulations—furriers, for instance, who were nonetheless numerous. Janice Archer has shown that silk work was a women's preserve, and that many single as well as married women made their livings in cloth and clothing-related occupations. Beguines (religious women living in loosely organized communities) often supported themselves through stitching, spinning, purse-making, and other types of textile production.[52] As professions became increasingly remunerative, men tended to enter them, as was the case for embroidery.[53]

Towns similarly grew in England, Wales, and Scotland from the eleventh to thirteenth centuries, from some 100 to 830 by 1300. As across Europe, there was a rural exodus as town employment or the hopes of attracting a broader clientele to one's craft attracted people seeking to better their position. Some English industrial villages consisted entirely of weavers, but lacked much variety in services, which had to be sought in market towns, where commerce was organized on a temporary basis on certain days of the week, attracting itinerant merchants. London, like Paris, was a center for luxury trades and goods, with some 175 crafts practiced in the later Middle Ages.[54] In such cities, one could shop any day of the week, evidenced by regulations enforcing closure on certain holidays or Sundays for various professions: there was constant demand for new hose, kerchiefs, and floral wreaths (Figure 2.12).

Shopping was rarely a one-stop process: fabric had to be taken to tailors and/or stitchers, and coordinated with finishing items. Some tailors were quite poor, but some distinguished themselves by producing flattering clothing and being trustworthy with expensive cloth, becoming quite wealthy: some of these could be found among the goldsmiths on the Great Bridge in Paris. In London, the tailors' guild was also associated with the linen-armorers, who provided the padded garments worn under metal armor. By the fifteenth century, their group included some wealthy merchants, showing how entrepreneurs might gain by connecting different crafts, industries, and clients.[55]

One type of merchant that emerged to better facilitate the shopping process for individual customers was the mercer. Itinerant mercers brought goods to nobles on their estates, and villages in the countryside. In the city, their shops offered a single place to choose accessories, as well as "notions" and decorative trims for finishing, updating, and personalizing garments made in the household, received as gifts, or bought used. In London, there was a large area called the Mercery, which held several *selds* or covered bazaars, as well as streets packed with small shops (as many as 200) and as taverns. Merchants and silkwomen there sold a wide range of goods: expensive silks and linens, worsted beddings, yard goods, and accessories. Some mercers rose to an increasingly dominant position among the Merchant Adventurers of England in the fifteenth century as they coordinated trade with Holland, Zeeland, Brabant, and Flanders, taking great risks in hopes of gain (this is the sense of "adventure"), later achieving a monopoly on English exports.[56]

Fripperers (French *fripiers*) also filled a significant shopping need. As nobles and wealthier bourgeois discarded wardrobes, often gifting items to servants, garments that did not fit or suit recipients might be sold to permit other purchases. For customers, this could be a way to get ready-made clothing quickly, bypassing the drapers and tailors. Parisian tax records show that some used clothing dealers were quite poor, paying the minimum tax contribution. They probably provided cheap clothing as well as repairs and alterations for those in a similarly modest social position. Some were quite wealthy, however. One such group was located in the streets facing les Halles in Paris. *Fripiers* with special rights granted by the grand chamberlain were called *haubaniers*. In London,

FIGURE 2.12: A tailor's shop, fourteenth century. The tailor takes measurements, while a male and female stitcher construct garments. Note the different garments on the clothes-pole: hoods, bags, hose, and coats. From an illustrated *Tacuinum Sanitatis*, Bibliothèque nationale de France. MS nouv acq. Lat 1673 fol. 95r.

certain fripperers were active in civic and social life.[57] This could be a highly remunerative and fairly respected occupation. Etienne Boileau's statutes do contain several pages of concerns about receiving stolen merchandize and fraud, but this testifies to a desire on the part of many to maintain good reputations.

Households had to be careful with resources. Although it was expected that nobles assert their social position with splendid dress, and with new garments for every great social occasion as seen in later medieval inventories, this came at great cost: they were constantly in debt to Jewish and Lombard lenders. Likewise, in more modest households, the renewal of wardrobes and coveting of pretty things presented constant challenges. In an advice book purportedly written by an older husband to a young wife c. 1393, the writer counsels the wife and her Beguine to constantly inspect the sheets, blankets, dresses, cloaks, and fur linings for damage, airing them in the sun in good weather and keeping them under cover in the damp season, protecting them from vermin, and treating grease and wine stains appropriately (II.iii.11). Stitchers and shoemakers fall into his second category of servants, those who work for the household for a precise period of time with a specific task (II.iii.1). The writer offers pages of recipes and home remedies, but there is no real sewing advice: he does not seem to expect the wife to sew for the household herself. Nor does he expect her to shop completely independently for fabric, shoes, or various other household provisions, but should consult with the men ("gens") in her service concerning price and payment negotiations (II.iii.3).[58]

CONCLUSION

The Middle Ages saw a broad range of production modes, from that of basic household needs in rural settlements in the early Middle Ages to sophisticated workshops specializing in large quantities of specialized textiles for the export market in the later medieval periods. Distribution methods shifted over time, but continuously employed sea vessels to move clothing materials around the Mediterranean and later around the North Sea. Over a thousand years, the population diminished and then gradually expanded again, with many towns growing or indeed created as cloth production and trade permitted new types of employment. While some clothwork was reserved for women throughout this period, as cities and wealth grew the females in the house were no longer directly responsible for all cloth or garment production. They could, however, make a living on their own by textile work, as could men. When there was significant money to be made in textile production and garment trades, we see men dominant in both production and leadership.

ACKNOWLEDGEMENTS

Eva Strand Andersson kindly thanks Ulla Mannering and Ulla Lund Hansen for their constructive criticism, Cherine Munkholt and Ariel Rosenblum for their excellent suggestions and proofreading, and a special thank you to Mary Harlow for her editorial advice. This chapter is written with the support from the Danish National Research Foundation's Centre for Textile Research, Copenhagen University (DNRF 64).

CHAPTER THREE

The Body

GUILLEMETTE BOLENS AND SARAH BRAZIL

The historian Jacques Le Goff writes that "the body provided medieval society with one of its principal means of expression . . . Medieval civilization was one of gestures." In the next paragraph, he adds, "Clothing was of even greater social significance."[1] Our purpose is to study the medieval body from the vantage point of these two most relevant aspects, gesture and clothing, linked together. Reminding us that "spectacles were only invented late in the thirteenth century," Le Goff also claims that the sense of touch was of central importance to medieval people.[2] Touch is a crucial sense if we are to better understand the way in which medieval people felt bodily. In her introduction to *A Cultural History of the Human Body in the Medieval Age*, Monica Green raises the question, "What did the medieval body look like?"[3] In turn, we wish to ask, "How did the medieval body feel (like)?" That is to say, what can we find in medieval documents, discourse, and art that may give us a sense of the way in which medieval people experienced embodiment sensorially and perceptually. We will grapple with this complex cultural question by considering issues of skin, clothes, and gestures; hygiene, care, and cure; silhouette, gait, and girdles. We will consider how clothing impacts the way humans move and relate to each other and to themselves.

BALANCE, TOUCH, AND CARE

Clothing shapes the way we perceive a body. It also fashions the way we sense our own body. To begin with, the nature of a fabric induces tactile perceptions that impact the way we feel in a most straightforward way. The *Tacuinum Sanitatis* ("Table of health") is a Latin translation (1254–66) of the health treatise written by the eleventh-century Iraqi physician Ibn Butlan, which was remarkably illuminated in northern Italy between the late fourteenth and early fifteenth century.[4] In it, the captions of two illuminated plates describe the sensation of wool and of linen on the skin.[5]

> Plate XLVI. Woolen clothing (*Vestis lanea*)
> *Nature*: Warm and dry. *Optimum*: The thin kind from Flanders. *Usefulness*: It protects the body from cold and holds warmth. *Dangers*: It causes skin irritation. *Neutralization of the Dangers*: With thin linen clothing. (*Casanatense MS*, f. CCVI)
> Plate XLVII. Linen clothing (*Vestis linea*)
> *Nature*: Cold and dry in the second degree. *Optimum*: The light, splendid, beautiful kind. *Usefulness*: It moderates the heat of the body. *Dangers*: It presses down on the skin and blocks transpiration. *Neutralization of dangers*: By mixing it with silk. *Effects*: It dries up ulcerations. It is primarily good for hot temperaments, for the young, in Summer, and in the Southern regions. (*Vienna MS*, f. 105v)

The version of the *Tacuinum Sanitatis* attributed to Ellbochasim de Baldach (another version of Ibn Butlan's name) states that "*Tacuinum Sanitatis* explains the six things necessary to clarify the benefits of food, of drinks, and of clothing, their dangers and the neutralization of those dangers, according to the advice of the wisest men among the ancients."[6] One of the pervading aims of medieval health and lifestyle is balance and moderation. Balance is a goal in the theory of humors, which dominates all medieval treatises on hygiene and health, including the *Tacuinum Sanitatis*. In the latter, the entries *Dangers* and *Neutralization of dangers* delineate this constant preoccupation, which applies indifferently to food, temperature, clothing, everyday life practices (such as making pasta or ricotta), or activities (such as fencing or taking a walk), or to emotions. For example, joy, *gaudium* (Vienna MS, f. 104v), is useful as it provides "a profound feeling of well-being." But it presents the danger of "causing death if experienced too often." Its neutralization comes from "living with wise people."[7]

In *The Regimen of the Body*, written in the thirteenth century by Aldobrandino da Sienna (d. c. 1287) at the request of Beatrix de Savoie, moderation and the right measure are the way to retrieve and maintain health.[8] All self-care and curing gestures must follow the measure adapted to one's temperament and complexion, whether in feeding, sleeping, or having sex—there is a danger in having too much as well as not enough sex.[9] As for bathing "*en estuves et en cuves*" [in steam rooms and in vats], one should "not stay too long in them, but just enough time to wash his body and clean himself from the dirt that Nature hides through the apertures of the flesh," *les pertruis de le char*, i.e., skin pores.[10] One should be clean but not excessively so.

Caring and curing involve touch, as appears in the illumination of a doctor palpating a patient in Figure 3.1. The patient, standing and fashionably clad in tight hose, sleeves, and hood, lifts his *cote* to allow a sitting physician to feel his abdomen. In Aldobrandino's *Regimen*, care for pregnant women includes massaging their feet and hands.[11] As for the newly born, advice concerning the umbilical cord (called *boutine*) suggests the use of a twisted thread of wool and a cloth dipped in oil.[12] This gesture of intimate care confers wool with the vital function of tying the umbilical cord until it dries up and falls off.

The *Trotula* is a Latin compendium of three Salernitan texts on women's medicine, which "circulated throughout Europe from the late twelfth century to the end of the fifteenth century."[13] It begins with a passage that articulates the question of care for gynecological patients, a question rarely addressed so explicitly in medieval written discourse, generally conscious of men:

> Women, from the condition of their fragility, out of shame and embarrassment do not dare reveal their anguish over their diseases (which happen in such a private place) to a physician. Therefore, their misfortune, which ought to be pitied, and especially the influence of a certain woman stirring my heart, have impelled me to give a clear explanation regarding their diseases in caring for their health.[14]

Among the numerous treatments (some for men as well) gathered in the *Trotula*, one explains how to sew a third-degree perineal tear with a silk thread after delivery.[15] Other treatments are cosmetic or hygienic, such as the recipe to whiten the teeth: "Take burnt white marble and burnt date pits, and white natron, a red tile, salt, and pumice. From all of these make a powder in which damp wool has been wrapped in a fine linen cloth. Rub the teeth inside out."[16]

Hippocratic and Galenic principles of humoral balance pervade the *Trotula* and serve to account for male and female fertility issues:

Conception is impeded as much by the fault of the man as by the fault of the woman. The fault of the woman is double: either excessive warmth or humidity of the womb. For the womb at times, because of its natural slipperiness, is unable to retain the seed injected into it. And sometimes from its excessive humidity it suffocates the seed. And sometimes she is unable to conceive because of the excessive heat of the womb burning the semen.[17]

Men's turn: "If conception is impeded because of the fault of the man, either this comes about from a defect of the spirit impelling the seed, or from a defect of spermatic humidity, or from a defect of heat."[18] Decoctions, unguents, fumigations, and specific food are then recommended—for instance, onions and parsnip, which are said to help generate more semen. Monica Green rightly stresses that the societies which produced these texts "saw a different body than we do, not necessarily because the physical body itself differed significantly, but because their intellectual structures of explanation and their social objectives in controlling the body differed. The task of the history of medicine is to reconstruct an image of the world that they saw, a sensation of the body as they experienced it."[19] Through the humoral system, the body is experienced, explained, and cared for in terms of a lost and regained balance.[20]

FIGURE 3.1: Physician examining a patient's abdomen, from *Liber notabilium Philippi septimi francorum regis, a libris Galieni extractus*, by Guy of Pavia, 1345. Vellum. Chantilly, Musée Condé (Ms. 334, f. 272). © RMN-Grand Palais (domaine de Chantilly)/René-Gabriel Ojéda.

GAITS AND GESTURES

Balance also shows in a person's look, gait, and general allure. In Jean de Meun's continuation of Guillaume de Lorris's *Roman de la Rose* (c. 1235/1275), the Old Woman claims that a woman should not shut herself up in her house but rather let people know about her beauty:

> Et quant a point se sentira
> Et par les rues s'en ira
> Si soit de beles aleüres,
> Non pas trop moles ne trop dures,
> Trop ellevees ne trop courbes,
> Mais bien plaisanz en toutes tourbes.
> Les espaules, les costez mueve
> Si noblement que l'en ne trueve
> Nulle de plus bel mouvement,
> Et marche jolivetement
> De ses biaus sollerez petiz
> Que faire avra faiz si faitiz
> Qu'el joindront au pié si a point
> Que fronce n'i avra point.[21]

> When she is well turned out and goes through the streets, she should carry herself well, neither too stiffly nor too loosely, not too upright nor too bent over, but easily and graciously in any crowd. She should move her shoulders and sides so elegantly that no one might find anyone with more beautiful movements. And she should walk daintily in her pretty little shoes, so well made that they fit her feet without any wrinkles whatever.[22]

The tongue-in-cheek style of Jean de Meun in his part of the *Roman de la Rose* suggests to take this advice with caution, all the more so that it is provided by the Old Woman, ever ready to compromise women's virtue. It remains, however, that the imperative of moving well, as vague as it may sound, was topical in the Middle Ages as in other historical periods.[23] The question, of course, is to decide what the meaning of *well* is, depending on the context, whether amorous or religious—of which more later.

In any case, sartorial and kinesic qualities were read together as vectors of personal and social distinction. This is perceptible in the illuminations of *Les Très Riches Heures du duc de Berry* (1411–16). In Figure 3.2, the backs of the nobles are emphatically straight—a fact enhanced by the perfectly vertical lines drawn by the long hanging sleeves and golden ornaments of the woman riding on the second horse. This highlighted verticality contrasts with the slanted posture of the peasant on foot, who twists his neck backwards and reverts his gaze up toward the first rider. In addition, the man's naked legs appear under his clothes. This type of partial nakedness is regularly associated with labor and the lower estate. In the background of the same image, peasants harvest in a field and cool off in a river. The swimmers' postures are stark counterexamples of aristocratic idealized postures: they are eminently non-vertical, and exposed in all possible ways (skin and posture), in particular that of the man with legs apart, swimming on his back.

The changes in sartorial styles that took place in fourteenth-century courtly milieus did not so much expose more skin as they exhibited the vertical lines of the limbs and

FIGURE 3.2: Pol, Jean, and Hermann Limbourg, The Calendar, the month of August, from the *Très Riches Heures du duc de Berry*, 1411–16. Vellum. Chantilly, Musée Condé (Ms 65, f. 8v). © RMN-Grand Palais (domaine de Chantilly)/René-Gabriel Ojéda.

stretched the body into elongated silhouettes.[24] In these stylistic variations, the shape (not the skin) of masculine legs is on display in a tight-fitting hose, extended into *poulaines*. The chest is held straight by a padded *pourpoint* (or quilted doublet) that flattens the belly, augments the rib cage, and makes it difficult to *not* hold oneself straight.[25] The male body expands upwards, starting from long and thin shoes evolving toward a bulging and erect upper chest, while the female chest is narrowed into a close-fitted corsage underlined by a high belt, and expands downwards into a prolific gown that ends in an ever longer *traîne*.[26] This gendered dynamic in clothing is manifest in the illustrations of *Renaut de Montauban*. In Figure 3.3, men's legs are strikingly thin, ending in *poulaines* so long that they trespass onto the lady's *traîne*. Tubular hats further lengthen men's silhouettes, and their walking sticks enhance the verticality of their posture. Towering *hennins* and padded horned headdresses equally elongate women's silhouettes.

In the fifteenth-century painted glass of the Hôtel de la Bessée at Villefranche-sur-Saône (c. 1430–40) (Figure 3.4), Édouard II de Beaujeu and the daughter of Guyonnet de La Bessée, a member of a wealthy Villefranche family, display an acute awareness of the latest fashion in town. The lady's divided *hennin* is a mix between padded horns and conic hennin, taking headdress fashion to striking heights.

FIGURE 3.3: David Aubert, View of a garden, from the *Renaut de Montauban Cycle*, 1462–70. Vellum. Paris, Bibliothèque nationale de France (Ms. 5072, f.270v). © BnF, Dist. RMN-Grand Palais/image BnF.

FIGURE 3.4: Painted glass depicting chess players, from the Hôtel de la Bessée in Villefranche-sur-Saône, c. 1450. Paris, Musée de Cluny—Musée national du Moyen Âge. © RMN-Grand Palais (Musée Cluny—Musée national du Moyen Âge)/Jean-Gilles Berizzi).

The man wears a *chaperon* covered with trendy dagged tails,[27] his sleeves are baggy with narrow cuffs, his shoes are apparently already becoming round-toed, and his leather pouch is on display.[28] This accessory, called an *aumônière*, was a locus of ostentation *as* accessory (here matching the rest of the outfit), linked to its function of purse, and "making spending money . . . a centerpiece of the toilette."[29] The lady wears a divided *hennin* on an extensively plucked forehead, the size and shape of which make it necessary to hold one's head up; she has an open collar, a high waistline, and an impractical gown made of a vast quantity of fabric—another signal of wealth. Most interestingly, the sitters are playing chess. While this iconographic motif is not new, the painted window exploits the erotic valence of the traditional motif (see the lady's central pleats in the early fourteenth-century example of this motif, Figure 3.5) with local jet-set people dressed in the latest fashion. The chess game iconographic code is used in new ways in this artwork, to elicit a semiotic understanding of the situation along with the perception of novel connotations associated with the fact that seduction is now also expressed via fashion statements.

The same is true of gesture in this representation. The man's typical hand under the chin posture and the lady's raised hand are coded signs pervasive throughout medieval

FIGURE 3.5: Mirror case depicting a game of chess, c. 1300, ivory. Paris, Musée du Louvre. © RMN-Grand Palais (Musée du Louvre)/Daniel Arnaudet.

art. The first conveys sadness and concern, and the meaning of the second ranges from increased attention to radical shock.[30] While this is the case, the other hand of both protagonists creates a more complex narrative. The lady's left hand touches the sleeve of her opponent, suggesting that her surprise is mild at best, and that physical contact is in order (a possibility apparently already enacted at the level of feet); while Édouard's leaning posture on his elbow seems to increase proximity rather than express sorrow—all the more so that he is taking his opponent's queen pawn, thus winning the day and, perhaps, his game partner's favors. This representation exhibits the way in which clothing organizes contact gestures and their narratives. Gestures and clothes have expressive valences. These valences are coded, and it is this very codification that provides a lever to communicate unexpected alternatives—in true fashion spirit.[31]

RELIGIOUS IMPERATIVES

In Psalm 14, the question is asked to know who will dwell in the Lord's tabernacle. The elect's first listed quality is, "He that walketh without blemish" (*Qui ingreditur sine macula*) (Ps 14:2).[32] The meaning of a "stainless gait"—another version of *moving well*—is metaphorical and refers to an irreproachable behavior. But metaphors always evince as well as impact cultural conceptions, and it was relevant to medieval mentalities to think that a person's ethical quality could show in his or her gait. Countenance and kinesis—by which we mean the style of a person's movements and gestures in interaction—were clearly seen as a paramount expression of personality.[33] Kinesis was thus a major focus of attention, as it linked such central concepts as *incessus* (gait), *vultus* (facial expression, countenance), *gestus* (gesture), *motus* (movement), and *habitus*.[34] Andrea Denny-Brown highlights the importance of the Aristotelian concept of *habitus* in relation to habit or clothing: "*habitus* connotes simultaneously the subject's garments and his overall condition of being."[35] The terms *habitus* and *vultus* are used together by Boethius and Alain de Lille to express a dramatic change of fate.[36] They also appear in a striking passage of the English *Life of Christina of Markyate* (first part of the fourteenth century), which synthesizes the correlation and extreme relevance of these notions in medieval mentalities.

The hermit Roger, finally convinced by Christina's religious excellence, consents to let her live in a cell near his, although he refuses to see or speak to her, owing to external suspicion and social pressure.

> Nevertheless they saw each other the same day; and it happened in this way. The virgin of God lay prostrate [*prostrata iacebat*] in the old man's chapel, with her face turned to the ground [*demersa facie ad terram*]. The man of God stepped over her with his face averted [*averso vultu*] in order not to see her. But as he passed by he looked over his shoulder to see how modestly the handmaid of Christ had composed herself for prayer [*sese composuisset ad orandum*], as this was one of the things which he thought those who pray ought to observe. Yet she, at the same instant, glanced upwards to appraise the bearing and deportment of the old man [*ad videndum incessum et habitum senis*], for in these she considered that some trace [*vestigium*] of his great holiness was apparent.[37]

This scene depicts in detail the kinesic event of a shared glance and presents it as a turning point in the narrative. Remarkably, the narrator provides a rationale for the protagonists' mutual peek: both consider that composure in such a gesture as prayer, as well as gait (*incessus*) and bearing (*habitus*) convey the signs or trace (*vestigium*) of the person's essential value and merit. Equally notable is the distinction between *facies* and *vultus*. *Facies* is the organ, the side of the head where the eyes, the nose, and the mouth are located, while *vultus* is the expressive space this area becomes when it moves, perceives, and communicates. For example, the three-word sentence "*vultus propalabat hilaritas*" calls for the following translation, "the immense joy [which filled her at the thought of her freedom] was displayed for all to see in the cheerfulness of her countenance."[38]

Facies is physical, *vultus* is kinesic, relational. The same distinction applies to clothing. Clothing is both and at the same times pieces of fabric stitched together *and* the manifestation of a person's *habitus*. As such, it can be the locus of crucial interactional events. In the *Life of Christina of Markyate*, clothing is highly expressive of events taking place between protagonists. After an empowering vision of the Virgin Mary, Christina walks past the man who persecutes her and wants to force her into marriage and intercourse.

> And where she had to go down, there lay Burthred prostrate on the ground [*iacebat prostratus super pavimentum*] swathed in a black cape [*atra circumamictus cappa*] with his face turned downwards [*versus faciem ad terram*]. And as soon as he saw her passing by he stretched out his hand to seize her and hold her fast. But she, gathering her garments about her and clasping them close to her side [*Illa vero colligens et stringens ad se vestimenta sua*], for they were white and flowing [*que habebat candidissima et subtus ampla*], passed him untouched [*pertransibat intacta*]. And as she escaped from him, he followed her with staring eyes, groaning horribly, and struck his head with repeated blows on the pavement to show his rage.[39]

The black cape of the wicked man and the immaculate garments of the pure woman are unambiguous signs, which are, however, interestingly dramatized by means of gestures. Indeed, prostration in Christina is read as proper composure in prayer, while in her persecutor prostration conveys threat, when a sudden hand extends from under his dark cloak to snatch the virgin's ankle as she passes. At this point, she stringently wraps herself in her super white garment (*candidissima*) in a cinematic and protective movement that brings its ample folds around her body and leaves her untouched, intact (*intacta*), while Burthred is reduced to banging his head against the floor in angered frustration. In stark contrast to the latter's emotionally debilitating display, religious conduct was associated with an authoritative sense of self-control, which could be not only expressed but also supported by specific pieces of clothing, such as Christina's white garment in this instance.

In this regard, an interesting case in point in monastic wear is the girdle. Monks such as John Cassian in the fifth century, who greatly influenced western monastic asceticism, wrote about the preeminent role clothing held in keeping the brethren from the temptation of illicit desire.[40] The girdle in particular is continually cited as the item which not only can achieve this for the body, but also for the mind.[41] The girding of loins, which in a biblical sense meant to make oneself ready for work or battle, implied securing clothing with a belt somewhere between the haunches and rib cage.[42] However, the loins in this Christian sense pointedly include the sexual organs, the area in most need of control subsequent to the Fall. And while the girdle itself would have been placed matter-of-factly around the waist, it was proffered as impacting both the mental and physical demeanor of the person.[43] Cassian writes:

As we are going to speak of the customs and rules of the monasteries, how by God's grace can we better begin than with the actual dress of the monks, for we shall then be able to expound in due course their interior life when we have set their outward man before your eyes. A monk, then, as a soldier of Christ ever ready for battle, ought always to walk with his loins girded.[44]

As Cassian outlines, the correlation between interior and exterior is efficiently communicated by the look of the monk, whose girding controls posture and behavior, and manifests his mental and bodily purity. The biblical—and more specifically Old Testament—senses of girding are here maintained and transformed when presenting the monk as "a soldier of Christ," with their fight being waged spiritually, and thus their girding also rendered in a context that locates it between the literal and figurative.

The monk Smaragdus wrote a commentary on the Benedictine Rule in the tenth century. He also premised the girdle as a vital accessory to the monk's daily struggle. In his *Prologue*, he describes the girdle as a double stranded item, outlining the dual function it performs:

Therefore with our loins girded with faith and the observance of good deeds. Here most elegantly and in prophetic fashion, the blessed father Benedict posited the double belt proper to monks. He knew *faith without works is dead* and works without faith are empty. And so he wanted the monks' belt to be, not simple but woven out of both of these.[45]

According to Benedict, who Smaragdus names as the designer of the girdle, the monk is never correctly performing a devotional act if the mind and body are not cooperating, with one being totally reliant upon the other in order to succeed. Belief and action are thus the dual aspects of the monk's commitment, with the girdle not merely signifying this, but also helping to realize it. Smargadus, like Cassian, furthermore mentions the importance of gait in this process: "For Sacred Scripture addresses as men those who walk the Lord's way with strong and not slack steps [*qui vias domini fortibus et non dissolutis gressibus ambulant*]. Now to gird one's loins manfully is to curb the impurity of the flesh and of the mind, whether in deed or thought."[46] The girdle is thus intended to affect gait, curb physical and mental desires, and overall promote self-control toward efficacious action.

The religious imperative of radical self-control could lead to self-inflicted violence. "Mortification of the flesh—wearing hair shirts, going barefoot, minimal washing, extreme dietary abstinence—might be self-inflicted or might be imposed as penance."[47] Women proved terribly efficient in this area, as their "body was seen as pervious and excessive and [their] character both corruptible and corrupting."[48] Through ascetic movements, models developed "of sanctity based on sealing the body within strict physical and spiritual boundaries" and on shutting it down entirely.[49] Mortification of the flesh often gave way to drastic skin mistreatments. However, an interesting passage from the early thirteenth-century West-Midlands *Guide to Anchoresses* shows an effort to channel such tendencies:

Nobody should wear linen next to the skin unless it is made of stiff and coarse fibers. Anyone who wishes may wear an undergarment of rough wool; anyone who wishes may do without one. You should sleep in a robe, and wearing a belt, but so loosely fastened that you can put your hands under it. Nobody should wear a belt of any kind next to her skin except with her confessor's permission, or wear anything made of iron or hair or hedgehog skins, or beat herself with them, or with a scourge weighted with lead, with holly or with thorns, or draw blood, without her confessor's permission. She should not sting herself anywhere with nettles, or scourge the front of her body, or mutilate herself with cuts, or take excessively severe disciplines at any one time in order to subdue temptation.[50]

In other words, moderation is in order in mortification as much as in other practices and self-treatments. Incidentally, it is noteworthy that, next to beating one's skin with hedgehog skins, drawing blood should be listed as a practice potentially used for mortification. The medical gesture meant to retrieve humoral balance could thus be abused by immoderate application.

The queen of the Franks and abbess of Poitiers, Radegund (c. 525–87) was not into moderation, and her biographer "shudder[s] to speak of the pain she inflicted on herself."[51] She chained herself so tightly that her flesh swelled up and enclosed the iron, forcing her to tear her bleeding body open to unchain herself. "On another occasion, she ordered a brass plate made, shaped in the sign of Christ. She heated it up in her cell and pressed it upon her body most deeply in two spots so that her flesh was roasted through. Thus, with her spirit flaming, she caused her very limbs to burn."[52] This is followed by even worse treatments, and it is explained how "she drew it to herself, so that she might be a martyr though it was not an age of persecution."[53] She devised "terrible agony to torture herself," which ultimately turned her into a saint capable of performing miracles. One of her miracles takes place in a bath:

> A certain *monacha* shivered with cold by day and burned with fire by night through an entire year. And when she had lain lifeless for six months, unable to move a step, one of her sisters told the saint of this infirmity. Finding her almost lifeless, she bade them prepare warm water and had the sick woman brought to her cell and laid in the warm water. Then she ordered everyone to leave, remaining alone with the sick woman for two hours as a doctor. She nursed the sick limbs, tracing the form of her body from head to foot. Wherever her hands touched, the sickness fled from the patient and she who had been laid in the bath by two persons got out of it in full health.[54]

The tortures Ragemund inflicted onto her body gave her the power to cure incurable illnesses. She is compared to a doctor, and her hand tracing and feeling the form and limbs of her bathed patient evinces the experience of caring and curing via gesture and touch in a mystical religious context: "Wherever her hands touched, the sickness fled from the patient."

Her superpowers were transferred to her haircloth, functioning as a relic.[55] Sorrowing parents decided to wrap their stillborn baby in the saint's haircloth, and "as soon as the infant's body touched the most medicinal garment and those noble rags, he came back from the dead to normal life. Blushing away from his tomblike pallor, he rose from the mantle."[56] As will be further discussed, contact with a saint's skin could transfer holiness to objects, thus turned into relics and made potent with curing capacities.

In the biography of St. Rupert written by the Rhenish abbess Hildegard of Bingen (1098–1179), clothing has a highly significant and expressive function. Once freed from the bond of marriage, St. Rupert's mother, Bertha, takes her son to a place "where now her relics and those of blessed Rupert rest. There she built a church. She cast off her expensive and showy clothes and gave no further thought to the prestige of her lineage and wealth. She wore poor clothing of rough material, tied with a cincture."[57] Raising her child in religion, the latter became a man who longed—literally, panted—for God very intently: *"homo, qui diligentissima intentione ad Deum anhelat."*[58] In his twelfth year, Rupert decided to abide by the biblical exhortation "When you see a naked person, cover him, and don't despise your own flesh" (Is. 58:7).[59] He had a dream where an old man was bathing boys in clear water, and dressing them in beautiful clothes. Because Rupert wishes to join the heavenly party straightaway, the man prompts him to first perform his mission for the poor. For, "by feeding and clothing them, you may be nourished by the food of life and put on the clothing that Adam took off through disobedience. By becoming a stranger to the world in your mind you may choose for yourself the better part."[60] The question of care is articulated in this *Vita* in three correlated ways: self-care consists in alienating oneself from the world by wearing the habit of religion; care for the poor means covering their nakedness; and self-care in the form of charity to the poor is a way of resuming Adam's primal clothing.[61] In the three instances, clothing is central and conveys the stakes of protagonists' spiritual and salvific goal.

THE MADONNA'S CARING TOUCH

Clothing was intrinsic to the identity and worship of the Virgin Mary in late medieval Europe, and was a central point of contact particularly between the Mother of God and her female devotees. Typically, Hildegard of Bingen compares Rupert's caring mother, Bertha, to the Virgin Mary: when Rupert was born, she "wrapped him in swaddling clothes, just as the blessed mother of God, Mary, did her son."[62] But more than just a figure of ideal motherhood, Mary was a Madonna in all modern senses of the name, and dominated iconography for her own sake, such was her power and status in the Middle Ages. She was principally recognizable through her regal apparel and signature blue *qua* celestial mantle, and gave medieval women more to aspire to than her traditionally lauded attributes of virginity, humility, and gentleness. In her they could also see elegance, poise, and beauty, which exceptionally was not suspect to patriarchal anxiety, moral treatises about excessive eyebrow and forehead plucking, or sumptuary regulations relating to the amount and quality of fabric worn. Mary was Queen of Heaven, and as such could pull off the most sumptuously decorated kirtle or daring red shoe, with the numerous folds of clothing announcing her proximity to the divine and her role in producing the savior of mankind, not excessive pride or vanity.[63] Miri Rubin attests to the power that was attributed to the Virgin from the earliest instances, noting that in Constantinople "Mary was presented as an imperial figure: finely dressed, frontal, central and sometimes surrounded by angels and saints as attendants; in Rome she emerged as *Maria Regina*, a queenly figure bedecked in royal costume."[64] Cloth continually signaled the central position that she held in Christian worship, and as Caroline Walker Bynum writes, "The gorgeous textile behind a medieval Madonna (whether it is painted or pasted on) is a frame for, a declaration of, her sacrality."[65]

It was the particularity and singularity of Mary's body that afforded her such advantages over her fellow woman. Mary's virginity, based upon the intact nature of her hymen, was theologically deemed to be so at all stages of her conception and delivery (*ante partum, in partu et post partum*) and provided her with the privileged paradox of being both virgin and mother.[66] As well as being proclaimed *Theotokos* (in Latin *Dei genetrix*), or Mother of God, at the Council of Nicaea in 431, the doctrinal acceptance of the Immaculate Conception in the twelfth century proposed Mary's own conception, as well as her son's, to be considered without fault, thus exempting her from all taint of Original

FIGURE 3.6: *The Virgin and Child*, Lorenzo Veneziano, between 1357 and 1379. Tempera on panel. Paris, Musée du Louvre. © RMN-Grand Palais (Musée du Louvre)/Gérard Blot.

Sin.[67] This Second Eve, typologically considered to be the redemptive counterpart to the fallen first mother, was the embodiment of feminine perfection, and this can be consistently seen in the flowing hair, aristocratic high brow line and elongated and exposed neck, all of which was reinforced by the luxurious fabrics that draped her precious body in painting and sculpture.[68]

Lorenzo Veneziano's *Madonna and Child*, or *Madonna della Rosa* (between 1357 and 1379) (Figure 3.6) perfectly encapsulates such aspects. In this painting the enthroned Virgin dominates the frame and is the only figure making eye contact with the viewer. A bright gold nimbus surrounds and accentuates her blond hair, and a row of multi-colored jewels at its base creates a crowned effect.

Mary's delicate features are further complemented by her outstandingly beautiful and intricately decorated clothing, with a pink kirtle covered in gold-leaf embroidery and lined at the neck, upper arm, and wrists by gold or blue bands. The deep blue mantle covering the kirtle is also painted with a similar gold design, and further color contrast is provided by the gold border and soft green lining which traverses the Virgin's lap. She gently holds her son who stands on her lap, his hands brushing against the rose and brooch.[69] The rose in particular is repeatedly linked to Mary throughout the Middle Ages. As Rosemary Woolf elucidates:

[T]he flower imagery [of the rose] . . . suggested her beauty as well as her humility and chastity. Biblical authority for this imagery lay in the Song of Songs, and in the interpretation of the tree of Jesse, according to which the Virgin was the stem or branch on which grew the flower, Jesus, though occasionally she was herself the flower.[70]

This symbol, coupled with the fact that Mary wears a ring on the fourth finger of her right hand, positions the Virgin as bride of Christ. Anne Winston-Allen outlines that the bride in the Song of Songs "had come to be popularly identified with the Virgin Mary, who is a type of the church . . . since she was seen as the first bride of Christ and, hence, the model for each individual believer."[71] Mary is thus Queen, Mother, Virgin, and Bride simultaneously, with Lorenzo Veneziano's masterpiece persuading the observer of this.[72]

Apart from the decorous paintings, illuminations, and sculptures in which women could encounter Mary, there were also relics of her clothing that offered them a means of caring for and coping with their own bodies.[73] Two key relics of the twelfth century, the *sainte chemise* held at Chartres Cathedral, and the girdle of the Virgin, most notably held at the Prato Cathedral, Tuscany,[74] were venerated by women for both style and health reasons. The chemise, posited by Jean le Marchant in the *Miracles de Notre-Dame de Chartres* as touching the Virgin's skin as she gave birth, was replicated in silk and worn by French queens, perhaps to help them through their own childbirths, perhaps as a "must-have" item they pictured their feminine idol wearing.[75] Le Marchant writes:

[. . .] Qu(e)'*en* meesmes l'enfantment
la dame ce seint vestement
Avoit vestu, celui meïsmes,
Si haut, si precïeus, si seintimes,
Quant le v(e)rai filz Dieu enfanta.
Domques di ge qu'a l'enfant a
Touchié celle seinte chemise,
Croire le devez sans faintise
Que la chemise, ce me semble,
Toucha a l'un et l'autre ensemble.
Donc c'est arguement necessaire
Que c'est plus haut saintuaire
Qu'en nul leu puise estre trovez;
Par miracles est esprouvez.[76]

[It is attested] that the lady was wearing this holy clothing when she gave birth, this very clothing, so high, so precious, so holy, when she gave birth to the true son of God. Therefore I say that the child touched this holy shirt, you must believe it without deceit that the shirt, it seems to me, touched the one and the other together (mother and child). Thus it is a necessary conclusion that it is the highest relic that can ever be found in any place; it has been tried and confirmed by the miracles (it produced).

The most pertinent feature of the chemise emphasized by le Marchant is the contact envisaged between the cloth, the Virgin's body, and Christ's body too ("*Que la chemise, ce me semble, Toucha la l'un et l'autre ensemble*"). The outstanding value of this item is linked to the fact that, while the Virgin was in the process of giving birth to the Christian savior, it touched both bodies. Relics, particularly when distinct from a saintly or divine body, gained power and force when in direct contact with that holy body. It is thus the intimate proximity to the skin of the Virgin (in an earlier poem her naked skin *"sa char nue"* is mentioned) and Christ, as well as the process to which the chemise was included in, that gave it such prestige and drew such crowds of faithful pilgrims.[77] Furthermore, the fact that both Mary and Jesus were believed to have ascended directly to heaven, thus leaving no *post-mortem* (or post-ascension) corporeal relics behind to venerate, made these secondary relics all the more important.[78]

Touch was the means of transferring power between animate (or formerly animate) bodies and objects such as the chemise, which were then believed to hold a power of their own. Even objects such as church bells and statues of saints were believed to carry the sanctifying abilities to transfer holy power to other objects.[79] A girdle, Mary Fissell points out, was often wrapped around a statue of the Virgin and then worn in labor, a practice which she cites as performed by Elizabeth of York, queen of King Henry VII, during her own pregnancy.[80]

Indeed, women, rich and poor, frequently used girdles throughout the process of labor. As David Cressy notes, such items were given out by monastic houses to protect expectant mothers and babies from the manifold dangers involved in childbirth, with the example of the monastery in Bruton, Somerset listed: "our lady's girdle of Bruton, red silk, which is a solemn relic sent to women travailing which shall not miscarry *in partu.*"[81] This was not a free service, however, and Roberta Gilchrist argues that this type of girdle was subsequently restricted to women who came from wealthier families. There were also other options, as "Poor women borrowed objects from their parish church, dress accessories which normally decorated the statues of saints. Or they might resort to using their own girdles as birthing amulets, first attempting to transfer sacred power to them by wrapping the girdle around church bells," again using this process to infuse the various items with a protective power.[82]

Girdles, whether thought to be worn by the Virgin, or blessed by her in some capacity, were crucial to women in labor. They were wrapped around the belly of the expectant mother, and prayers written by a priest were often inserted into them to lend a further type of intercessory power.[83] They were equally important for the comfort of a woman during pregnancy, as shown in Margaret Paston's letters to her husband, John. Margaret writes to her absent husband to ask that he firstly buy her a new, lighter dress, as her current winter wardrobe has become too heavy for her to wear in her advancing state of pregnancy. On December 14, 1441, Margaret writes to John:

> Entreating you to know that my mother sent to my father in London for a cloth of muster-de-vilers to make a gown for me . . . I ask you, if it is not out of your way, that you will agree to buy it and send it home as soon as you can, because I have no gown for this winter other than my black and green a Lierre, and that is so cumbersome that it makes me weary to wear it.[84]

The cloth known as *muster-de-vilers*, a woolen cloth, usually gray, originating from Montivilliers in Normandy, is here preferred to the cloth of Lierre (from Brabant), typically black, and seemingly composed of heavier material, as it is described by Margaret as being too cumbersome (*comerus*) for her to continue wearing.[85] Margaret then proceeds to insist that her husband not forget to bring her a new girdle, there being only one that currently fits her:

> As for the girdle that my father promised me . . . I entreat you, if you will take it upon yourself, that you will agree to do so before you come home; for I have never needed

this more than now, for I am growing so fat that I may not be girt in any of my girdles but one.[86]

Margaret's admittance of her bodily changes and discomfort is an intimate one, only likely to be found in such exchanges as between family members. The urgency of her letter highlights the importance of wearing the right items in terms of fit and comfort, and points to the fact that women adjusted their clothing to their bodies during pregnancy.

Gilchrist further evidences that there were specific garments made for pregnant women, although this does not appear to be what Margaret had requested: "A woman's transition to motherhood was marked by special apparel ... Pregnant women wore "stomachers," a piece of triangular fabric attached to the front of the bodice to conceal the lacing of their expanding bellies."[87] An example of this can be seen in a stained glass image of Mary and Elizabeth at a scene of the Visitation, in the parish church of St Peter Mancroft, Norwich (c. 1450–5) (Figure 3.7).

In this image, Mary typically has unveiled, flowing blond hair, delicate facial features, and wears her customary blue cloak. Her slender neck, too, is bare, unlike Elizabeth's, who is covered entirely except for her face and hands. Her pregnancy is much more apparent than Mary's, and the lacing which covers the clearly visible stomacher extends

FIGURE 3.7: *The Visitation*. Stained glass, church of St. Peter Mancroft, Norwich, c. 1450–5. © Mike Dixon, photographer.

from the hip area right up to the top of her gown, allowing for growth in the areas most likely to need it.

Through art, monastic and cathedral records, as well as poetry in the case of le Marchant, there is clear evidence that women used clothing connected to the Virgin for both physical and spiritual sustenance, particularly during times of uncertainty such as pregnancy and childbirth. The Virgin's body, as well as her clothing, provided protective and intercessory guidance, while her beauty and elaborate dress could have inspired women in more aesthetic, and less practical, capacities, convincing them perhaps that their own beauty was not necessarily bound to be a token of primal guilt.

CONCLUSION

Throughout this chapter, we have attempted to outline the relationship between clothing and body in medieval culture, with a focus on the two pertinent criteria of sensation and perception. Because of its shaping proximity to the body, clothing is more than just pieces of fabric, as it transforms the bodily experience of the wearer, and in turn is a crucial facet in the external perception of that body. It is through these positions that we have come to explore the connection between skin and cloth, as mediated by touch, by theories of balance (which have included all manner of health care, hygiene and healing), and by considerations of gait as well as pregnancy.

Clothing is both material and ideological; it has a practical impact on the body, but can also denote abstract concepts indicative of the particularity of an embodied subject, as for instance in the case of a monk's girdle. Gestures play a key role in the intersection between body and clothing, as they often induce the very narratives that elaborate the notion of *body* acknowledged by a given culture. Perceptions and sensations flesh out such narratives of gesture and clothing, which create the ever-transitional coherence that grounds the experience of embodiment.

CHAPTER FOUR

Belief

ANDREA DENNY-BROWN

Ideas about dress and fashion influenced medieval belief systems in a variety of ways, from ambitious philosophical questions about human existence, moral virtue, and well-being to everyday concerns about social propriety, bodily self-maintenance, and self-fashioning. This essay traces one dominant theme in the medieval period, which ties contemporary clothing and fashion to the original garments of skin created by God in Genesis 3:21. What this example reveals is that specific biblical garments served, perhaps unsurprisingly, as a kind of genealogical starting point for many cultural beliefs about clothing and fashion in western Europe. Importantly, tracing the meaning of Adam and Eve's garments through the medieval centuries also shows the crucial role that the mere *idea* of clothing was understood more generally to play in organizing beliefs about human life. In the case of the garments of skin, a connection emerges between the use of clothing as the primary material marker to distinguish human from divine nature in Genesis 3:21 and the way clothing comes to mediate and dominate codes of distinction and relationality across human life: between life and death, moral and immoral, proper and improper, summer and winter, civilized and uncivilized, courtier and Wildman, or player and audience.

SKINS, THORNS, TUNICS

The invention of tools or weapons is often given primacy in discussions of human evolution, and yet, as geographer and economist Jane Jacobs has pointed out, metallurgy "began with hammering copper into . . . ornaments long before 'useful' knives and weapons were made."[1] The fundamental role that clothing or bodily adornment plays in western creation myths furthers this point, testifying not only to its significance as a primal instinct, but also to the importance of clothing to basic concepts of and narratives of humanness. In Genesis, famously, Adam and Eve make themselves fig leaf garments when they first become aware of their nakedness (Gen. 3:7). Less well-known to modern readers is the story of their second set of garments, the "garments of skin" (*tunicas pellicias*) that God makes to replace their fig leaf aprons and in which he clothes them immediately before expelling them from the garden of Eden:

> And the Lord God made for Adam and his wife garments of skin, and clothed them. And he said: Behold Adam is become as one of us, knowing good and evil: now, therefore, lest perhaps he put forth his hand, and take also of the tree of life, and eat, and live for ever. And the Lord God sent him out of the paradise of pleasure, to till the earth from which he was taken. And he cast out Adam; and placed before the paradise

of pleasure Cherubims, and a flaming sword, turning every way, to keep the way of the tree of life (Genesis 3:21–4).[2]

For the Christian Middle Ages, the dramatic turning point in human fortune signaled by the garments of skin in Genesis 3:21 would forever tie clothing and dress to the concept of the fallen world, and specifically to ideas about human mortality and morality. Beginning with the earliest Christian and Jewish translators and interpreters of Genesis and extending to the late Middle Ages and beyond, writers and thinkers seized on the symbolism of these garments as a key to understanding human nature. At issue was not only the curiously active role that God was said to play in the creation of Adam and Eve's garments—in effect, taking up the role of tailor—but also the specific material he was said to have used: skin, *pellis*.[3] Early biblical exegetes from different traditions postulated that these garments of skin were not to be understood literally, as garments made from animal skins, but rather metaphorically, as the mortal bodies that God created for Adam and Eve after they sinned, which replaced the glorious Paradisical bodies they had enjoyed prior to this event.[4] As Gary A. Anderson points out, for early Christian thinkers especially, the donning of these (human) skins was often interpreted as not just one punishment among the list of punishments enacted by God when Adam and Eve sinned, but rather as *the main* punishment through which all other punishments at the moment of their expulsion—toiling, childbirth, suffering, death—should be understood.[5]

Because these thinkers took the garments of skin from Genesis 3:21 to represent the origins of the mortal body, they sometimes described the skins as physically uncomfortable or painful. The important fourth-century Syrian poet and theologian Ephrem imagines the epidermic transformation to be instantaneous, happening before Adam and Eve have finished making their own fig leaf aprons, and yet he also likens the creation of the skins to the creation of thorns and thistles (from Gen. 3:17), implying their rough, punishing materiality.[6] Other early thinkers imagined the donning of skins as a slower and more overtly tangible process. The fourth-century apocryphal *Cave of Treasures*, for example, imagines the skins being stretched over Adam's and Eve's bodies and bringing an immediate experience of bodily suffering:

> At the turn of the day, Adam and Eve received the penalty; he made for them garments of skin and clothed them. That is, skin, which was stretched out over their body, that brought about diverse sorts of bodily pains.[7]

The idea of the *tunicas pellicias* as the human body that brings with it somatic pain and suffering is further elaborated in texts such as the apocryphal *Life of Adam and Eve*, which enumerates seventy different painful diseases that will afflict the newly-donned body.[8]

The fourth-century Church Father Ambrose also interpreted the garments of skin from Genesis 3:21 to mean the mortal and suffering human body, "the garment of decay," while at the same time expanding the definition to conceptualize and materialize affective experience itself—the skin garment as "the garment of affection." As Hanneke Reuling points out, Ambrose also saw the garments as real garments—specifically, as a kind of penitential garb. As he states in his *De paenitentia*: "God threw Adam out of Paradise immediately after his sin; he did not postpone it, but separated him immediately from the delicious things, so that he could do penance; immediately he clothed him in a garment of skin, not of silk."[9] The idea that Adam and Eve's garments were meant simultaneously to convey and effect repentance has a strong draw for later moralists, as we will see in the next section. Relatedly, the distinction Ambrose makes between these first skins and other luxury materials, such as silk, demonstrates an important and early conceptual link between clothing and propriety that continues throughout the Middle Ages and into the modern world.

Deeply influenced by Ambrose, Augustine (354–430) likewise demonstrates a double understanding of the biblical garments of skin, simultaneously interpreting the skins as the acquisition of the human body and as actual garments of animal skin that symbolize the mortal condition of that body:

> For all of us who are born from Adam have begun to owe to nature that death with which God threatened us when he gave the command not to eat the fruit of that tree; that death was prefigured by the garments of skin. For they made for themselves aprons from the leaves of the fig tree, but God made for them garments of skin. That is, having abandoned the face of truth, they sought the pleasure of lying, and God changed their bodies into this mortal flesh in which deceitful hearts are hidden . . . For what could more clearly signify the death that we experience in our body than skin which we get from dead animals? And so, when against God's command man desired to be God, not by legitimate imitation, but by illicit pride, he was cast down to the mortality of the beasts.[10]

Augustine's focus on the *tunicas pellicias* as a cause and symbol of human deception—from the Latin *mentior*, "to lie"—introduces another important cultural belief cultivated in the Middle Ages and that, moreover, remains one of the most entrenched ideas about clothing in western belief systems.[11] This is the fundamental belief that our truest selves, our modes of being and existing, are deep and internal, rather than external, and correspondingly, that surfaces, and the clothes that mark the body's surface, are trivial and untrustworthy. Clothing is not merely the symbol for Adam and Eve's deception; it is inherently deceptive itself and was invented for its properties of concealment.

Cultural anthropologist Daniel Miller argues that this idea that clothing and other surface materials are inherently deceptive—and that what is internal in inherently truthful, what he calls "depth ontology"—has long been misunderstood by western cultures to be a universal truth, when it is in fact particular to certain cultures, and especially to cultures that have a history of institutional rigidity with regard to notions of race, class, and gender.[12] Miller uses as an example the primary importance of contemporary clothing ownership and display in Trinidad, where homeless squatters without water or electricity usually own at least twenty pairs of shoes, to demonstrate that some cultures in fact hold to the opposite belief: a kind of *surface* ontology in which the hidden interior is considered to be the place for lies, and the surface is the place for truth, honesty, and revelation. The link between clothing and deception epitomized by the biblical story of the first garments offers a useful starting point for rethinking and untangling one of the most powerful beliefs in western culture involving internal and external truths.

ALB, HAIRSHIRT, PILCH

The moral symbolism of *tunicas pellicias* from Genesis 3:21 and its interpretations by late antique biblical exegetes and patristic thinkers had a profound impact throughout the Christian world during the medieval period and beyond. While the following sections deal primarily with examples from late medieval England, interest in the biblical garments of skin can be found throughout medieval Europe in historical and literary documents, in artifacts from the visual, plastic, and decorative arts, and in the vestimentary belief systems more generally that emerge during this period of heightened attention to clothing and fashion.

In England, while the theological notion that the garments of skin symbolized the human body persisted, the garments were more often associated with the changing materials and styles of contemporary attire. The fifteenth-century Benedictine preacher Robert Rypon follows a tradition in homiletic literature when he describes the garments of skin as the starting point for an evolution of dress materials that becomes more morally fraught with each new invention:

> Where before sin the naked body was without natural shame, immediately after sin was committed, the whole naked body was encompassed with the shame of its nakedness: wherefore, because it lacked clothing, there was thus fashioned for it a tunic of skins at the first, in token that through his sin man was become like the beasts which by nature are clad in raiment of skins alone. But later, as their pride grew, men used garments made of wool. Thirdly, through the more ample nourishing of carnal delight, they used garments made from plants of the earth, namely, of linen, and fourthly silken garments which are fashioned from the entrails of worms; all of which kinds of raiment are now rather for vain-glory and worldly pomp than for the necessity of nature, diversely decorated as it were in an infinite variety of ways, and assuredly most of all to excite lust alike in men as in women.[13]

The moral problem posed by clothing was so intrinsic to human nature that all clothing had the capacity to be morally suspect; for those in the religious orders, therefore, new divisions were required to distinguish sacred attire from secular. In his *Rationale Divinorum Officiorum* (*Rationale for the Divine Offices*), a monumental liturgical treatise influential throughout the late medieval period and into the sixteenth century, French theologian and bishop William Durand (1230–96) repeatedly used the symbolism of the garments of skin from Genesis 3:21 to help articulate the current ritualized distinctions between sacred and secular dress. Describing the meaning of the *tunica alba*, or alb, the traditional floor-length white tunic worn by clerics as well as by the newly baptized, Durand states:

> the alb—which is a linen vestment that, from a long distance, looks like a tunic made from the skins of dead animals, with which Adam was dressed after his sin—signifies the newness of life that Christ had, taught, and conferred in Baptism, about which the Apostle says: *Strip off the old man with His deeds and put on the new one* [Col 3:9], *and put on the new man which has been created according to God* [Eph 4:24].[14]

Here Durand relies on the belief that the baptismal garment both opposes and replaces the archetypal garment of skin inherited by every human from Adam. Yet at the same time, he clearly suggests that the alb itself still carries the residual trace—the semblance—of the very garment it is supposed to replace. As this passage suggests, at its heart it is not the style of clothing, nor even the material of clothing, but rather the *fact* of clothing that caused moral tension in medieval culture.

Later medieval moralists did not always agree about the meaning of Adam and Eve's first garments, nor were they always negative about the moral lessons generated by them. One influential fourteenth-century English preacher, for instance, the Dominican John Bromyard (d. c. 1352), describes these garments of skin as an early ideal of sartorial simplicity, a clothing standard free of finery and precious stones that corresponds to the nakedness of Christ on the Cross and from which people should learn to cast away their own luxurious attire.[15] Likewise, in his popular vernacular sermon collection, the *Festial*, Augustinian Canon John Mirk (d. c. 1414) describes the garments of skin as a material indicator of God's compassion for the first humans: "for Adam and Eue weron nakud, God hadd compassion of ham and clothed ham wyth pylches, that is, a cloth makud of dede bestus" (because Adam and Eve were naked, God had compassion for them and clothed them with pilches, that is, a cloth made from dead beasts).[16] As can be seen in Figures 4.1–4.5, the iconography of these garments was frequently represented throughout the medieval period and varied greatly, ranging from rough, untreated animal skins with heads and tails intact worn over the shoulders (Figure 4.3), to simply-sewn garments in a range of colors and lengths (Figures 4.1, 4.2, 4.4), to hairy, belted tunics with few signs of tailoring (Figure 4.5).

For the most part, the Middle English word "pilche" used by Mirk and other English writers when translating or discussing the *tunicas pellicias* from Genesis 3:21 had morally positive connotations. A generic garment made of skin or fur and worn by both men and women in winter months, the pilch was often associated with hair shirts or other garments worn by ascetics, most likely because of its association with simple or coarse clothing.[17] Middle English versions of Aelred of Rievaulx's rule for anchoresses, *De institutione inclusarum*, written in the late fourteenth and fifteenth centuries and used by both anchoresses and laypeople, identify the pilch as the one garment that anchoresses are allowed to wear in the winter.[18] Similarly, in her autobiography the English mystic Margery Kempe (1373–1438) mentions the same garment at one of her most desperate moments: during the long cold winter when she is planning her pilgrimage to Santiago de Compostela in Spain and when she is ill enough to think that she might die, she reports that a "good man" suddenly gave her forty pence, with which she promptly "bowt hir a pylche" (bought herself a pilche), an event that looms large in her memory.[19] In one final example from popular culture, the fifteenth-century *Prose Merlin* mentions the same garment as donning the "savage man" Merlin, who has been living as a recluse in the forest; when he is finally caught, he is filthy, rumpled, bearded, barefoot, and "clothed in a rough pilche."[20]

Yet in the realm of medieval fashion even the simple pilch could be misused, as Chaucer suggests in his short, trenchant, late fourteenth-century poem known simply as "Proverbe." In this poem the pilch's biblical symbolism adds moral fuel to what seem to be implicit criticisms about the latest London fashion for wearing winter furs in the summer:

What shul these clothes thus manyfold,	What shall be done with so many clothes
Lo this hote somers day?	On this hot summer's day?
After grete hete cometh cold;	After great heat comes cold;
No man caste his pilche away.	No man casts his pilch away.
Of al this world the large compass	The world's large circumference
Yt wil not in myn armes tweyne;	My two arms cannot contain;
Who so mochel wol embrace,	Whoever tries so much to embrace
Litel therof he shal distreyne.[21]	Little he shall retain.

As I discuss in more depth elsewhere, in this poem Chaucer addresses a common criticism in England in this period that people are owning and wearing too many clothes at once, and in too many different varieties of styles. His singling out of the pilch is especially interesting since it allows him to discuss current fashions, a particular interest of his, while

FIGURE 4.1: Adam and Eve are clothed by God, with Adam wearing blue and Eve green. Leaf, by William de Brailes. England, 1230. Musée Marmottan Monet, Paris, France/Giraudon/ Bridgeman Images.

FIGURE 4.2: Left: Adam and Eve are expelled from Paradise, wearing fig leaves. Right: Adam and Eve are clothed by an angel in light brown tunics, as they delve and spin. England, 1305–10. Spencer MS 002, f. 3. New York Public Library.

FIGURE 4.3: Left: God clothes Adam and Eve in coarse animal skins, heads and tails intact. Right: expulsion of Adam and Eve from Paradise, wearing skins. France, 1372. The Hague, Meermanno Museum, Koninklijke Bibliotheek, MMW, 10 B 23, f. 11v.

FIGURE 4.4: Adam and Eve are expelled by an angel from Paradise, carrying white garments. The Netherlands, 1479–80. MS Royal 14 E V, f. 13v. © British Library.

also invoking Adam and Eve's vestimentary heritage—a rare moment of what seems to be straightforward Chaucerian moralizing.[22]

WHITELEATHER, WINDING CLOTH, SHROUD

Because of their use of creative costuming and their generic dramatization of key biblical events, the medieval cycle plays performed throughout England from the fourteenth to the sixteenth centuries offer wonderfully instrumental examples of the extent to which Adam and Eve's original garments were not only imagined, but also materially produced and performed for early audiences. It was conventional for those playing evil or morally repugnant biblical characters such as Pontius Pilate and Christ's torturers to be costumed

Caucat tamē diligentissime ne faciat excessium
In omni re semper debitus modus est tenendus

FIGURE 4.5: Adam and Eve wear hairy gray garments of skin as they delve and spin, with children in the background. England 1485–1509. MS Harley 2838, f. 5. © British Library.

in excessively stylized garments; these costumes were meant to symbolize the twisted morals of the characters, but they were also no doubt meant to comment on the fashionable clothing worn by audience members or by the players themselves.[23] Chaucer's famous portrait of Absolon, the parish clerk and *galaunt* who dresses in the most fussy, fashionable attire of the *Canterbury Tales*—including having the design from a window of Saint Paul's Cathedral carved into his shoes—also has him playing the flamboyant tyrant Herod in the local mystery play: "He pleyeth Herodes upon a scaffold hye."[24] The association between biblical scoundrels and high fashion was furthered by contemporary moralists and chroniclers, who commonly complained that fashionable attire made people "look more like torturers, or even demons, than men."[25] In plays depicting Christ's Passion, the dramatic costuming of the characters surrounding Christ was also meant to contrast excessively fashionable attire with the nakedness of Christ on the cross, whose sacrifice was typologically connected to the nakedness of Adam and Eve.

In plays depicting events from Genesis, the traditional costumes used to simulate Adam and Eve's prelapsarian nakedness were white leather bodysuits made by tanners or makers of whiteleather, known as whittawers.[26] The leather material of these bodysuits would have enhanced the early theological associations of leather skins with mortal flesh discussed earlier, especially when the play in question not only dramatized the nakedness of Adam and Eve with white leather costumes, but also subsequently staged Genesis 3:21 and God's reclothing of Adam and Eve with the archetypal leather skins, as does the fifteenth-century Chester play *The Creation, and Adam and Eve*, which I will treat at some length now.

The Chester play, whose thematic emphasis on clothing and skins is underscored by the fact that it was produced by the powerful Drapers' Guild and possibly also the Tanners' Guild, includes a speech in which God explains at length to Adam and Eve the symbolism of the *tunicas pellicias* as he dresses them in those garments. The first two stanzas of the speech, divided by Latin stage directions, are reproduced and translated here:

Deus: Now shall ye parte from this lee.	God: Now shall you depart from this protection
Hilled yow behoves to be;	Covered it behooves you to be;
Dead beastes skinnes, as thinketh me,	Dead bests skins, I think,
Is best yow on yow beare.	Are best for you to bear/wear.
For deadlie bothe now bene yee,	For deadly both of you now are,
And death no way may you flee;	And you may in no way flee death;
Such clothes are best for your degree,	Such clothes are best for your degree,
And such now ye shall weare.	And such now you shall wear.
Tunc Deus induet Adam et	*Then God shall clothe Adam and*
Eva tunicis pelliciis.	*Eve with garments of skin.*
Adam, now hast thou thy willing,	Adam, now you have your wish,
For thou desiredst over all thinge	For you desired over all things
Of good and evill to have knowing;	To know good and evil;
Now wrought is all thy will.	Now wrought is all your will.
Thou woldest knowe both wayle and woe:	You would know both joy and woe:
Now is yt fallen to thee soe.	Now it has fallen to you so.
Therefore hence thou must goe	Therefore hence you must go
And thy desire fulfill.[27]	And fulfill your desire.

In God's speech we see many of the themes apparent from the earliest interpretations of the biblical verse in question, especially the idea that the garments of skin symbolize death, bestiality, and the destructiveness of human desire. Less overt are the processes by which the scene claims dramatic attention, highlighting not only the pivotal importance of this sartorial event but also its cultural implications. In the first two lines of God's speech, for example, the explicit causal connection between Adam and Eve's departure from God's immaterial protection, "lee," and their need to be covered or protected, "hilled," by clothing, is not only poetically resonant but also practically so, since as discussed in the previous section, the garments of skin invoked in Genesis 3:21 were often understood to be a kind of everyday pilch worn for protection from winter weather.

Another point of concentration is the speech's stress on immediacy—the manner by which the urgent instantaneousness of Adam and Eve's expulsion from Paradise and their accompanying change of apparel is verbally recreated through repetition of the word "now," which recurs throughout the speech. This emphasis on immediacy, however, offers a glaring contrast to the protracted nature of the speech itself, which continues for three stanzas before Adam and Eve are driven from Paradise and which would conceivably have been further prolonged by the mid-speech action of dressing the performers in their costumes. The combined temporal effect of the speech's verbal emphasis on "now" and its protracted words and actions is to dramatize the very idea of protective clothing as it is first conceptualized, and then materialized, by God.

Another potential reading of the careful treatment given to Adam and Eve's garments of skin in *The Creation, and Adam and Eve* is provided by the fact that the play was produced by some of the most powerful makers of clothing in Chester: the drapers and possibly, in the earliest history of the play, the tanners.[28] Both guilds were made up of craftspeople who worked to create clothing out of raw materials—drapers producing finished cloth out of wool, tanners producing leather out of cow hide. In this sense their ability to produce the materials for the play's costumes overlapped with the ability of their professions to stand in as powerful agents of vestimentary creation analogous in many ways to God's own originary act in Genesis 3:21. From this perspective, to dramatize the scene of the *tunicas pellicias* on stage is to accentuate a divine lineage for the cultural authority possessed by Chester's cloth-makers and clothing industry. Moreover, if we consider the Tanners' Guild more specifically, to emphasize this scene is effectively to ensure the audience's undivided attention to the Guild's two-fold display of merchandize— in the form of both the leathered nakedness of Adam and Eve's bodies, dressed as they likely were in finely-crafted whiteleather, and also the rough leather "skinnes" in which God subsequently dresses them. The direct association of this play with either guild would have made the scene depicting Genesis 3:21 especially evocative as a commentary on more mundane uses of clothing as a material concern in everyday medieval life.

Two other themes from God's speech in the Chester play likewise link Genesis 3:21 to distinctive registers of material meaning in this period: the idea of wearing clothing that explicitly marks a person's socio-economic status, and the idea of clothing as a manifestation of human design, or "will," tied to human artisanry—that which has been "wrought." In the first stanza quoted, the garments of skin are twice described by God as the "best" choice for Adam and Eve's new circumstances; the word takes part in the alliterative clustering of several ideas—beast, best, (to) bear, (to) be—and its usage suggests that the garments of skin are being recast in terms of social propriety and social organization. More explicitly, God's statement that "[s]uch clothes are best for your degree" (367), which on the surface reminds Adam and Eve of their newly fallen status, also invokes the language and intention of the European sumptuary laws. From the thirteenth century onward, sumptuary laws throughout France, Italy, Iberia, Germany, and elsewhere sought to regulate what they saw as social disorder brought on by new access to different kinds of clothing and new forms of vestimentary display.[29] More particularly, the laws written in late medieval and early modern England when this play was performed strove to regulate materials and styles of clothing according to specific socio-economic categories; importantly, they inculcated these ideas by reproducing formulaic language about the proper attire necessary for each person's "degree." This rhetoric initially emerged with the substantial English sumptuary law of 1363, which opened its sartorial regulation with a statement about numerous people wearing outrageous and excessive apparel "against their estate and degree" (in the original French, *contre lour estate & degree*).[30] This verbiage was subsequently repeated almost verbatim throughout two centuries of English clothing regulation: for example, in the 1463 legislation of Edward IV, in which people were told to dress "only according to their degrees" (*soulement accordant a lour degrees*); in Henry VIII's sweeping 1533 legislation, which likewise urged people to dress "according to their estates . . . and degrees"; and in the numerous sumptuary proclamations put forth during the reign of his daughter, Elizabeth I, which concerned themselves with "the confusion of degrees of all estates."[31] What the audiences in Chester during this period would have heard and understood when they listened to Adam and Eve being told that the garments of skin were "best for your degree," therefore, was likely an echo of, and perhaps a play on, current-day sumptuary legislation. Such a performance would have been made all the more potent by the fact that the people putting on the play were many of those same craftspeople making and selling the wares under regulation.[32]

Finally, this focus on cloth-making continues with the use of the word "wrought" in the second stanza of God's speech in the Chester play. The word signals its importance in the passage through alliterative links with other key words—"willing," "will," "wayle and woe" (joy/comfort and woe), as well as "now" and "knowing." When, directly after clothing them in the garments of skin, God says to Adam "Now wrought is all thy will," a fascinating connection emerges between the shaping of Adam's capacity for self-directed choice and the fashioning of his first garment.[33] That the word had a previous association with the garments of skin from Genesis 3:21 can be seen in the thirteenth-century poem known as the *Middle English Genesis and Exodus*, which describes the garments made for Adam and Eve as having been "wrought" by angels: "Two pilches weren thurg engeles wrogt, / And to adam and to eue brogt." (Two pilches were by angels wrought, / and to Adam and Eve brought).[34] Considering the guildsmen associated with this play, moreover, the Middle English word "wrought" is especially appropriate, as it carried connotations not only of artisanal shaping and fashioning more generally, but also of the making and finishing of clothing and textile materials more specifically. Whereas throughout the medieval period the verb form of "wrought" was used to mean "to sew" and "to weave," by the fifteenth and sixteenth centuries when the Chester play was written and performed, the adjective form was used to identify raw materials that that had undergone some form of artifice or manufacturing, such as silk that had been spun or plain broadcloth that had been embroidered or decorated—that is, the finishing processes undertaken by drapers.[35] That England's 1463 sumptuary legislation spends a great deal of its protectionist energies outlawing "ready wrought" clothing and craft goods manufactured outside of England for the stated purpose of helping "impoverished, and much hindered" English artisans suggests how loaded the notion of clothing "wrought" without permission could be for local craft cultures and economies.[36]

In closing this section let me make clear that while the Chester play *The Creation, and Adam and Eve* dedicates a substantial amount of verbal and performative energy to the symbolism and meaning of the *tunicas pellicias* from Genesis 3:21, many other cycle plays addressing the same biblical events ignore the garments of skin altogether, preferring to focus on the artisanal symbolism of the fig leaf garments. These plays also often employ the charged keyword "wrought," such as in the York *Fall of Man* when God, upon first seeing Adam in fig leaves, delivers the line "This werke, why hast though wrought?"[37] The N-Town play, for which no particular guild association is known, delivers one of the most stark examples of postlapsarian sartorial symbolism, in which God not only neglects to make the garments of skin but also banishes Adam and Eve to "Goo nakyd, ungry, and barefoot" for the rest of their lives.[38] At the end of this play, the act of cloth-making becomes Eve's own distinctive punishment, as Adam and Eve each articulate in separate speeches:

ADAM But lete us walke forth into the londe:
With ryth gret labour oure fode to fynde,
With delvyng and dyggyng with myn hond;
Oure blysse to bale and care to pynde.
And wyff, to spynne now must thu fonde,
Oure nakyd bodyes in cloth to wynde
Tyll sum comforth of Godys sonde
With grace releve oure careful mynde.
Now come, go we hens, wyff.

ADAM But let us walk forth into the land
To find our food with right great labor,
With delving and digging with my hand;
To grieve our bliss and pinch our care.
And wife, now you must try to spin,
To wind our naked bodies in cloth
Until some God-sent comfort
With grace, relieves our careful mind.
Now come, go we hence, wife.

EVA Alas, that ever we wrought this synne
Oure bodely sustenauns for to wynne.
Ye must delve, and I shal spynne
In care to ledyn oure lyff."[39]

EVE Alas that we ever wrought this sin,
For which we win our bodily sustenance,
You must dig, and I shall spin,
In care to lead our life.

The characterization of Adam delving and Eve spinning (also captured in Figures 4.2 and 4.5) is one of the most well-known portrayals of the postlapsarian biblical couple in late medieval England, famously used by the rebel leader and cleric John Ball to protest socio-economic disparities during the Uprising of 1381.[40] When read with an eye toward the sartorial belief system generated by the fall, however, we can see another set of associations here. Most overtly, the verb "winden" in line 327 implies that Eve's future acts of spinning yarn and making clothing are inherently associated with the enshrouding of human bodies that have suddenly become mortal and open to decay; because of its intrinsic association with death, therefore, all subsequent human clothing is portrayed here as being inherently connected with death shrouds.[41] Related to this idea is the play's statement that Eve will make clothing to cover their human nakedness until God sends "some comfort" to relieve them of their cares, a statement that projects forward to the coming of another kind of protection in the form of Christ.[42]

GARLANDS, GLOVES, SOFT CLOTHING

Bringing the symbolism of Adam and Eve's garments of skin typological completion, Christ's intervention on behalf of the human race—the Incarnation, from Latin *incarnare*, to cover with flesh—was specifically conceptualized as a kind of protective skin or garment. This popular imagery is demonstrated by Middle English lyrics such as "I would be Clad in Christis Skin" (I would be clad in Christ's Skin) or, as the English mystic Julian of Norwich puts it, using the same double meaning of the verb "to wind" as the N-Town play, "He es oure clethynge, for loove wappes vs and wyndes vs" (He is our clothing, that for love wraps us and winds us).[43] This vestimentary association, however, also meant that people who wore the wrong kinds of clothes were said to be in danger of offending Christ; in Chaucer's *Canterbury Tales*, for example, the moral Parson preaches that "Wyues that ben apparailled in silk . . . ne mowe nat clothen hem in Iesu Crist" (Wives who are dressed in silk . . . must not clothe themselves in Jesus Christ).[44]

Relatedly, the vice of wearing fashionable clothing—the vestimentary descendent of Adam and Eve's garments of skin—was cast in direct opposition to Christ's fleshly existence. In the lyric known as "Jesus doth him bymene" (Jesus does Bemoan) (c. 1400), Christ compares the attire of the fashionable person to his own appearance on the cross; in the following passage he asks that sinners compare their beautiful garlands and fine white gloves to his own crown of thorns and nailed hands:

Jesus doth hym bymene,	Jesus does bemoan,
And speketh to synful mon;	And speak to sinful man:
"Thi garland is of grene,	"Your garland is of green,
Of floures many on;	Of many flowers;
Myn of sharpe thornes,	Mine [is] of sharp thorns,
Myn hewe it maketh won.	It makes my hue wan.
Thyn hondes streite gloved,	Your hands are tightly gloved,
White and clene kept;	Kept white and clean;
Myne with nailes thorled	Mine are pierced with nails
On rode, and eke my feet."[45]	On the cross, and also my feet.

In a subsequent stanza Christ contrasts his own side wound to the male fashions for wearing ornamental knives and doublets with stylishly slit sides:

"Opyne thou hast thi syde,	Open you have your side,
Spaiers longe and wide,	Slits long and wide,
For veyn glorie and pride,	For vainglory and pride,
And thi longe knif astrout—	And your long knife sticking out—
Thou art of the gai route;	You are of the fashionable crowd;
Myn with sperë sherpe	Mine with spear sharp [is]
Y-stongen to the herte,	Stabbed to the heart,
My body with scourgës smerte	My body with painful scourges [is]
Bi-swongen al aboute."[46]	Beaten all about.

Just as meditating on the wounds of Christ offered a moral counterweight for the sin of wearing fashionable attire, so meditating on the clothing that Christ wore offered a way to resist the temptation of wearing fashionable clothes or to retroactively protect a person who has already done so. In the Middle English *arma Christi* poem "O Vernicle," readers are meant to visualize Christ's seamless garment and the purple robe from the biblical scenes of his mocking to request protection from the moral ramifications of the use (or in some versions of the poem, the "misuse") of luxurious clothing. The poem is written from the point of view of the sinner:

The white cote that had seme none	The white coat that had no seams
And thee purpure that laid opone,	And the purple that [they] laid [lots] upon,
Thai be my socour and myn helpyng	They are my succor and my helping
That my body hate used soft clothing.[47]	That my body has used soft clothing.

An alternate version of the poem directly requests healing and pardon for sartorial misdeeds:

Lorde, be thou my helinge	Lord, be my healing
Yf I haue vsed my clothing	If I have used my clothing
By vayneglory and vanyte.	With vainglory and vanity.
Gracyous Lorde, pardon me.	Gracious Lord, pardon me.

As these examples suggest, in medieval culture the act of clothing oneself was never entirely singular or isolated; it was implicitly understood within certain symbolic systems. Like the earlier examples from the Chester play and other texts previously discussed, these lyric poems invite readers or listeners to interpret their habits of dress in terms of vestimentary typology—as acts that must be understood within the rich symbolism of sacred history in general, and of Adamic and Christological artifacts in particular.

This belief in the relational, associative quality of clothing symbolism and meaning plays out nicely in the double drama of clothing invention that occurs in Genesis, where a decidedly two fold enactment—first fig leaves, and then skins—ensures that the very idea of clothing, and that every subsequent act involving clothing, always already points to a prior act of covering. The conceptual link between Adam and Eve's garments of skin and Christ's Incarnation furthers this perception, building a system of moral comparison into the act of choosing which materials to wear on one's body.

In these ways, clothing becomes a symbol for the practice of choice itself—moral and otherwise—in medieval culture. The Chester play *The Creation, and Adam and Eve* emphasizes the way the theme of choice implicitly underlies the Genesis scene; there, tensions between God's choice, what he "thinks" is best, and Adam's choice, the actions driven by his "will" and "desire," develop as an inherent part of the genealogy of clothing and clothing symbolism. Late medieval moralists can be seen to rely on the same implicit connection, imploring people, for instance, to use their "witte, skill and free will" to choose appropriate attire for themselves.[48] Sumptuary laws likewise attempted to regulate vestimentary choice, restricting materials and ornaments according to socio-economic categories so that the most freedom of choice was assigned to the top tier of the aristocrats and the least choice to the poorest laborers; that these regulations often failed through non-compliance or repeal, moreover, demonstrates even more acutely the exceptional charge that clothing carried in this culture. Across these different registers as the medieval period drew to a close, clothing, and the belief systems involving clothing and fashion, were made to mediate complex cultural shifts in the understanding of human autonomy and responsibility. By the end of the period, as social philosopher Gilles Lipovetsky has argued, the conflicts involving fashionable attire revealed "the effort of human beings to make themselves masters of the conditions of their own existence."[49] By framing the medium of clothing in terms of the human capacity for artistic, material inventiveness on the one hand, and the human experience of high moral stakes, on the other, the running medieval commentary on Adam and Eve's garments of skin helped create one of the most enduring beliefs about the struggle for human autonomy in the material world.

CHAPTER FIVE

Gender and Sexuality

E. JANE BURNS

In her fifteenth-century *Book of the City of Ladies*, Christine de Pizan includes an anecdote about a man who falls asleep and wakes up wearing a dress. The tale is used to convey the importance of not allowing ignorance to blind the author to what she knows for certain.[1] But it also shows the extent to which a simple article of clothing can actually create gender. When the sleeping man awakes and sees the dress, he is convinced he has become a woman. Although the man is the victim of a prank and told by those who taunt him that he has switched genders, the dress plays a key role in his new perception of what the author calls "his own being." The very sight of the garment on the man's body overrides everything else: his past history, his physiology, and any identities of gender and masculinity that he had previously believed to be his. His categorical reaction to seeing himself in a woman's dress offers a compelling paradigm for understanding how gender operates both in the Middle Ages and the current moment. Indeed, this anecdote underscores not only the power of clothing to communicate and even create gender, but also the key role played by sight in that process. One is reminded here of contemporary gender theorist Kate Bornstein's observation that "gender itself can't be seen" but requires modes and metaphors to help us visualize it.[2] One such mode, in fact perhaps the most easily recognizable one, is dress.

By this I do not mean that clothing accurately reflects the pre-established gender of its wearer. My argument, on the contrary, is that gender does not in fact exist separately from the modes and metaphors, acts and interpretations that call it into being. As a result, clothes can evoke, convey, and indeed create gendered identities of many sorts along a wide spectrum of possibilities that are not necessarily conditioned by assumed foundational differences in anatomy.

Medieval literary texts provide a host of examples that bear out this claim. We might consider, to begin, two medieval heroines: the cross-dressed fictional character, Silence, in the thirteenth-century romance, *Le Roman de Silence*, and the fifteenth-century historical figure Joan of Arc. Although both wear men's clothing, neither believes that "she" is a "he," even if others do.

The heroine Silence is cross-dressed as a boy by her parents who wished to protect their inheritance from a royal decree banning all female children from inheriting wealth or title. The parents' plan aims at strategic deception: with the application of boy's clothes, we are told, ". . . de mescine avront vallet,/ Et de lor fille un oir mallet" (they will have a boy instead of a girl, and a male heir instead of their daughter, vv. 2209–10).[3] And indeed, once Silence has "les dras et le contenance" (the clothes and the *look*) of a male (vv. 3644–6), the visual effect is so convincing that the queen falls in love with Silence, now described as "le valet ki ert meschine" (the boy who was a girl, v. 3704). Although the transformation is only temporary and Silence resumes her so-called "natural" gender as the tale concludes, we have witnessed during the course of the narrative a female body dressed in men's clothing that has socially, professionally, and legally "become" a man. The cross-dressed Silence has gained a reputation as a highly capable knight and an expert minstrel. Indeed, he/she explains the complexity of his/her situation by saying: "Donc, sui jo Scilentius/ Cho m'est avis, u jo sui nus," (vv. 2537–8), which can have at least two meanings in Old French. First, "I am Scilentius or I am no one" meaning my name "Silence" reflects that my gender assignment at birth as "female" has been hidden or silenced so that I could assume the gender and legal status of a "somebody," a male child. Or alternately, taking the second meaning of the Old French "nus," we can understand this heroine's remarks as "I am Silentius or I am nude," meaning that I must retain the clothing and disguise of a male because, if not, my female body will be revealed. Deprived of her highly generic "clothes of a young man" (*wallés dras,* v. 6536), Silence will lose everything it seems: not only her legal right to inherit but, more important for our purposes, her ability to perform as a superior knight, and her exceptional skills as a minstrel. How can this be?

Silence's dilemma only makes sense within a world of binary oppositions that structure the body as either clothed or unclothed, understanding gender in terms of two mutually exclusive categories: male and female. And yet this heroine's remarks also suggest that there might be a way of reconstructing or reimagining gender beyond the either/or dyad of nature and culture that so conditions her existence. While Silence categorizes her dilemma as having to hide her female body in order to be seen as a social subject, her story also suggests the possibility of a third term standing between the binary pairs of dressed and undressed and between the rigid dichotomy of male and female that so flummoxed the sleeping man in the folktale with which we began. After all, Silence "was" a successful knight and minstrel, she "was" the hero Silence. For the bulk of the romance, she "was" visually, socially, and professionally a "he" *while still being* a "she."[4]

The possibility of a third gender identity is exemplified perhaps even more cogently by the historical Joan of Arc who doggedly annoyed her inquisitors by retaining her male garb and refusing to wear a "woman's dress." Joan's intent was never to deceive those who observed her slight, androgynous body clothed in typically male attire. Rather, Joan identified herself throughout the trial as a woman in man's clothes. It was the very indeterminacy of her position, according to Marjorie Garber, the fact that she insisted on being both a woman and a man simultaneously, visibly and publicly, that so disturbed her accusers.[5] The trial record bears this out on nearly every page, explaining how "she" dressed openly as a "he":

> The said Jeanne put off and entirely abandoned woman's clothes, with her hair cropped short and round in the fashion of young men, she wore shirt, breeches, doublet, with hose joined together" (*chemise, braies, gippon, chausses*).[6]

The sartorial duo of "*chemise* and *braies*" typically appear together in medieval literary accounts, as we will see later, as requisite undergarments for men. The *gippon* and *chausses* (doublet and hose) provide an outer layer of clothing that conforms closely to the body, creating a distinctively male silhouette in stark contrast to the shape of a woman's floor-length gown in this period.

The heroine Silence too wears a recognizably masculine doublet and hose. In her case, they form part of her armor: a *ganbizon de soie* (silk doublet, v. 5336) designed to fit under a chain mail hauberk (*obierc malié,* v. 5337) and *calces de malle* (chain mail hose, v. 5342).

FIGURE 5.1: Late medieval "male" silhouette: *gippon* (pourpoint) and *chausses*, Eugène-Emmanuel Viollet-le-Duc, *Dictionnaire raisonné du mobilier français de l'époque carlovingienne à la renaissance*. Paris: Gründ et Maguet, 1854–75. Vol. 3, 271.

FIGURE 5.2: Late medieval "female" silhouette: floor-length fitted gown, Eugène-Emmanuel Viollet-le-Duc, *Dictionnaire raisonné du mobilier français de l'époque carlovingienne à la renaissance*. Paris: Gründ et Maguet, 1854–75. Vol. 3, 275.

FIGURE 5.3: *"Ganbizon de soie,"* as worn by Silence. Viollet-le-Duc, *Dictionnaire raisonné du mobilier français de l'époque carlovingienne à la renaissance.* Paris: Gründ et Maguet, 1854–75. Vol. 5, 441.

FIGURE 5.4: *"Chausses de maille,"* mail hose as worn by Silence. Viollet-le-Duc *du mobilier français de l'époque carlovingienne à la renaissance.* Paris: Gründ et Maguet, 1854–75. Vol. 5, 275.

Beneath these garments, Silence also wears *braies* as a key indication of her transformation into maleness (v. 2056).

Whereas these items of dress are used to cover and obscure Silence's female body, the *gippon* and *chausses* worn by the fifteenth-century Joan perform a different function. Throughout her trial, Joan openly defies the prevailing cultural assumption that the sexed body should be matched by appropriately gendered clothing. Indeed, when Joan, the young military heroine who raised the siege at Orléans and won a significant victory for the King of France, insists on retaining both her military garb and the title of "la Pucelle d'Orléans" (the maid of Orléans), the typically male clothes she wears no longer convey unquestionable masculinity. Neither do they connote a "woman" cross-dressed as a man. As Marina Warner argues persuasively, Joan was not perceived by the soldiers surrounding her as a sexualized woman. Nor was her goal to fool them into thinking she was a male soldier. Her male garb, in this instance, enables her to move into a third, hybrid category of gendered being.[7] While the doublet and hose worn by Silence as part of her knightly armor can be understood as potentially redefining the body of a "maiden" (*mescine*) hidden beneath, similar articles of clothing worn by Joan result in a more thorough expansion of gendered categories altogether. She is openly both "male" and "female" at once.

Whatever medieval garment we might consider, from underwear or everyday attire to wedding dresses or coronations robes, items of dress can either reinforce or disrupt and challenge the predictable categories of gendered identities they are ostensibly designed to convey. Literary texts are particularly useful in revealing the more nuanced functions of medieval dress because they give us glimpses of garments within specific, if imaginative, cultural contexts. Literary representations of medieval clothing allow us to see, for example, how items of dress could be used to communicate rank or political advantage, how they might be worn to display wealth or status, manipulated to gain influence or power, or gifted to convey a range of emotions. Depictions of medieval clothing in literary texts are especially useful for understanding gender and sexuality, not because they record accurate historical uses of medieval dress, which they may or may not do, but because they express cultural patterns of desire, anxiety, or concern. Indeed, the kinds of ambiguity and gender fluidity that medieval literary texts often stage are not easily rendered in visual representations. The sole surviving image of Joan of Arc, for example, gives us a highly feminized female torso wearing the bodice of a dress. Whereas the image, made by a clerk who had never seen Joan, reflects gendered assumptions that might derive from her name alone, it tells us nothing of the complex gender assignment she understood herself to occupy.[8]

Curiously, the static drawings of the fanciful French architect Eugène Viollet-le-Duc that I have included in this essay actually convey few gendered restrictions. To be sure, his encyclopedic images representing both medieval architecture and household items are problematic on many counts, most notably because they often provide a highly romanticized version of life in the Middle Ages seen through the lens of nineteenth-century medievalism. I have chosen to incorporate Viollet-le-Duc's images, nonetheless, because of their usefulness for understanding expressions of gender in the Middle Ages. Indeed, many of the garments illustrated in the *Dictionnaire raisonné* are especially striking because they stand alone without a gendered wearer.

Consider, for example, the unisex chemise in Figure 5.5, worn by both women and men, or even the purportedly male *chausses de maille* pictured in Figure 5.4. Without a human subject, neither of these images conveys gender or sexuality in and of itself. What, then, if we were to view these and other illustrations of medieval clothing in

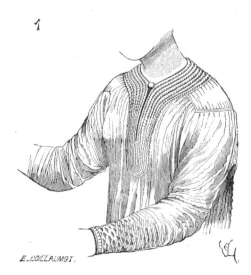

FIGURE 5.5: Chemise, Viollet-le-Duc, *Dictionnaire raisonné du mobilier français de l'époque carlovingienne à la renaissance*. Paris: Gründ et Maguet, 1854–75. Vol. 3, 175.

Viollet-le-Duc's catalog as potentially ungendered? What would we see? If the floor-length *chemise* can cover any body, might not the chain mail *chausses* be worn by individuals of any gender or sexuality as well? And what of the *gantelet* in Figure 5.6?

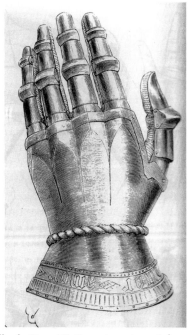

FIGURE 5.6: Gauntlet, Viollet-le-Duc, *Dictionnaire raisonné du mobilier français de l'époque carlovingienne à la renaissance*. Paris: Gründ et Maguet, 1854–75. Vol. 5, 456.

Could this garment not potentially be worn by a range of individuals possessing, in Denise Riley's term, "different densities of sexed being?"[9] This is certainly not the way Viollet-le-Duc intended his images to be read. Nor is it the way we have been trained to read them. And yet, in light of the diversely gendered items of dress depicted in many medieval literary texts, Viollet-le-Duc's schematic images might be understood as providing the shapes of raw materials from which gendered acts and identities can be created. In this vein, we might even reconsider the image of the person wearing the doublet and hose in Figure 5.1 with which we began. Viollet-le-Duc's illustration of the clothing itself does not convey gender or sexuality apart from the head he adds to the garments. If we were to suspend our own assumptions that only men wear armor or doublets and hose, we might see this image differently. We might see the garments themselves as potentially ungendered.

A number of years ago Christine Delphy suggested that "perhaps we shall only really be able to think about gender on the day when we can imagine nongender."[10] This has proven to be a difficult task. And yet we as medievalists might consider drawing on Viollet-le-Duc's illustrations of *chausses* and *chemise* in Figures 5.4 and 5.5 along with images like the *gantelet* in Figure 5.6 to help us begin to reimagine the range of gendered options that medieval clothing can offer.

To be sure, some garments in literary accounts are more clearly sexed than others: the late medieval floor-length gown for women, for example, or the earlier medieval *braies* for men. However, in many literary scenarios, even clothes that might initially carry a gendered designation are shown ultimately to promote a wide range of gendered identities and sexualities.

Consider, for example, Robert de Blois's twelfth-century tale of Floris and Lyriope, star-crossed lovers who succeed in being together solely because of a generic "robe."[11] Indeed, Floris sneaks into the all-female living quarters of his beloved after changing clothes with his twin sister, Florie: "Ta robe, fait il, me donras,/ Et tu la moie vestira. La irai en guise de toi./ Tu remaindras en leu de moi" ("Give me your robe" Floris says to Florie, "and you will wear mine. I will go there appearing to be you and you will stay here in my place," vv. 830–3). This sartorial transformation has more far reaching implications than Silence's temporary and strategic disguise or Joan of Arc's individual challenge to the socially sanctioned exclusion of doublet and hose from the realm of woman's dress. The exchange of "robes" in Robert de Blois's narrative actually facilitates amorous encounters, enabling Floris to stay in Lyriope's company as a "maiden," we are told, smiling with her, holding hands, lying in her lap, and touching her skin (vv. 909–12). The two kiss and embrace, prompting Lyriope to declare "Onques mais n'an oi novales/ Que s'entramassent dous puceles./ Mais n'ameroie pas, ce croi,/ Nul hom tant con je fais toi,/ Ne tant, ce cuit, ne me plairoit/ Li baisiers, s'uns hons me basoit" (I have never heard of two maidens loving each other so much. But I don't think I will ever love any man as much as I love you, nor would a man's kiss please me as much as your kisses, vv. 1010–15).

This love tryst, occasioned by the hero's donning of his sister's robe, provides a scene of heterosexual union that is infused with a range of negotiable gender identities. If Floris's kisses are not those of a man any more than are his garments, and if, as the text relates, "he's now a she" (v. 878) one must ask, what precisely creates or determines gender identity in this tale of courtly coupling? In this instance, courtly love seems to thrive on if not require a lack of alignment between "naturally" sexed bodies and the garments they wear. Lyriope falls in love with a woman whom she loves more than she could love any man. She then continues to love this same individual once he resumes his identity as Floris. What lies beneath the gowns of these courtly lovers—the anatomical differences contributing to their "diverse nature"—as we are told, appears in this sense to be of little consequence.

Indeed, Floris, dressed as a woman, first declares his/her love for Lyriope by casting him/herself as the male lover Piramus, drawn from a story the couple are reading together (vv. 992–7). Then speaking as a female lover, Floris describes the uncanny strength of the bond that unites two women in love, ". . . nos en nostre fole amor/ Sentons andui si grant doucor./ Mout est cele doucor plus granz,/ Plus saverouse et plus plaisanz/ Que cil ont qui ainment a droit" (. . . we, in our mad passion, both feel such intense pleasure, more agreeable and more delicious than the pleasure felt by straight lovers, vv. 1030–4). We might ask whose pleasure is in question here: the love between two young women or the desire joining a woman and a man? Most important for our purposes, it is clothing that plays a key role in shaking gender lose from its anatomical moorings in this tale.

Certainly, one could cite any number of medieval literary examples in which clothing helps facilitate more standard heterosexual amorous coupling: the *trouvère* woman poet who claims to feel her male lover under her cloak,[12] the hero in Jean Renart's romance *Galeran de Bretagne* who lavishes kisses on the embroidered sleeve his beloved has sent him as if it were her physical body,[13] the women in the *chansons de toile* who sing and sew to express their desire,[14] or the heroine Soredamor who sews her hair into a *chemise* she sends as a love token in *Cligès*.[15] In all of these instances, binary gender positions remain intact.

In *Floris and Lyriope*, by contrast, we confront the possibility of a spectrum of gendered subject positions and amorous liaisons based on a conception of the courtly body itself as more sartorial than anatomical.[16] At one point the cross-dressed hero Floris even suggests "Si li une de nos estoit/ uns damoiseaux, nostre solas/ Ne porroit nuns dire sanz gas" (If one of us were a young man, no one could speak of our delight without boasting, vv. 1035–7). We as readers of the tale understand that hypothetically changing Floris into a "man" would produce a heterosexual pair of lovers. But if Lyriope, an equally viable referent for "one of us," were to become a young man (presumably by donning men's clothing much as Floris's own sister did earlier when she agreed to wear her brother's "robe,") the resulting couple would feature two "men." All of these different ways to "be" male or female, masculine or feminine lovers are made possible in this tale and other early medieval literary texts because of what characters wear. Indeed, these examples provide a cogent illustration of Judith Butler's now-famous assertion that "there is no gender identity behind the expressions of gender."[17] For Butler, gender is created by performative acts that are regulated by cultural norms and practices but not dictated by bodily configurations.[18] So too in *Floris et Lyriope* the lovers come together in unexpected amorous configurations through acts of dressing and undressing that often challenge assumed categories of anatomical difference.

THE DAMSEL'S SLEEVE

A small article of clothing, the damsel's sleeve, featured in the closing volume of the thirteenth-century Lancelot-Grail Cycle, *The Death of King Arthur*, provides a particularly telling example of the ways clothing can complicate gendered desire.[19] The Lady of Escalot who has fallen hopelessly in love with Arthur's best knight, Lancelot, gives him her sleeve to wear on his helmet at a tournament. Typically, knights have everything to gain from wearing a beloved lady's sleeve since the garment, standing in for the ladylove herself, provides inspiration and increased strength for the aspiring knight. In this instance, however, Lancelot does not love the lady of Escalot and only consents to wear her sleeve because he is bound by a prior oath. The results are unexpected.[20]

Whereas this article of clothing typically reinforces normative gender assignments in which knights establish their masculinity by fighting for ladies, the Lady of Escalot's sleeve actually undermines the viewer's ability to define Lancelot's prowess as an armored knight apart from an item of women's dress. Lancelot is known during this tournament only as "cil chevaliers . . . qui porte cele manche desus son hiaume" (the knight who wears the lady's sleeve on his helmet, 17). His public identity as a prized and proven chivalric champion, his masculinity, rests, in this instance, not on his own name or valiant deeds but on an article of clothing belonging to a woman who has imposed her request, her desire, and her will on the world's best knight. Her gesture creates gender trouble in a number of ways. It defies a long standing courtly convention, articulated in both lyric and romance, that only men should initiate the love suit: women's assigned role is to concede.

And yet, what is recorded in the public display of this damsel's sleeve, what is *seen* by the viewers at the Winchester Tournament, is the inordinate influence she has wielded over him. Wearing so visibly and publicly the sleeve of a woman who has "dressed" him in this garment, Lancelot becomes marked as "hers" against his will. While his chivalric performance at the tournament attests to his incomparable skills as a knight, the sleeve attached to his helmet signals his helplessness against a damsel who, at this point in the tale, is hardly in distress. To be sure, this heroine's passion and pleasure are brutally displaced from the courtly scene later in the tale when she is made to die Ophelia-like of love sickness. However, before that calamitous moment, she has succeeded in dressing the world's best knight in an item of her clothing that publicly announces her desire not his.

The knight Gauvain crosses proscribed gender lines even more flagrantly in this episode by imagining himself in the role of a damsel with a sleeve to give away. Recounting Lancelot's extraordinary feats at the Winchester Tournament, Gauvain tells the lady of Escalot, "Si ge estoie damoisele, je voudroie que la manche fust moie, par si que cil m'amast par amors qui la manche portoit (If I were a damsel, I would want that sleeve to be mine and the man wearing the sleeve to be in love with me, 23). If we too can imagine Gauvain in a damsel's dress, giving his/her sleeve to a knight in combat, the established meaning of knights "fighting well" because they are inspired by a courtly ladylove changes significantly. It seems from this example that knights wearing women's sleeves could in fact be fighting for the affection of other knights as well as for ladies.

The episode demonstrates that something as small as a damsel's sleeve, whether worn physically by Lancelot or imagined metaphorically by Gauvain, has the potential to challenge and disrupt the codes of gendered desire that typically structure the world of Arthurian romance.

ACCESSORIES: AUMOSNIÈRE AND CEINTURE

Other small items of clothing that can confound expectations of gender and sexuality include the well-known duo of the almspurse and belt (*aumosnière* and *ceinture*). The Old French *aumosnière* described in romance texts and trade accounts of the thirteenth century is fashioned typically from costly silk and hung from a belt that is itself made of rich silk fabric. Although these small almspurses can serve the practical function of holding anything from herbs, unguents and medicines to holy bread or even sewing

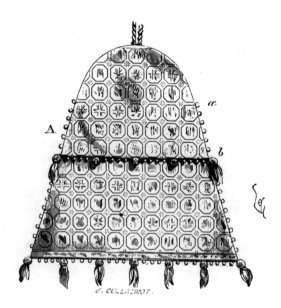

FIGURE 5.7: *Aumosnière*, Viollet-le-Duc, *Dictionnaire raisonné du mobilier français de l'époque carlovingienne à la renaissance*. Paris: Gründ et Maguet, 1854–75. Vol. 3, 27.

supplies, Old French literary texts also often feature richly embroidered silk purses as receptacles for carrying valued rings, brooches, and jewels. At times the silk *aumosnière* becomes the signifying mark of the male courtly lover, as in Guillaume de Lorris's *Roman de la Rose*; courtly ladies typically wear the costly accessory atop other articles of lavish attire.[21] Medieval manuscripts often depict *aumosnières* for sale in merchants' stalls where they appear as ungendered accessories as in Figure 5.8.

In general the aristocratic *aumosnière* can be distinguished from the leather money pouches or small satchels called *bourses* that hang from the belts of peasants and tradesmen. Leather *bourses* designed to carry coins are portrayed in the Old French fabliaux as being used by merchants at fairs, customers in the marketplace, clients at the tavern, or shopkeepers and tradesmen in town settings.[22] The term *bourse* also often appears in comical and ribald tales accompanying visual images of male sexual potency and lustful gaming. Its erotic connotations emerge clearly, for example, in one fourteenth-century manuscript image of a merchant's stall where the *bourses* and belts displayed for sale are juxtaposed with an image of a fornicating couple.[23]

Against this backdrop, we see the heroine Lienor in Jean Renart's thirteenth-century *Roman de la rose ou de Guillaume de Dole*, deploy an *aumosniere* and *ceinture* during a legal trial as material evidence to prove her innocence against false charges of sexual misconduct.[24] Accused of not being a virgin by a devious seneschal who claims to have seen an image of a rose on her thigh, Lienor exonerates herself through the deft manipulation of intimate items of her own clothing: her belt and its attached almspurse. Before the trial, she had shrewdly arranged to have them planted on the seneschal's person as if they were love tokens from the Chastelaine de Dijon. Lienor sends these items of clothing along with a brooch to the seneschal with instructions that if he wishes to meet the ladylove he must wear the belt under his *chemise* against his flesh. When the

FIGURE 5.8: Twelfth-century Minnesanger poet, Dietmar von Aist, pictured as a peddler in the Manesse Codex, University of Heidelberg Library, early fourteenth century, f. 64 r.

FIGURE 5.9: A "*ceinture*" or belt, as used by Lienor, Violet-le-Duc, *Dictionnaire raisonné du mobilier français de l'époque carlovingienne à la renaissance*. Paris: Gründ et Maguet, 1854–75. Vol. 3, 107.

seneschal claims falsely in court to have robbed Lienor of her virginity (vv. 3585–6), she asserts that he also took her *aumosniere*, *ceinture*, and her jewelry (vv. 4783–7). In fact, the seneschal took none of these items, and in claiming his innocence of the charge— asserting that he has not "taken" her virginity or her belt or almspurse "by force"—he disproves his own earlier claim to have "taken" her virginity, presumably with her consent, at all.

Whereas the seneschal can provide no tangible proof of his allegation, Lienor has the material evidence of items of dress on her side. Although she fabricates the story of the stolen belt and purse, the items themselves can be produced in court. The narrator observes crucially that, as "everyone could see," the seneschal was wearing the belt tightly fastened around her bare body. In this instance it is the combined *aumosnière* and belt, here called most often by the single term *ceinture*, that enable this heroine to demand justice. When the Emperor Conrad's barons express skepticism that the belt it so commonplace it might belong to anyone, Lienor demonstrates that the embroidery decorating the cloth belt's surface is unequivocally hers.

In the end, Lienor succeeds in using everyday items of aristocratic dress, the *aumosnière* and *ceinture*, worn by both men and women in the courtly world, to provide indisputable proof of her status as a marriageable virgin. Shifting the focus from her own hypersexualized body to the body of the seneschal, she sheds the gender stereotype of the vulnerable, ravishable young woman and imposes a different kind of sexualized vulnerability on her male accuser. And she does so by deploying an article of clothing that she herself has embellished and marked as her own.

CORONATION ROBES AND WEDDING DRESSES

Some garments tell stories. Two highly gendered examples that come to mind are the coronation robes of King Erec in the twelfth-century romance *Erec and Enide*[25] and the wedding dress worn by the heroine Lienor in the tale we have just discussed: *The Romance of the Rose or Guillaume de Dole*. Both garments have a magical provenance—they are said to have been made by fairies—and both make reference to figures in the Classical world. The gendered messages they convey could not be more distinct or more conventional. When Erec is crowned at King Arthur's court he assumes the metaphorical mantle of power wearing a robe embroidered with images of Classical learning from the Trivium and Quadrivium: Geometry, Arithmetic, Music, and Astronomy. Representing the skills needed to govern wisely, images of these disciplines have been woven with gold thread into the cloth of Erec's "costly, elegant, and beautiful" robe. Although we hear that before the coronation "Quanque pot, d'Enide atillier/ se fu la reine penee" (the queen had put her finest efforts into the adornment of Enide, vv. 6762–3), no description of a historiated robe even approaching the scope and authority of Erec's mantle accompanies Enide's coronation. Her investiture is rendered in a single brief phrase "Puis ont Enyde coronee" (v. 6824; Then they crowned Enide).

When Lienor marries the Emperor Conrad, after successfully proving her innocence and virginity in the trial, as we have seen, her gown is decorated curiously with a story of rapt and ravishment. The motifs embroidered by the queen of Puglia on fabric woven by fairies tells the story of Helen of Troy, her capture by Paris and the Trojan War it provoked when the Greeks came to retrieve her (vv. 5332–50). This extended account of abduction and ravishment, well known to medieval audiences from Benoit de Saint Maure's *Romance of Troy*, could not be more different from Lienor's own story. We have already witnessed her inordinate skill and intelligence in the trial scene where she extracts justice from an *aumosnière* and *ceinture*. Her equally lavish and costly wedding dress, adorned with visual images completely embroidered in gold thread, wraps this courtly heroine in the trappings of a borrowed and dissonant mythic past. It seems in a sense that Lienor's deft performance in the trial scene, now covered over and occluded by the ornate imperial wedding gown, offered a glimpse of an alternative narrative to the story of Helen's rapt and sexual violation. While the knight-hero of *Erec et Enide* assumes the mantle of kingship embroidered with a story of knowledge and authority, the heroine Lienor in Jean Renart's tale is expected to wear a wedding gown depicting women as vulnerable creatures in a greater scheme of war and revenge.

These are some of the most highly gendered stories that medieval clothing tells. They provide examples of garments that literally enact and reinforce a gendered status quo.

UNDERWEAR

So too does underwear in many instances. Less visible than elite robes and gowns, medieval underclothes are no less significant in articulating gendered social identities. Their usage in literary texts tends to emphasize the extent to which standards of masculinity require covered bodies while acceptable femininity requires exposed skin.[26] The *chemise*, worn by both women and men as we have seen, is most often made of linen and sometimes pleated. It serves both as a nightshirt and an undergarment, always worn next to the skin. In the case of women, the *chemise* is often partially visible above the upper edge of the outer layer of dress. Most distinctive of women's underwear, however, is the complete absence of any garment equivalent to the male *braies*. Indeed, the courtly lady is often described as appropriately "nue en sa chemise" (naked in her *chemise*).

By contrast, the words *chemise* and *braies* often appear together as a linguistic pair to describe an ensemble of male underclothes. In the French *Prose Lancelot*, Lancelot rebuffs the advances of a temptress by refusing to remove both his *braies* and his *chemise*.[27] Indeed, in many instances, the man's *braies* become a visual locus for the margin of safety between social acceptability and social disgrace. In the *Queste del Saint Graal*, for example, when Perceval finds himself in bed with a naked temptress, he wounds himself in the thigh and then sees that he is "toz nuz fors de ses braies" (completely naked except his *braies*, 111). The undergarment alone stands between him and the nudity that would signal moral perdition. By contrast, when King Arthur allows himself to be duped by the wiles of the enchantress Camille in the *Prose Lancelot*, underwear offers no protection from social nudity. Shortly after arriving at his night time rendezvous, the king, dressed only in *braies*, is unable to defend himself against forty armed knights who break into the bedchamber with swords drawn, "li rois saut sus si com il puet, car il n'avoit que ses braies" (the king leaps up as well as he can because he is wearing only his "braies," Micha 8: 443). These examples reflect a logic of partial denuding in which the male protagonist is seen as either clothed or unclothed; that is to say he is either properly socialized and visibly operative as a member of a specified cultural group, or he is desocialized and visibly marginalized from the locus of acceptable social activity.

Whereas exposed skin spells vulnerability and danger for knights in particular, courtly ladies gain status to the extent that their skin is on view. Rather than conveying a protective distance from nudity, the woman's *chemise* often connotes just the opposite: seduction and nudity itself. Even aristocratic women who are fully and lavishly clothed, appear curiously to be fundamentally naked. The standard literary portrait of twelfth-century

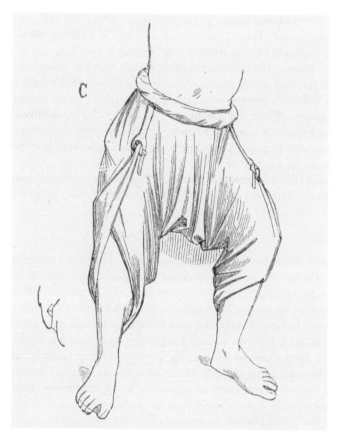

FIGURE 5.10: *"Braies,"* Viollet-le-Duc, *Dictionnaire raisonné du mobilier français de l'époque carlovingienne à la renaissance.* Paris: Gründ et Maguet, 1854–75. Vol. 3, 78.

heroines begins with the lovely face, often commenting on the hair, forehead, eyebrows, eyes, nose, mouth, teeth, and chin, while also describing the seductively white skin of her throat and chest. And the description often continues by detailing parts of the body that are actually hidden from view: the round breasts, elegant waist, delicate hips and what is euphemistically called "all the rest" (*le sorplus*). This is yet another example in which the literary text has an advantage over visual images in effectively conveying the culturally potent ambiguity of women being understood socially as clothed and unclothed simultaneously.

The marked difference in male and female underwear is significant during an era when outer clothing revealed little differentiation in gender. In courtly literature of the twelfth and thirteenth centuries the standard indoor costume for both men and women is a highly unisex ensemble known as the "robe." For elite members of the courtly world in France, the "robe" would typically include an outer loose-fitting tunic with sleeves, termed either a *bliaut* or *cotte*, and a long cloak or mantle fastened at the neck. Sometimes a sleeveless garment called a *surcot*, was worn over the *cotte* or *bliaut* but under the mantle. Figure 5.12 shows the heroine Silence learning to become a jongleur while wearing the unisex *cotte* and *surcot*.

Starkly different from the tight-fitting doublet and hose that distinguished men from women who wore long dresses in the later Middle Ages, the ensemble of *chemise, bliaut,*

FIGURE 5.11: The courtly "robe," Viollet-le-Duc, *Dictionnaire raisonné du mobilier français de l'époque carlovingienne à la renaissance*. Paris: Gründ et Maguet, 1854–75. Vol. 3, 288, s.v. "cotte," fig. 7, after an image of king Philip III the Bold in a manuscript, *Histoire de la vie et des miracles de Saint Louis*, end of the thirteenth century.

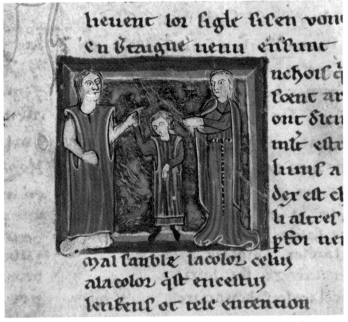

FIGURE 5.12: Silence learning to become a jongleur, from a collection of romances and fabliaux, c. 1200–50. Manuscripts and Special Collections, The University of Nottingham, WLC/LM/ 6, f. 203 r.

and *mantel* creates a strikingly similar silhouette for aristocratic men and women whose clothing actually proves interchangeable at times. We hear, for example, in the *Prose Lancelot* that the knight Bors arrives at court "vestuz dune robe d'un samit vermeil foree d'ermine dont il avoit cote et mantel" (dressed in an outfit composed of *cote* and *mantel*, all of red silk lined with ermine, 4:374). Queen Guenevere is said similarly to wear a "robe de porpre qui toute estoit batue a or, si en avoit cote et mantel forré d'ermine" (dark-colored silk outfit composed of a *cote* and *mantel*, both lined with ermine, 4:385). The outermost component of the unisex *robe*, the mantle, actually passes regularly between knights and ladies, as traveling knights stop for lodging at castles where they shed their armor in exchange for more comfortable indoor clothes. In the *Prose Lancelot*, Hector is greeted by a young woman who removes his armor and offers him a "court mantel" (short cloak) identical to her own indoor attire (8: 303). In a more extreme example, the young lady who welcomes the Duke of Clarence actually dresses him in an item of her own clothing, removing the "un mantel d'escarlete" (a dark-colored wool cloak) from her shoulders and placing it "au col" (around the neck and shoulders) of her male guest.[28]

In the courtly world, women's distinctive social identity resides less, then, in what they wear than in how they wear it. A passage from the *Prose Lancelot* reinforces the importance of men's flesh being covered while ladies' skin should be open to view. The scene contrasts ".II. routes de chevaliers *tous armés*" (two columns of fully-armed/armored knights) and "une dame" on horseback "vestue d'un samit vermeil, cote et mantel a pene d'ermine; si fu *toute desliie* et ele estoit de merveilleuse biauté" (dressed in a red silk gown and a cloak lined in ermine. She [her head] was *completely uncovered* and of wondrous beauty, my emphasis, 7:358). While the helmeted knights are fully encased in armor, the lady's costume is characteristically open (headdress undone) so that her beautiful face can be seen. It is not that this lady is unclothed per se but that skin itself constitutes a key element of the aristocratic woman's requisite attire.[29]

There are intriguing exceptions to the rule, of course. One maiden in the *Prose Lancelot* who has dutifully guided Lancelot through the forest suddenly switches rhetorical modes and begins to entice the unsuspecting knight by unveiling her skin, "De totes les choses le semont de quoi ele le cuide eschaufer, si se deslie sovent por mostrer son vis et son chief qui de tres grant bialté estoit et chante lais bretons et autres notes plaisans et envoisies" (Everything she said to him was designed to heat him up; she repeatedly unlaced her headgear to reveal her very beautiful head and face as she sang Breton songs and other pleasing and seductive tunes, 1:317). And yet, this damsel is not reduced to fetishized skin alone, for she has moved tentatively into the position of the desiring subject, constructing an amorous scenario between herself and Lancelot. Later in the scene, when she slips into bed next to the timorous and incredulous Lancelot, he rejects her advances saying he had "onques mes n'oi parler de dame ne de damoisele qui volsist prendre chevalier par force" (never heard of a lady who tried to take a knight by force, 1:323). That is to say, in effect, "ladies don't wear armor and can't cross-dress as knights," at least not as long as they follow the courtly code that polices this kind of unmarked transvestism. According to the dominant rules of courtliness, ladies should wear only one outfit: a loose and flowing gown which, diametrically opposed to the knight's armor, is tied typically to her exposed and gendered flesh. However, the lady escorting Lancelot through the forest has injudiciously stepped over the hypothetical line dividing armor from skin. In cross dressing metaphorically as a knight, she has made gender trouble in the courtly world, not by donning actual armor, as Silence does, but by "being" a lady while *acting* as if she wore arms and armor, as if she were, as Lancelot charges, able to "take a knight by force." This scenario encourages us to consider other ways in which physical arms and armor might confer social value across gendered identities.

ARMOR

Typically, it is squires who arm knights for combat, but any number of configurations are possible. In the twelfth-century romance *Erec and Enide*, the future ladylove herself arms the knight, dressing him in iron greaves, a hauberk, helmet with chin guard, a shield hung around his neck and a lance in his hand (vv. 709–26). In fact, it is only through a process of continual dressing and undressing that the courtly knight's body achieves and maintains the requisite level of masculine identity.[30] The point is driven home perhaps most clearly in another twelfth-century romance, *Perceval ou le Conte du Graal*, which shows that arms and armor are not necessarily separable from the properly chivalric body. After killing the Red Knight in this tale, the hero Perceval explains that he will have to cut the dead man into pieces to remove the armor he now feels is rightfully his. The Red Knight's armor, he explains, ". . . se tiennent si au cors/ Que ce dedens et che defors/ Est trestot un, si com moi samble" (is so stuck to the body that the inside and the outside are one, vv. 1139–41). It seems, indeed to Perceval "Qu'eles se tiennent si ensamble" (that they are joined together, v. 1142). The incident provides a particularly cogent example of a sartorial body, formed as much from fabric as from flesh. Indeed, Perceval's comments suggest the extent to which all knightly armor functions as a kind of social skin that creates as it clothes the chivalric body.

The point is made in a very different way in one of the earliest Old French poems to address theories of knighthood, the *Ordene de Chevalerie*, which stages the historical capture of French knight Hugh of Tiberias (here called Hue de Tabarie) by Saladin in 1179.[31] Negotiations between the two rivals lead ultimately to Saladin's request to learn "comment l'on fet les chevaliers" (how knights are made, v. 80). Curiously, Hugh does not respond with words but begins instead to enact an elaborate ritual of dressing. In response to Saladin's request for information, Hugh actually "makes" him into a knight (though not a Christian) by enfolding him in a series of garments, followed by golden spurs, a sword, and a cloth head covering (*coiffe*) typically worn beneath a helmet. Individual garments include white linen underclothes, a red robe, black silk leggings, and a narrow white belt around his waist. Indeed, it seems that Hugh is unable to "teach" Saladin "how knights are made" without actually putting clothes on the eastern king's body, clothes that are not dissimilar to the garments worn by Hugh himself and other western courtly knights. In this case we see the extent to which chivalric bodies on both sides of the Mediterranean are construed as sartorial bodies.

Armor is perhaps most significant for questions of gender because although it functions ostensibly as the quintessential marker of medieval masculinity, armor is the only garment in the medieval wardrobe that covers the entire body. As such, armor can potentially contain any kind of gendered being. And how would we know? The question is articulated near the end of the *Roman de Silence*, when King Ebains calls on Silence, now known as "the best knight in France" (vv. 5209–10) to quell a revolt. "She" is armed as follows: with a quilted silk doublet, a fine chain mail hauberk, lightweight and impenetrable, with leggings made of the same chainmail, golden spurs, and a sword belted at the waist (vv. 5336–48). Just before the armed knight departs, the assistants close the ventail and lace on the helmet which has no equal in any land: it is studded with gemstones, a circlet of

FIGURE 5.13: Helmet, Viollet-le-Duc, *Dictionnaire raisonné du mobilier français de l'époque carlovingienne à la renaissance*. Paris: Gründ et Maguet, 1854–75. Vol. 6, 111.

gold worth more than a treasure and a carbuncle decorating the nasal (vv. 5352–60). This fully covered character has all the appearance of a knight and all the skill to be victorious in the upcoming battle.

What then of all the other knights in the Arthurian world, we might ask, who acquit themselves honorably in battle and tournament? Could they too be potentially "women" like Silence? Or perhaps the more appropriate question might be, if they excel as Silence does in chivalric skills, if they establish their prowess irrefutably and in public as all knights do, might they too at times possibly be examples of a hybrid gender, lying somewhere between the supposedly uncontestable categories of masculinity and femininity? Indeed, this is the question that many medieval texts ask repeatedly, even while promoting and endorsing more rigid categorizations of masculinity and femininity. If in the world of courtly encounter, knights wear armor and women display skin, what happens when that female skin becomes so encased in chainmail and metal gear that we see it no longer? If a "woman" whose skin is covered and concealed beneath a shell of masculinity that she does not remove in the public eye, we cannot "know" or define her/his gender apart from the sartorial body we see.

This does not mean that clothes "make her into a man" any more than Gauvain's imagining himself as Lancelot's ladylove makes him into a "woman." Rather, dress is used in these examples and in many others we have discussed to loosen and expand the very categories of "men" and "women." Indeed, we have seen the extent to which medieval literary representations of clothing can offer singularly potent ways of creating gender apart from anatomy. Literary accounts of the clothes worn, displayed, and manipulated by fictional characters often pose fundamental challenges to our assumptions about gendered identities and gendered beings, assumptions that we may share with the sleeping man who wakes up wearing a dress. Is he a "he" or a "she," he wants to know. Reading gender through clothes can help us understand that there are other more productive questions to ask.

CHAPTER SIX

Status

LAUREL ANN WILSON

Every form of dress carries some indication of the status of its wearer. Status, defined most simply as social difference, is a social relationship which dress effectively makes visible to others.[1] In the period from Late Antiquity through the late Middle Ages, the relationship between dress and status was renegotiated many times. During the early Middle Ages, status divisions became broader and less detailed than they had been under the Roman Empire, and dress became correspondingly simpler, as well as somewhat less important as a status indicator. In the later Middle Ages, as finer gradations developed in the spectrum of ranks and statuses, dress became more complex in ways that enabled the display of subtler distinctions.[2] In the twelfth century, the everyday dress of aristocratic men, after remaining largely unchanged for centuries, was replaced by longer, relatively unisex garments, which by the thirteenth century were being combined in *robes*, or ensembles.[3] In the next century, more complex forms of dress developed, often in separate pieces, requiring choice and assembly. This new complexity, together with the incessant and rapid changes in style that began in the fourth decade of the fourteenth century, indicated an increasing importance given to dress as a status marker, and, in my view, marked the transition from dress to fashion.[4] The primary focus of this essay is thus an examination of the changing relationship between dress and status in the period from the twelfth century through the fourteenth.

The evidence for medieval clothing has its limits. Much of the evidence is representational—that is, artistic or literary—which in itself is limiting (see Chapters 8 and 9). Some of the best documentary evidence for how clothing conveys status, such as sumptuary laws, livery rolls, and wardrobe accounts, most often describes clothing materials rather than actual garments. The surviving evidence also makes it difficult to see beyond the aristocracy and the wealthier bourgeoisie. When working class or peasant dress appears in art or literature it is generally stereotyped.[5]

I have focused this discussion primarily on men's clothing, since men's clothes changed drastically during the Middle Ages, while the changes in women's clothes were far more incremental. This is not to suggest that women's clothes remained entirely static, or that women were not interested in changes in dress, but male dress was the leading force in European fashion until the eighteenth century.[6]

CHANGE IN CLOTHING

The visual evidence of men's clothing from the early Middle Ages can be roughly divided into long clothing, reserved for aristocrats, and short tunics, generally depicted as featureless except for a defined waistline, which were long used by artists to designate workers or peasants. The most common long style is a draped garment, with a cloak or mantle over it. Biblical figures, saints, and kings were most often depicted dressed this way: long robes, generally made of precious fabrics, have signified majesty and gravitas in many cultures, and are often used for coronations and other investment ceremonies for this reason.[7] For similar reasons, as clerical and secular clothing began to diverge in the early Middle Ages, clerical clothing generally remained long even when secular clothing had become shorter.[8] Artistic representation further amplified the significance of long robes by using them to signal not just majesty and gravitas, but holiness and heroism as well.[9]

A second type of short secular male attire appeared sometime in the early Middle Ages, and remained in use for centuries thereafter. Consisting of a knee-length belted tunic, slightly flared and often decoratively edged at the bottom, worn over colored, decorated, or cross-gartered hose, frequently with a large square mantle, or *penula*, over it, what I will term the "tunic ensemble" began to appear in artistic representations as early as the sixth century, and was still represented in the twelfth century.[10] Unlike the peasant tunic mentioned earlier, this ensemble was often depicted in detail, making it possible to discern variations in fabric, color, and decoration.

While the silhouette remained largely unchanged, its significance as a status indicator changed considerably over time. Until the ninth century, the tunic ensemble, in addition to being used consistently to depict military dress, was represented as ordinary dress, in contrast both to the robes worn by men of high status and clerics, and to the worker/peasant tunic. Charlemagne's counselor Einhard, writing a few years after Charlemagne's death in 814, describes the tunic ensemble as Charlemagne's preferred clothing, and classifies it as similar to that worn by "the common people."[11]

Over the course of the ninth century, the significance of the tunic ensemble changed. In an illumination created c. 850, the men flanking the enthroned Charles the Bald are dressed in it, while in a manuscript created for him in 870, Charles the Bald is shown wearing the tunic ensemble himself, in an allegory of royalty by divine right.[12]

Over the next several centuries, increasing numbers of kings, saints, and even angels were depicted in some version of the tunic ensemble, while at the same time it remained the ordinary dress of a wide range of men.[13] Figure 6.1, from an eleventh-century French manuscript, depicts, according to the accompanying text, "kings, princes, and merchants," as well as musicians in the bottom register, and all are wearing the tunic ensemble, though the materials vary according to the status of the wearer.[14]

In the twelfth century, dress took on new importance as a status marker. The silhouette of men's clothing shifted: the primary garment was still a tunic, but it was long, draped, and tightly fitted. In artistic representations, the clothing is so closely molded to the body that the contours of the stomach are visible, a style of painting which art historians refer to as "dampfold" because it gives the appearance of damp clothing. Actual clothing was tightly fitted, probably by lacing, but it is difficult to know how much the revealing nature of the painted clothing was simply a convention.[15] Garments often had wide sleeves, and side slits exposing men's legs and hose, showing off a new type of shoe with exaggeratedly long toes (Figure 6.2). Like most draped clothing, the new clothing was somewhat unisex in appearance, more than the tunic ensemble had been, and, perhaps because of this, there were some corresponding changes in women's clothes, such as tighter fit, dropped waists, and emphasized body contours.

There is visual evidence of the new clothing from roughly 1130 on, along with confirmation in the form of chronicles written by horrified clerics.[16] The moralistic

FIGURE 6.1: Kings, princes, and merchants lamenting the fall of Babylon, Beatus of St. Sever, late eleventh century. MS lat. 8878, fol. 195r. Bibliothèque nationale de France.

FIGURE 6.2: Hawking (calendar page, May). English, first quarter of the twelfth century (detail). Shaftesbury Psalter. Lansdowne 383, fol. 5r. © British Library.

hysteria had actually begun in the eleventh century, prompted largely by changes in hair and beard styling, but also inflamed by what the chroniclers perceived as the new *shortness* in clothing. In the twelfth century, when clothing became longer, clerical chroniclers were equally disturbed by the new *long* clothing, which "swept up all the filth from the ground," and prevented men from walking properly or doing anything useful.[17] It is clear that they are talking about young men, and the visual evidence backs this up: the wearers are shown not just as young, but as engaged in noble, i.e., idle, pursuits such as hawking.[18] The new styles were also used to depict those engaged in bad or sinful behavior, as in a mid-twelfth century illustration of Psalm 1 produced in England, in which the "ungodly man" is dressed in the newest clothing, contrasting with the godly man in his robes.[19]

The vehemence of these reactions suggests that dress had taken on new meaning, and literary evidence backs up this conclusion (see Chapter 9). Twelfth-century romances often dress the high-status characters in fantastical clothing, e.g., the ceremonial robe worn by Erec at the end of Chrétien de Troyes's *Érec et Énide*, described as having been made by four fairies, who embroidered on it complete representations of geometry, mathematics, astronomy, and music.[20] The implication is that dress is so important that supernatural intervention is required to adequately indicate extremely high status.

In this literature, the state of being clothed or naked, the acts of dressing and undressing, and the act of clothing someone are also imbued with status significance. Giving clothing, or the materials for clothing, to someone is an act which establishes or reinforces relative status, since the gift of clothing always goes from the higher-status individual to the lower-status individual, often raising the recipient's status. Regular princely gifts to members of their households, termed "liveries," appear in this period (see later).

Judging from the visual evidence, both the tunic ensemble and the new clothing existed in parallel. The illuminations in the *Life of St. Edmund*, from mid-twelfth century England, suggest that the silhouette of the new clothing had been partially incorporated into the tunic ensemble; they also give a very clear picture of the different status categories the tunic ensemble could represent, as shown in Figure 6.3. King Edmund, enthroned, is wearing long robes, which appear to be standard royal dress rather than the new clothing. He is distributing alms to beggars, three of whom are wearing versions of the tunic ensemble, some barelegged and some with knee-length leggings; two of the beggars are wearing wraps made of hides with the fur still attached. By contrast, the courtier at the left, who is obviously of high status, wears a tunic ensemble, but it resembles the new clothing rather than the traditional tunic ensemble, except in length.

By the thirteenth century, longer clothing for men generally prevailed—exceptions included some knights' clothing, and, as always, the lower class and peasants—and the tightly fitting silhouette of the twelfth century had evolved into looser clothing, often worn in layers. Most often, these clothes were made in an ensemble called a *robe* or a pair of robes, consisting of several matching garments (see Figure 6.4): a long-sleeved cotte, surcot (often sleeveless), and a mantle, fur-lined if one could afford it (as shown on the clothespole), shorter and rougher for workers (such as those driving the beasts, lower right).[21]

Although the pictured clothing of the late twelfth and thirteenth centuries still gives the impression of relatively broad status groupings, other sources indicate the beginning of profound changes in the meaning of dress and in its uses as a marker of status. Increasing attempts to control who could wear what, such as sumptuary laws, and the growing importance of clothing as a literary symbol both indicate the newly prominent relation between clothing and status.

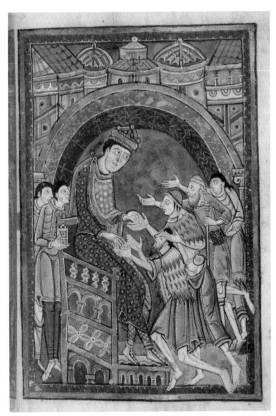

FIGURE 6.3: King Edmund distributing coins to beggars, Miscellany on the life of St. Edmund.
Bury St. Edmunds, c. 1130. Morgan Library, MS M 736, fol. 9r. © 2016. Photo: Pierpont
Morgan Library/Art Resource/Scala, Florence.

Thirteenth-century literature paid increased attention to clothing, and the clothing
was often depicted more realistically. *Le Roman de la Rose*, for example, a popular
thirteenth-century poem, is permeated by an awareness of clothing. Dress is repeatedly
used in the poem as an allegorical symbol or to represent a character trait, demonstrating
the expressive qualities ascribed to dress at the time.[22]

Major changes in actual clothing took some time to respond to changes in meaning. It
was not until well into the fourteenth century, after subtler gradations of status had begun
to appear in European societies, that men's clothing changed in a way that made it
infinitely more capable of displaying difference. Figure 6.5, from an early fourteenth-
century English manuscript, shows a number of these changes: note the decorative
buttons, the individual hoods, and the pleated slits in the front of the garments. It is
possible to see in this illumination changing attitudes as well: with their elegant poses,
their gloves, their fancy shoes, it seems clear that the artist intends these men to be seen
as fashionable, possibly foolishly so.

Truly radical change in men's clothing began in the 1330s, when the long, draped
garments of the previous two centuries were replaced by garments which were short,
tightly fitted, and tailored. A French manuscript of Guillaume de Machaut's *Remède de
Fortune* from the mid-fourteenth century makes it clear how sharply these clothes

FIGURE 6.4: The thirteenth-century "robe" ensemble. Detail from scenes from the Life of David, Absolom with the royal concubines, c. 1250. Tempera colors and gold leaf on parchment. MS Ludwig I 6, recto. The J. Paul Getty Museum, Los Angeles,

underlined sexual difference by displaying men's legs, and later in the century their buttocks.[23] The increasingly modular nature of men's clothing can be seen in this illumination as well. Although detachable elements of clothing had been in existence for some time, many more elements of clothing could now be mixed and matched: upper garments, lower garments, sleeves, hoods, capelets, hose, and shoes might be both separable and in separate colors and/or patterns.

Another fashion element newly prominent at this time may be seen in Figure 6.6, as well as in the illuminations of Machaut's manuscripts: decorative cutting into clothing, such as slashing, fringing, and dagging (the cutting of shaped or scalloped edges into fabric). Represented in earlier centuries as a mark of low status, dagging and fringes, along with tippets, long strips of fabric dangling at the elbows, were now a mark of fashionability, condemned by moralists and often banned or controlled in clothing regulations.[24]

The suddenness with which this completely new silhouette came to dominate men's clothing was so rapid that the English manuscript known as the "Smithfield Decretals," illuminated over the course of the years from 1338 to 1342, illustrates the actual movements of change, both in clothing and in the ways in which it was used to denote

FIGURE 6.5: Men fleeing the gates of Babylon (detail), Queen Mary Apocalypse. English, early fourteenth century. Royal MS 19 B XV, fol. 34v. © British Library.

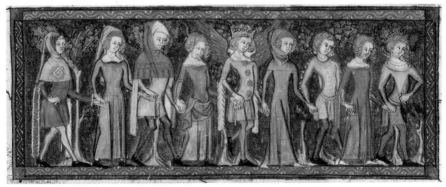

FIGURE 6.6: Carole, *Roman de la Rose*. French, mid-fourteenth century. MS fr. 1567, fol. 7r. Bibliothèque nationale de France.

FIGURE 6.7: King being led away by two men. Decretals of Gregory IX, the "Smithfield Decretals". Royal MS 10 E IV, fol. 308v. © British Library.

status.[25] The shortness of the new clothing was crucial to its fashionable status, but these illuminations suggest that the changes were so rapid that for a period of time the status implications were in flux and difficult to parse. In one illumination (fol. 310v), two knights are embracing while their attendants wait with their horses; one knight's clothing is long, though fashionably accessorized with tippets, while his counterpart's clothing is short and tight. In another illumination from the same section (Figure 6.7), a king is being led away by two knights, and each of the three high-status men has clothing of a different length.[26]

Not only was the change in clothing sudden and profound, it ushered in an era of constant, rapid change in clothing, which lent yet another layer of status expression to dress, since it now required both money and knowledge to keep up with the changes. As a result of all of these developments, the new garments could be used to express status distinctions far more finely graded than those expressed either by the tunic ensemble or by ensembles of robes. The new expressiveness of clothing, its increased importance as a marker of status, and the increased levels of status themselves, combined with a newly available range of choices in clothing, triggered what one scholar called "an explosion of regulatory activities" around clothing, such as sumptuary laws, dress codes, and changes in the practice of livery.[27]

SUMPTUARY LAW

Sumptuary laws intended to regulate public consumption and display in accordance with social status. They are found in many societies, and, although the emphasis of the laws varies with culture and context, they typically target food consumption, banquets, and ceremonies such as births, weddings, and funerals, in addition to their primary focus on dress.[28] Since it reflects the imagined status hierarchy of a given society, sumptuary law is an ideal vehicle for examining the relationship between dress and status. The laws that appeared in both Iberian kingdoms and Italian cities in the thirteenth century were the first non-ecclesiastical sumptuary laws in roughly 750 years.[29] From then on, sumptuary laws multiplied across Europe. The rapid development of medieval European sumptuary laws is a clear indicator of the intensification of the connection between dress and status.[30]

Concern that dress should transparently reveal social status is universal in medieval sumptuary law, as is regulation of luxurious and/or expensive materials such as cloth of gold and furs. The targets and structures of the laws vary widely, however. At one end of the spectrum is the intense focus on the materials and ornamentation of dress found in the Spanish and Italian sumptuary laws.[31] In the case of those from Florence, for example, the focus might be described as obsessive.[32] Taking the comprehensive Florentine *Pragmatica* law collection issued in 1356 as a case study, although there are the standard prohibitions and restrictions on valuable furs and cloth of gold and silver, the real energy seems to have gone into proscriptions and regulations of ornamented clothing, belts, and headwear. Paragraphs are devoted to the size and placement of permissible fringe and a list of the garments on which it may be worn; sleeve lengths are specified; and the function, appearance, and location of buttons is regulated to the point where it has been suggested that the placement of sleeve buttons was the clearest sign of a woman's status.[33]

Social status is not really the focus of the Italian laws, however. It is clear that dress had become newly significant in Italy during the thirteenth and fourteenth centuries, but the increasing social categories visible in other contemporaneous sumptuary laws (see later) were not found in these. The only ranks mentioned, other than female servants and prostitutes, are those which are specifically exempt from the laws: knights, judges, and doctors.[34] More accurately, since Italian sumptuary laws were directed almost entirely at women, it is actually the wives of knights and doctors who were exempted for the most part. There were a few laws which did apply to men, but they were still included under the rubric *de ornatus mulierum*, "on the ornaments of women," and enforced, when they were, by the *uffiziali delle donne*, the ladies' officials. With rare exceptions, then, Italian men could dress richly and fashionably with impunity.

And, in a way, so could women: although the Italian laws are generally thought to have been strictly enforced, the records of actual prosecutions are relatively few. Creative resistance certainly played a part, but economic interests often trumped status as well. The prohibitions had a tendency to evolve into a licensing arrangement, particularly when the commune needed money. In Florence, there was a registration and fine system in place from the first law, in 1299, and by 1373 what had been described in previous laws as "forbidden ornaments" (*ornamenta vetita*) became simply "robes and clothing and other things subject to tax" (*robe et vestimenta et res gabellate*).[35] Although there are no specific references to status as it relates to taxable clothing, it is possible that owning such clothing was in itself an indicator of status, since the garments in question were extremely luxurious.[36]

The Italian laws emanated from the governing bodies of individual communes, while Spanish laws came from the king.[37] Nonetheless, the Spanish laws resemble the Italian in their focus on ornamentation and decorated cloth, in addition to the standard prohibitions and regulations of luxury materials. The Spanish laws also limit the amount of clothing acquired per year. In a Castilian sumptuary law from the mid-thirteenth century, it is specified that no noble may have more than four "pairs of robes" per year, and the ornamentation on those is strictly limited.[38]

The king is exempted from all the limitations described, and he is also the only person permitted to wear a scarlet (*escarlada*) rain cloak, which reflects the unique fixation on dye and color in the Spanish laws. They specify not just what colors may not be worn and by whom, but also what *must* be worn in certain cases. For example, while "no squire [*escudero*] may wear . . . scarlet stockings, or wear scarlet, green, dark brown [*brunet*], pale green [*pres*], brown [*morete*], orange [*narange*], pink [*rrosada*], blood-red [*sanguine*], or any dark-colored clothing," it is the duty of young knights to wear bright colors, such as red, green, and purple, because they confer lightness of heart, and avoid darker colors because they bring sadness, a notion similarly expressed in some Italian laws.[39]

The specific objects and dyes in these laws are carefully regulated by rank. There is no single graded list like those described later in the English and French laws, but the hierarchy is clear. At the top is the king, and although he is granted special privileges he is also subject to certain prohibitions, particularly those pertaining to food.[40] Below the king are his brothers—not his sisters, gender is a relative afterthought in much of this legislation—plus dukes, marquesses, princes, counts, and viscounts, all grouped together as *ricos omes*, and below them are the nobility and the *caballeria*, the knightly class. Knighthood is, in fact, the preoccupation of large portions of Spanish sumptuary law, possibly stemming from the constant need for defense against Islam. The law delimits the behavior expected of knights, both prescribed and prohibited, including colors to be worn, and even the manner in which a *manto caballeroso*, or knight's cloak, was to be made, worn, and fastened.[41]

By the thirteenth century, the military ranks had developed political power as well, and, as elsewhere, additional ranks were emerging. Originally the *caballeria* had consisted simply of knights (*caballeros*) and squires (*escuderos*), but ultimately multiple ranks developed: there were noble knights of various degrees, knights of the lesser nobility, and, as in Italy, knights from the wealthy bourgeoisie, the *caballeria urbana* or *villana*, meaning urban/city knighthood. Urban elites were increasing in power between the thirteenth and the fifteenth centuries as well, leading to the development of additional urban ranks such as *burgueses*, *ruanos*, and *ciudadanos*.[42]

Knights are prominent once again in the English laws, though their chronology is quite different from either the Spanish or the Italian laws.[43] The earliest sumptuary law in England was not enacted until 1337, and it was a relatively minor one with a strong protectionist slant, containing, among other things, a restriction on the wearing of imported cloth by anyone other than the royal family; it also restricted the wearing of rich furs to the royal family and the upper nobility. This was followed by a comprehensive sumptuary law in 1363 (see Table 6.1 for a breakdown of the content of this law).

At the very next Parliament, however, that law was repealed, having been in effect just over a year, and, despite repeated attempts, no comprehensive sumptuary law was passed again until 1463, exactly one hundred years later.[44] As in Florence, it would seem that economic interests won out over the need to make status transparently visible, possibly because in both cases the laws were emanating not from a ruler, but from a representative body including merchants.[45]

The originating force of the English laws belongs somewhere between the Spanish laws, emanating from the king, and the Italian laws, promulgated by municipalities. The English laws originated from petitions in the Commons, the lower house of Parliament, and then required the consent of both the upper house of Parliament and the king. The laws occupy a middle ground in terms of content as well: social gradations are far more finely parsed than in the Spanish laws, and the cloth matched to those gradations is sorted by maximum allowable price rather than decoration, but they also include some detail of forbidden or regulated clothing and ornaments.

In the law of 1337, the ranks listed below the royal family are those which are exempt from the restriction on fur, presumably those considered the higher nobility: prelates, earls, barons, knights, and churchmen with at least £100 per year from their benefices. By contrast, in the law of 1363, no higher nobility is listed at all. The thirty or so levels which

TABLE 6.1: The English Sumptuary Law of 1363

Knights	Esquires	Clergy	Commoners	Best Cloth Allowed	Forbidden Items
			carters, ploughmen, oxherds, "all manner of people of the estate," all those who have less than 40 shillings in goods	blanket, russet (12 pence)	by implication, everything else.
			grooms, servants of lords, as of misteries and artificers	2 marks (= £1.6.2/3) per piece	cloth of higher price, accessories of gold or silver, or embroidered or enameled, or of silk; women the same, with no veils costing over 12 pence per veil.
			craftsmen, artificers, yeomen (possibly including servants of rich merchants and artificers)	40 shillings per piece	precious stones, silk, cloth of silver, girdles, clasps, buckles, rings, garters, broochs, ribbons, chains, seals, and other accessories of gold or silver, anything embroidered or enameled or of silk, etc.; for women, no silk veils, but only those made of domestic thread, no rich fur or budge; only lamb, rabbit, cat, or fox.
	esquires and all sorts of gentle folk below the estate of knight with land or rents worth up to £100 per year	clergy with less than 200 marks per year[1]	merchants, citizens, and burgesses, artificers, craftsmen, in London and elsewhere, who clearly have goods and chattels worth £500	4 1/2 marks per piece	silk, cloth of gold or silver, embroidery and other decorations, rings, clasps, gold brooches, ribbons, girdles, other accessories of gold or silver or precious stones, no rich fur. Women and children the same, with no fur trim

(Continued)

TABLE 6.1: Continued

Knights	Esquires	Clergy	Commoners	Best Cloth Allowed	Forbidden Items
	esquires with land or rents of £200 per year or more		merchants, citizens, and burgesses, artificers, craftsmen who clearly have goods and chattels worth £1,000	5 marks per piece	*specifically permitted:* silk and cloth of silver, ribbons, girdles, and other accessories reasonably ornamented with silver; women may wear furs except ermine and lettice, and fur trim, but no jeweled accessories except on their heads.
knights with lands and rents of 200 marks per year[1]		clergy with more than 200 marks per year[1,3]		6 marks per piece	cloth of gold, clothes furred with miniver, ermine sleeves, clothes embroidered with precious stones; for women and children, fur trim is okay but no ermine nor lettice, and precious stones only for their heads. Knights and clerks in this category who may wear fur in the winter, may wear linen in the summer.
knights and ladies with land or rents from 400 – 1,000[2]				no limits	no limits except no ermine or lettice, and no jeweled accessories except on their heads.

All information from "Parliament of 1363," in Given-Wilson, *Parliament Rolls of Medieval England.*

[1]equivalent to £133/6/8
[2]equivalent to £266/13/4 – £666/13/4
[3]Clergy of rank in cathedral or collegial churches or schools, as well as royal clergy of an estate which requires furs, are to be guided by their own institutional rules.

are listed, carefully classified by a combination of birth and/or social rank with income, begin with wealthy knights and their ladies, and go down the social scale from there all the way to oxherd, specifying the maximum amount which each level is permitted to pay per piece (a standard measurement of cloth).

As elsewhere in Europe, in England finer social distinctions were emerging at this time, both within the nobility and below it. Only two noble ranks, earl and baron, existed at the accession of Edward I in 1272; by the mid-fifteenth century there were five. The creation of new ranks began at the same 1337 Parliament which passed the sumptuary law mentioned in Table 6.1, when Edward III created the first English duke along with six new earls.[46] It is notable that none of these ranks were mentioned in the 1363 law, though it treats much lower ranks, from oxherds and carters up through craftsmen. The primary focus of this law, though, is "the upper-middle level of the social spectrum—the knights, esquires, gentlemen, and burgesses," to a degree far greater than their share of the overall population would suggest.[47]

Since the House of Commons at that time was composed of these very groups, this is perhaps not surprising.[48] Within these middle groups, finer gradations of rank were also developing just as they were among the nobility: the rank of esquire appeared for the first time in the law of 1363, and gentleman appeared in the early fifteenth century.[49] Given the friction that was an integral part of the increasing number of divisions within social groups, particularly the specific social groups just mentioned, it is perhaps not surprising that the law sank out of sight so swiftly and for so long.

There is a similar gap in the chronology of the French sumptuary laws, though they began earlier: two comprehensive laws were implemented at the end of the thirteenth century, one in 1279 by Philip III and one in 1294 by Philip IV.[50] There was then a gap of more than one hundred years before the next comprehensive royal law was passed in 1485.[51] In terms of content, the French laws are at the other end of the spectrum from the Italian laws: the social gradations are as complex as the Italian gradations of dress, but specific items of dress are never mentioned. What matters are the number of garments permitted to each category per year, and the maximum amount each category was permitted to pay per *aune* (measure of cloth).

Here too, the number of social categories was increasing. The law of 1279 lists fourteen categories, from duke down through the upper nobility, the knightly levels, and the bourgeoisie, including various categories of clergy. By 1294, the number of categories had more than doubled, to thirty-two. The increase is mainly in the ranks of knights, expanding from two groups of *escuiers*, divided on the basis of income, to eleven knightly categories, ranging from knight and banneret down to squires. Divisions had increased among the clergy as well, from two categories to six.[52]

Although the laws span a spectrum between emphasizing material detail and emphasizing gradations of rank, the common thread is the insistence that the two should match. "Should," because there is also a striking commonality in the lack of enforcement evidence, suggesting that sumptuary laws were not meant as a form of actual social control. They need to be studied alongside other negotiations between dress and status, such as dress codes and livery.

DRESS CODES

Dress codes and sumptuary laws are often treated as a single phenomenon, since both position dress as a means of status identification, but they differ in significant ways.

Whereas sumptuary laws are proscriptive, dress codes are prescriptive. Sumptuary laws are often addressed to the legislators themselves, and frequently unenforced; dress codes are imposed from above and generally enforced. Sumptuary laws had a more symbolic purpose, whereas dress codes are more instrumental: they are a form of ingroup/outgroup identification, positive or negative.

Many medieval dress codes were negative ones, intended as visual distinction identifying inferior status groups such as Jews, prostitutes, and lepers. These groups were often branded in similar ways, and there are suggestions of the fear of pollution and contamination in many of these regulations.[53] There had been dress codes for both Jews and Christians in Muslim areas since the ninth century; by the thirteenth century identification of outsiders had been increasingly associated with the fear of pollution in many Christian countries.

In the Fourth Lateran Council of 1213, Pope Innocent III imposed unspecified distinctive dress on Jews and Muslims to prevent Christians from unwittingly having sexual relations with them.[54] Following the papal edict, dress codes for Jews (and Muslims, where appropriate) multiplied across Europe, making them roughly contemporaneous with sumptuary law, although they did not fade away in the same way that sumptuary laws did.

The details of the required signs for Jews varied: it might be a specific piece of clothing, such as red tabards for men and red skirts for women, required in Rome, or a symbol which was to be worn on all clothing, such as yellow badges (made notorious by the Nazis, but medieval in origin), or a shape representing the Tables of the Law, imposed in England, or merely a specific color, which might change over time.[55] Accessories played a part as well: earrings for women and specific hats for both women and men, worn proudly at one time, became signs of shame when imposed from outside.[56]

The question of Jewish dress codes is complicated somewhat by sumptuary laws imposed by Jews on themselves. Jews were thought by envious Christians to be wealthy and to display their wealth ostentatiously on their person, and it is not uncommon to see fashionable clothing used in art as a negative signifier for Jews (note the pleating on the Jew's tunic in Figure 6.8, for example). The self-policing laws promulgated by Jewish leaders appear to have arisen from a desire to dispel negative stereotypes. Those promulgated by the council of Jewish leaders held at the Italian city of Forli in 1418, for example, prohibited clothing trimmed with fur, unless the fur was on the inside.[57]

Prostitutes were repeatedly required to identify themselves by their dress, particularly from the fourteenth century on. In England in the 1350s, laws, applying first to the City of London and then to the realm as a whole, required prostitutes to wear hoods of striped cloth, while forbidding them to wear most furs.[58] In Pisa, prostitutes were to identify themselves by wearing a yellow band around their heads; in Florence, veils, gloves, high platform shoes, and bells were mandated. In many Italian cities, including Siena, Ferrara, and Padua, prostitutes were specifically permitted the fashionable clothing denied to "respectable" women, apparently in the hope that the latter would reject fashionable dress for fear of being taken for prostitutes. Such regulation could have effects opposite that intended: San Bernardino relates the story of a woman who had her dressmaker copy the clothing of a prostitute, in order to be more fashionably dressed.[59]

Clerical clothing conveyed another set of status distinctions via its dress code. A recent study makes the point that clerical clothing in the Middle Ages is not simply a subcategory of lay clothing, but rather a distinct culture, with different chronology and development.[60] Distinctive dress for the clergy, generally based on Roman civil clothing, began to emerge in the fourth century, and was well established by the sixth century.[61] The clothing was quite plain at the beginning, but in the ninth century clerical clothing became more

FIGURE 6.8: The Jew of Bourges, "Miracles of the Virgin," the Neville of Hornby Hours. English, c. 1330. Egerton MS 2781, fol. 24r. © British Library.

elaborate and luxurious, presumably as a way of displaying the elevated status of the upper clergy. In the eleventh and twelfth centuries, the relationship between clerical clothing and status began to shift. Elaborate vestments could be worn only in church, setting up a distinction between luxurious clothes in liturgical settings and plain clothes in others. At the same time, greater sartorial distinctions were being introduced within the church hierarchy, leading to more variations in vestments.

This precedes, but parallels, the increasingly fine gradation in clothing appearing in lay society a century or so later. In both cases, the changes arose from the same factors: more interest in status definition through dress, coupled with increases in gradations of status and rank. It took longer for the changes to become visible in society as a whole, since clerical dress is a classic example of a dress code: imposed from above, enforceable and enforced, as opposed to the non-centralized nature of dress in the larger culture, making change slower and messier.

LIVERY

Liveries of clothing can reveal as much about the entanglement between dress and status as sumptuary laws. In a sense, they are the complementary opposite of sumptuary law, reflective of actual practice rather than ideal conceptions. Liveries were goods, most often food and clothing or the raw materials for clothing, distributed by princes and nobles to their households and officers in lieu of or in addition to wages. They were carefully allotted to individuals in quantities and values calculated according to finely graded degrees of status.[62]

In the twelfth century, livery was primarily a manifestation of *largesse*, a specific kind of generosity lauded in twelfth-century literature. *Largesse* was expected of the upper ranks of knights: Marie de France's *Lanval*, for example, describes the joy of a magically-enriched knight in being able to dispense *largesse* to his household in the form of beautiful clothing and luxurious gifts.[63] The virtue of *largesse* was on display in the real world as well, perhaps in response to the literary depictions of it, and distributing rich gifts came to be an action constitutive of nobility, and thus a privilege.[64] In the thirteenth century, an English knight, on trial for raiding, was also accused of *largesse*, having been issuing liveries "as if he had been a baron or an earl."[65]

The distribution of livery was reserved for the wealthy in any case, since it was an enormously expensive undertaking requiring a large and efficient organization: in the greatest courts distributions might involve several hundred people. There were factors in addition to *largesse* that motivated this enterprise, primarily the need for royalty and nobility to present the correct image. Well-dressed retainers were considered so important for the image of the king that a treatise prepared for the future Edward III of England illustrates a passage on the appearance of the king not with the king in majesty, but with the king distributing livery to his knights (Figure 6.9).[66]

Livery worked to the benefit of the recipient as well as of the giver: to be seen in the lord's robes was considered an honor by all levels of society.[67] It was a powerful tool, and

FIGURE 6.9: Knights receiving livery from the king, "Secretum Secretorum." English, c. 1326. Addl MS 47680, fol. 17r. © British Library.

was often made use of in that way, as Edward I of England did in 1304 to force attendance at a Parliament held in a remote place. In his instructions to the keeper of the Great Wardrobe on the livery which was to be issued, he added, "we want you to understand that no one will have robes or cloth except those who are with us."[68] Edward was able to use livery as a tool because he, his retainers, and the keeper of the wardrobe all understood that liveries were due and expected for such an occasion.[69] Because livery so clearly carried reciprocal obligations, it could also be used as a technique of power from the bottom up. It was not unheard of for the noble holder of a hereditary office, should he not receive the expected liveries, to refuse to perform the necessary service *propter defectum vestium*, as one late twelfth-century case put it.[70]

The function and uses of liveries changed over time. In courts and great households, social status began to separate from function and, as in other contexts, increased stratification began to develop, so that there was a growing need to codify the visible signs of status more precisely into livery distribution.[71] In addition to the careful matching of the amount and type of cloth and fur distributed to the rank of the person receiving it, more visible distinctions could be made by color and/or pattern, primarily stripes, and increasingly by the use of *mi-parti* clothing, that is, clothing made of two or more types of cloth which differed in color and/or pattern.[72]

Initially the visible distinctions were internal identifiers only. There was no particular significance to the colors chosen, and the resulting clothing did not identify the wearer to an outsider as a member of a particular household. Over the course of the fourteenth century, livery began to take on an additional dimension, ultimately becoming a sign of allegiance and affiliation clearly recognizable to outsiders.

Technical developments as well as social factors led to livery becoming a more consistent means of identification. Livery had long depended on, and perhaps encouraged, a reliable supply of textiles of distinguishable and consistent values. Once dye techniques became more consistent, it was easier to buy large quantities of cloth of the same color; once techniques for weaving many variations of stripes, checks, and other patterns had developed on an industrial scale, it was possible to create different categories that were separately identifiable. The fine gradations of identification were applied particularly to the lower echelons of the household, and certain patterns and arrangements ultimately became associated with specific statuses: striped cloth, or ray, became associated with servants, while *mi-parti*, originally worn by those of high rank, also became identified with lower ranks.[73]

CONCLUSION

Between the twelfth and the fourteenth centuries, as social divisions in western Europe became more finely graded, status also became more fluid. The increasing slipperiness of status coincided with, and was in part caused by, the increasing commercialization of western Europe, the so-called commercial revolution of the later Middle Ages.[74] The growth of trade, and the new industries which arose in the later Middle Ages, particularly the cloth industry, affected the social structure of society, increasing the social and political presence of wealthy merchants and producing new forms of social groupings such as craft guilds, while ultimately lowering the status of weavers and other workers. There was increased friction between various strata of the social system, as groups rose and fell, gained or lost political power, and became conscious of themselves as groups.

This was particularly true in the middle and upper-middle levels of the social spectrum. While the upper nobility became more formalized, the ranks of the lower nobility, knights, and wealthy merchants were constantly in flux, changing places in a kind of giant game of musical chairs. The growth of commerce and industry also made a much larger range of goods available and produced the wealth with which to buy them, so that commodities which had once been the signs of nobility could now be purchased by anyone with sufficient means, while at the same time much of the nobility was struggling to make ends meet.

As social fluidity grew and status categories proliferated, visible markers of status took on greater and greater significance. Since a correspondingly greater variety of clothing and sartorial goods was developing at the same time, dress and clothing became of primary importance as status markers, leading, ultimately, to the dynamic we call "fashion."

CHAPTER SEVEN

Ethnicity

MICHÈLE HAYEUR SMITH

Visual appearance lies at the basis of the expression of cultural identity,[1] and dress can be considered as articulating one of the more fundamental dimensions of human experience: "belonging."[2] While the body is said to lack distinctive physical characteristics to distinguish it from others, by deliberately altering its appearance humans are successful at stating who belongs and who does not.[3] More specifically, however, dress can also come to symbolize subtle information within a given culture about social status and rank, gender roles and attitudes, sacred and/or secular affiliations, as well as age and whether the individual plays an active or passive role in society.[4] The effects of cultural interaction can produce amalgamations of symbols: through acculturation; through the maintenance of tradition; or, far more subtly, through hybridity.[5]

In what follows, Scandinavia and its colonies are examined as a case study for dress practices that marked medieval ethnicity. Their separation from the rest of Europe, combined with the connections of trade, warfare, and colonization, focus our attention on the ways dress was implicated in the articulation of ethnic identities—in the marking out of the categories of "us" and "others." While the particular sartorial expressions of culture that are revealed are unique to Scandinavia and the North Atlantic, it is important to remember that similar processes were at work throughout the medieval world. Where different groups interacted, acculturation, persistence of tradition, and hybridity occurred, in dress practices as in other cultural expressions. Here we will unpick the threads of such interactions in the Scandinavian world.

SCANDINAVIA AND THE SETTLEMENT OF THE NORTH ATLANTIC, 793–1050

The raid on the monastery at Lindisfarne in 793 has traditionally been used in the English-speaking world to mark the beginning of the Viking Age. This was a period characterized by an outward expansion of Scandinavian peoples toward the rest of Europe.[6] Preliminary voyages involved raiding and trading, targeting monasteries and other wealthy and vulnerable locations. In the second half of the ninth century, the lure of piracy was replaced by colonization. From Norway, settlers made their way to the British Isles: the Orkneys, Shetland, the Hebrides, Ireland, and eventually westward into the North Atlantic toward Iceland, the Faroe Islands, and Greenland.

Norwegian Vikings settled in Iceland starting around 874, bringing with them domestic animals from Europe and an agricultural lifestyle. There were no towns or cities and, until the 1740s, Iceland's settlement pattern was one of single farms scattered evenly across the

FIGURE 7.1: Map of Scandinavian settlement from the eighth to eleventh century, by Max Naylor.

landscape, with the exception of larger seasonal aggregations after c. 1250 at important coastal fishing locations.[7] Arriving in Iceland, these Norwegian settlers encountered a new, unoccupied country, and claimed as much available land as possible (Figure 7.1). A century later, around 985, Greenland was settled from Iceland, at the instigation of the famous outlawed Viking, Erik the Red.

While the dominant culture in these Norse colonies of the North Atlantic was Norwegian, Iceland was also home to many other settlers from other parts of the Viking world, including the British Isles, the Hebrides, and Ireland. Some of these were slaves, some the spouses of Norwegian settlers, and some were independent farmers in their own right. Christian churches dedicated to "Celtic" saints were founded during the first decades of settlement,[8] and mitochondrial DNA studies on modern Icelanders have also demonstrated a significant Celtic component among Iceland's female settlers.[9] Strontium isotope analyses on skeletal material from Viking Age burials of Iceland's earliest settlers have demonstrated that out of ninety early burials at least nine, and probably thirteen, of these individuals could be distinguished as migrants to Iceland coming from other not-yet identified places.[10] The emerging picture is one of cultural mixing, and this is apparent as well in Icelandic Viking Age dress and material culture.

DRESS AND CULTURAL IDENTITY IN VIKING AGE SCANDINAVIA, 793–1050

Viking Age women in Scandinavia wore long dresses with long sleeves, made of pleated linen, closed at the neck with a brooch.[11] A pair of oval brooches were worn on the chest, fastening the straps of a sleeveless apron (Figure 7.2), sometimes called a *smokkr*, worn on top of the longer dress.

FIGURE 7.2: Reconstructed Viking female dress and oval brooches from the Viking festival at Hafnafjorður, Iceland. Photo: M. Hayeur Smith.

A string of beads or a pendant was frequently hung between the brooches along with other useful implements: knives, scissors, and sometimes keys.[12] The textiles worn by women in Scandinavia varied greatly according to social status (and presumably task), from coarse woolens to fine oriental silks.[13] A wrap or shawl could be been worn over this outfit; and from evidence recovered at Hedeby, well-to-do women often wore an ankle-length coat over their dress. Cloaks were also worn and could be lined with fur, embroidered with silver thread, or edged with decorative ribbons or *posaments* (a metal appliqué, the more prestigious being of gold or silver wire spun around a silk core and fashioned to create diverse knotted motifs).[14] Poorer women's or slaves' clothing consisted of simple, ample, ankle-length long-sleeved dresses made of a rough woolen fabric.

The oval brooches, worn in pairs, are so widespread in Scandinavian burials that they are generally considered the most typical item of female Viking dress.[15] They are so standardized that they have been used as gender identifiers in Viking burials even where skeletal observations of sex are impossible.[16] Their designs are equally standardized, and it is not uncommon to find identical brooch types in areas as remote and distant as Iceland or Russia, wherever the Viking presence was felt. These brooches may have been symbols of married status, not unlike the wedding ring today, as they are not found in all women's graves but occur regularly with adult women of a restricted social stratum within society, potentially representing married women who ran an independent household.[17] The recovery of pairs of oval brooches on women's chests in Viking Age graves confirms that this was their intended placement on the women's attire, where they clearly resemble a stylized and accentuated pair of breasts. This visual statement was manifest in their placement directly on or slightly above the breasts, and reinforced by their decoration with multiple bosses (frequently nine—a recurring number in Viking Age religious art and mythology) that make allusion to nipples.[18] The goddess Freyja, who oversaw all issues relating to female reproduction and fertility, was frequently given the name of "sow" (or *bitch* by slanderous Christian missionaries in Iceland), and the similarity between the appearance of these brooches and the belly of a lactating pig or other animal is striking.[19] The brooches' hyper-emphasis of stylized female sexual traits could be direct reflections of female sexuality, or may have expressed notions of femininity, fertility and lactation, as well as associations with Norse divinities.

Male dress in Viking Age Scandinavia was no less lavish than female dress, indeed it was frequently more so, featuring elaborate textiles embroidered in gold or silver thread on silk.[20] Breeches or pantaloons were worn with a tunic that fell from mid-thigh to below the knees, held by a belt from which was suspended a knife, comb, and purse. A cape was frequently worn with a brooch or clasp on the right shoulder so that the right arm was free to carry a sword.[21] In some instances, men found in Scandinavian burials wear headbands or thin diadems of gold and silver from which hung small pendants that fell to the neck.[22] The most common form of adornment found in men's graves is weaponry, including swords, spears, axes, arrowheads, and shields.[23] Decorative elements of weaponry served a social function in addition to their practical purposes, conveying messages of ethnic affiliation, alliances, or external contacts, as well as denoting the social status of the wearer among other men.[24]

While Viking dress primarily appears to have denoted social hierarchy, there is evidence from the artistic styles of adornment that it also expressed regional variation.[25] Archeological evidence also shows regional variations where certain members of society practiced teeth filing. In Sweden, 557 skeletons were analyzed from four major Viking period cemeteries. It was found that 10 percent of the younger male skeletons had intentional horizontal grooves cut across the upper front incisors, cut deep into the enamel and arranged in pairs or triplets in a very precise fashion. They may have served to mark certain men as tradesmen, or as warriors possibly able to withstand pain. In short, what may have been a regional or ethnic marker was likely polysemous, also demarcating specific categories of people within society.[26]

Much of our information on dress in Viking Age Scandinavia comes from archeological and specifically mortuary analyses. However, medieval tales and stories also provide insights. Icelandic sagas were written down two to three centuries after the end of the Viking Age, recounting events that occurred during the settlement of the island. Information more immediately contemporary with the later literary descriptions can be obtained from the narrative of the Arab traveler Ahmed Ibn Fadlan, dated to 921. He formed part of an embassy sent by the Abbasid Caliph al- Muqtadir (caliph of Baghdad, 908–32) to the King of the Bulgars along the Volga.

In his travels, Ibn Fadlan encountered the Rús (Swedish Vikings and Slavs). His testimonials describe one event and one funeral, one of the only eyewitness accounts of the Vikings and their cultural practices. Although it is unknown from any other source, Ibn Fadlan recounts the Rús as being heavily tattooed: "from the extremities of their fingers to their necks they are covered with greenish blue tattoos of trees, figures, etc."[27] His descriptions of male dress fit the funerary data, stating that none of them wore caftans but wore a garment that covered their body on one side leaving one arm free (presumably the sword arm), and each one had an axe, a sword, and a knife that never left them.

As an outsider, Ibn Fadlan's comments implicitly show ethnic comparisons. The women's jewelry must have appeared striking to him. He remarked on the wearing of oval brooches or box-shaped brooches. He mentions that all women have on their breasts a circular box (brooch) of iron, copper, gold, or wood, depending on the wealth of their husbands: "Each box is circular in shape, and from it they suspend a knife. They wear from their necks necklaces of silver and gold, because as soon as a man possesses 10,000 dirhems, he buys for his wife a necklace and if he has 20,000 he buys her two necklaces, etc., and each time his wealth increases he adds another necklace."[28]

Color is an aspect of dress often described in the Icelandic sagas, and which has been given ethnic interpretation since antiquity. For instance, chapter 63 of *Laxdaela saga* describes men wearing a variety of colors: blue cloaks, tunics of scarlet and green, black breeches. Blue is a common color mentioned in the saga literature. Kirsten Wolf argues blue and black semantically overlapped in the Norse worldview and were the color of ravens, Hel—the goddess of the realms of the dead, and Óðin, the king of the gods but also the master of death.[29] In *Laxdaela saga* among other texts, blue is often worn before a killing, further enhancing associations with death.

Is blue an ethnic marker for Scandinavia? Blue garments are found in Viking Age burials in Scandinavia, notably at Birka (Sweden) and in Norway, but the color's significance is not absolutely clear. Scandinavians may simply have made use of blue due to the abundance of woad in northern Europe. However, this cultural practice was passed on and is prominent in Icelandic Viking Age women's burials.[30] In contrast, the Romans considered blue a "barbarian" color, dyeing primarily in shades of red. The Merovingian use of blue is ascribed to Celtic and Germanic influence. Its use diminished in the Carolingian period, not to return to fashion until the thirteenth century on the continent.[31]

In summary, then, while overall garment construction is similar across Scandinavia, permanent body modification such as teeth filing and tattooing may reflect cultural distinctions between the areas known today as Sweden, Norway, and Denmark, or may reflect specific markers of social affiliation or hierarchy within Scandinavian society itself. The most striking of these elements of dress, particularly for women, is the oval brooch, which stands out as a quintessential item of Scandinavian female gender and identity, in distinct contrast with brooch forms identified with other ethnic groups.[32] It is the inclusion of such jewelry types combined with other non-Scandinavian items that will be the focus of the following examination of Icelandic dress.

ICELANDIC VIKING AGE DRESS

We know from burial evidence that dress in ninth- and tenth-century Iceland was the same in basic construction as that of the mainland Scandinavians. Similar garments, decorative features, weaponry, and jewelry were worn, although preserved textiles tend to be less lavish and consist of woolen and linen weaves. However, analyses of the Icelandic mortuary corpus has revealed that the ways these items were arranged and combined with foreign—especially Celtic—objects and design elements, known to scholars as the Hiberno-Norse style, established features and fashions unique to the Norse colonies in Iceland and Scotland.[33] This hybrid form of dress was clearly the direct result of the amalgamation of individual traits familiar to these different population groups, living side-by-side in the North Atlantic colonies, to create something new and distinct.

However, it appears that multiple processes were in play during the settlement period in Iceland, as these hybrid fashions are found only in select burials. Others strongly display Norwegian affiliation, through the use of classical Scandinavian jewelry without any admixture of Hiberno-Norse elements, possibly stating their linkages to what clearly,

FIGURE 7.3: Oval brooch from Skógar í Flókadal, dated to the ninth century but recovered in a tenth-century context. Photo: National Museum of Iceland.

by the mid-tenth century, became Iceland's dominant cultural group. These women were buried with oval brooches, but in many instances these were stylistically older than the grave itself, suggesting that they may have been heirlooms when buried or objects that maintained links with ancestral families in the homeland. One such example is a set of brooches from Skógar í Flókadal (Figure 7.3), which have design elements dating to the ninth century, yet were recovered from a tenth-century burial.[34]

Many of the oval brooches found in Icelandic Viking Age graves were indeed in very poor condition, having undergone repairs that suggest they may have been heirlooms, deeply valued for their connections with Scandinavia. They may have been highly praised and valued, perhaps more so than they were in Scandinavia where they fell out of fashion by the late tenth century.[35] But in Iceland, the oval brooch may have come to signify much more than simply a woman's status, likely symbolizing where her kin group came from and to which emerging community she belonged.

In addition to these cases of "hyper-Scandinavian" emulation, other settlers clearly marked themselves as outsiders from the British Isles—possibly of mixed cultural background—while others still were adorned in exclusively Celtic jewelry but were given a Norse burial. The Hafurbjarnarstaðir burial is an example of this category. Located in

FIGURE 7.4: Trefoil brooch from Hafurbjarnarstaðir, the shape of the brooch emerged in the Frankish world generally decorated with acanthus leaves. Viking raiders brought the style back to Scandinavia where it was reinterpreted by local jewelers and decorated with Norse animal art. In the British Isles, this style of brooch was modified further to incorporate, such as this one, Celtic motifs. A parallel to this one can be found in Jarlshof, Shetland. Illustration: M. Hayeur Smith.

Gullbringusýsla, not far from Iceland's modern capital, Reykjavík, it contained the remains of an adult female placed in a flexed position and buried with an Irish ringed pin, a trefoil brooch worn on her chest (a style adapted from Frankish models, decorated with Norse animal art instead of foliage), along with a knife, a comb, two pebbles of unusual shape, three clam shells, and some iron fragments.[36] A stone slab had been placed on the upper part of her body and a whalebone plaque on the lower half.[37] Neither of the items of jewelry are typically Scandinavian in origin. The ringed pin is an Irish polyhedral head variant unknown in Scandinavian contexts, while the trefoil brooch (Figure 7.4) has parallels elsewhere in Iceland and intriguingly at Jarlshof in Shetland, where it may have been produced in the British Isles under Scandinavian influence.[38]

At the site of Kroppur, in Eyjafjarðarsýsla, two burials—male and female—were found. The female burial contained a bronze ringed pin of Scandinavian type (Patersen C), as well as a strap end (Figure 7.5) similar to another found in a Viking burial at Kneep in Scotland's Outer Hebrides.[39]

The tradition of integrating a small belt into female dress may have originated in the British Isles and have been brought to Iceland by settlers from Scotland.[40]

Other Hiberno-Norse material found in Iceland include Irish ringed pins, small copper alloy bells with parallels found across the British Isles, jewelry made of shale from England, belt straps and strap ends, and sword hilts decorated with Anglo-Saxon ornament and silver inlay.[41]

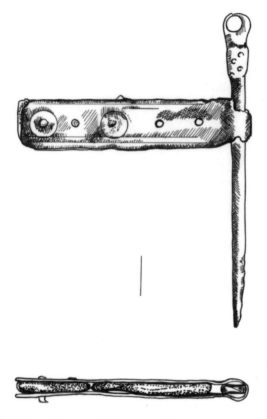

FIGURE 7.5: Burial finds from Kroppur. This strap end is similar to one from Kneep, Scotland. Illustration: M. Hayeur Smith.

Burials occasionally reveal regional Scandinavian variations combined with Hiberno-Norse elements. For example, two tongue-shaped brooches with Jelling-style decoration (Figure 7.6) were found in a burial at Kornsá in Austur-Hunavatnsýsla. These appear to have been worn in a fashion similar to oval brooches but would have been visually distinct and rarely seen in Iceland. These brooches appear to have been uncommon in Scandinavia, and to have had an eastern, or Baltic, regional distribution. On the other hand, a bell found in this burial finds parallels in other Iceland graves and in the British Isles.[42]

Hiberno-Norse elements like these were frequently found alongside typical and distinctly Scandinavian items of jewelry, such as the oval brooches, round brooches, and beads. It is tempting to consider that this mixture of elements of dress constitutes a distinct North Atlantic assemblage that reflects the cultural amalgamation described earlier. This style of dress expressed a dominant Scandinavian view, but incorporated elements of the subordinate cultural group while maintaining elements of the culture of origin.

Textile assemblages also point toward similar cultural interaction and processes. Landnám (Settlement) Period (c. 870–950) textiles from mortuary contexts show a strong connection with the textile traditions of Norway, in color, cloth production methods, and the diversity of weaves used. Microscopic analysis even reveals they have been spun

FIGURE 7.6: Tongue-shaped brooch from Kornsá. Illustration: M. Hayeur Smith.

identically to Norwegian textiles. The decision to spin yarn either clockwise (z-spun) or counter-clockwise (s-spun) is technologically neutral: either direction will produce usable yarn. Yet in many archeological studies, spin direction seems to remain constant over broad geographic regions, as do decisions whether to use counter-clockwise-spun or clockwise-spun yarns for warp or weft threads, and whether to use differently spun threads for different tasks. These consistencies suggest that such choices and decisions were elements of daily production passed down as part of the way new textile producers were trained.[43] As a result, spin direction and the combinations in which differently spun threads are used are non-random, culturally informative attributes of textile assemblages. Conversely, major changes in regional patterns of spinning and weaving are similarly socially informative acts.

Z/z-spun cloth appears to have been the norm in Scandinavia from AD 200 onwards, and has been linked to the adoption of the warp-weighted loom in Roman Iron Age Scandinavia along with the weaving of 2/2 twills.[44] By the Viking Age, z/s-spun fibers are noted on some Scandinavian sites, although Norwegian and Gotlandic traditions remained more conservative with a persistent use of older spinning methods and the continued production of z/z-spun twills.[45] In Iceland, z/z-textiles produced in a manner similar to contemporary Viking Age Norwegian textile traditions dominated at the time of settlement, but z/s-spun twills quickly came to replace z/z-textiles in the Icelandic assemblages. By the eleventh to twelfth centuries, twills and tabbies woven with z/s-spun yarns became the norm. This pattern became ubiquitous and continued (Figure 7.7) until the flat loom was introduced to Iceland in 1740.[46]

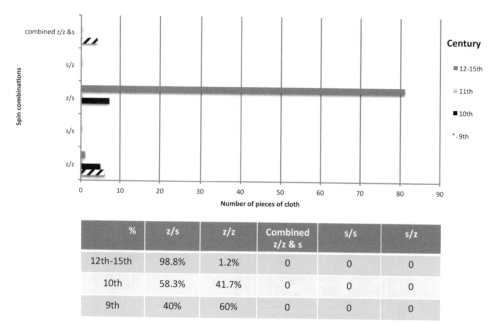

%	z/s	z/z	Combined z/z & s	s/s	s/z
12th-15th	98.8%	1.2%	0	0	0
10th	58.3%	41.7%	0	0	0
9th	40%	60%	0	0	0

FIGURE 7.7: Changing proportions of spin combinations in textiles from the Viking Age to the fifteenth century, Iceland. M. Hayeur Smith, 2015.

It is unlikely that the shift or desire to spin z or s had much to do with technological concerns, as from AD 200 spinners and weavers used the same tools in northern Europe to spin equally well in one direction or the other.[47] The most likely explanation for this shift in Icelandic spin direction involves the ethnic origins of the spinners who were producing the yarn and introducing different textiles traditions into Iceland.

We know that textiles from ninth- to tenth-century Anglo-Saxon contexts across Great Britain were generally z/s spun, contrasting significantly with textiles recovered from contemporary Viking Age grave finds from Scotland, Ireland, and the Isle of Man, where settlers were presumably Norwegian. There, weavers were producing z/z-spun textiles.[48] While this observed difference between Scandinavian spinning traditions and those of the British Isles may not fully explain why Icelandic women eventually adopted z/s spinning for the production of all cloth, it suggests that ethnic origin and the transference of shared production traditions had some influence.

Both textile data and the elements of dress found in Icelandic Viking Age mortuary assemblages therefore suggest this colony's settlers made deliberate attempts to follow Norwegian traditions by including in these burials Norwegian textiles and jewelry that were most likely heirlooms from mainland Scandinavia. Yet alongside these apparent attempts at being hyper-Scandinavian, elements of Hiberno-Norse and Celtic dress found their way into the assemblages, as well. The dominant Norwegian settlers determined most of the infrastructure of the society and they may have used dress to mark themselves apart. It is also clear that subaltern groups had influence though, and that hybridization made its way into various cultural practices, some of which, such as weaving, were very significant and were soon to prove critical to the survival of Iceland's economy.

THE NORTH ATLANTIC IN THE MEDIEVAL PERIOD

Iceland's Landnám (or Settlement) period ended roughly c. 930–60, by which time sources suggest that all available land had been claimed. Around 1000, Christianity was adopted as Iceland's official religion, and slavery abolished. Icelanders had created an independent republic by 930, integrating its scattered chieftainships under one general assembly, the *Althing*. The period from 930–1262 is known as the Commonwealth Period, for the decentralized but integrated political system that Icelanders established. While short lived, the Commonwealth sparked a cultural fluorescence known today through a massive corpus of indigenous, vernacular medieval literature, histories, clerical texts, and related documents produced between c. 1125 and 1300. Culturally speaking, the Viking Age divide between Norwegians settlers and others diminished.[49]

Unlike Europe, the Norse North Atlantic colonies from 1200 to 1500 became ever more remote, isolated, and poor. While they had contact with Europe and traded both cloth and fish with European customers, primarily through Norwegian and later English and German/Hanseatic merchants, only a very select few had access to the fashions and fineries of Europe. Furthermore, from 1300 to c. 1900 the cooling period known as the Little Ice Age affected the North Atlantic particularly severely, eventually resulting in the disappearance of the Greenland colony. Iceland suffered increasingly colder winters, starvation, poverty, volcanic eruptions, and epidemics from the fifteenth through the eighteenth centuries. From a political standpoint, 1262 marks a significant turning point in the history of the North Atlantic, with the beginning of Danish colonial rule.

Evidence for dress and textiles for the post-Viking Age Middle Age (1050–1550) is scarce. Archeological data of any kind is sparse, few garments of this period remain other than episcopal robes, and textual evidence of what Icelanders might have worn and what defined them to the rest of the world, is rare. Surviving manuscript illustrations reproduce stylized forms of European dress styles copied from other documents, rather than showing what the Icelanders actually wore.[50]

However, recent research is beginning to shed some light on the dress of this period.[51] Emerging from the middens of Norse farms are neglected archeological textile collections—overwhelmingly brown fibers, predominantly of coarse woolen 2/2 twills, with the occasional imported fragment originating from England or the European mainland.[52] They appear to lack dyes or color of any sort and were produced and used from the late eleventh to sixteenth centuries as a form of currency known as *vaðmál*, or legal cloth.[53] From the Commonwealth period, production intensified as it became the main currency in Iceland through which all economic transactions were carried out. While this cloth was used to pay taxes and tithes, settle legal disputes, and traded overseas for commodities that Icelanders needed, once acquired, it was frequently transformed into clothing and reused and recycled until it was discarded.

Behind the production of this important national product were women, who were responsible for all aspects of textile work.[54] This production was not the result of elite-supported specialists, but was carried out on every farm across Iceland. It was clearly significant enough that its production nearly eliminated all other textile types from the island's woven corpus, suggesting that women's efforts were channeled almost exclusively to the creation of this product.[55] *Vaðmál* was legally regulated in successive medieval law codes, and the cloth itself was made to fit guidelines stipulated by law and evaluated by regional authorities.[56] From a perspective of cultural identity, *vaðmál*—

as currency, export product, or commodity transformed into garments—formed a unique cultural trait and marker of Icelandic identity. Once sold to Norway or Britain it came to be known as a distinct Icelandic product suitable for clothing the urban poor.

Trade in *vaðmál* began early on during the settlement period, and Iceland turned toward Norway for supplies—where long-standing kinship relationships and networks still existed—and established trade relationships with that country. Bruce Gelsinger argues the vital commodity sought was grain, perhaps among resources unavailable in Iceland, for which the Icelanders traded woolen cloth, sulphur, as well as other North Atlantic exotics such as falcons, arctic fox fur, and walrus ivory.[57] During the tenth century, Norway was heavily invested in breeding cattle, their own supplies of woolen cloth were low, and the country's population was expanding quickly. Consequently, Norwegians were willing to acquire Icelandic wool products in exchange for the goods Icelanders needed. Norway became Iceland's first and most important trading partner. By 1022, Iceland and Norway established their first reciprocal commercial agreement.

Norwegian merchants also forged ties with England to satisfy both Icelandic needs and their own. Gelsinger suggests that the need for Icelandic cloth in the British Isles was a direct outgrowth of the English specialized production of high-quality woolens for export to the Low Countries. In rural areas, people producing sufficient amounts of wool for their own households' consumption would have had little need for Icelandic *vaðmál*. In urban centers, however, textile merchants and craftsmen would have sought to produce cloth that brought them the highest revenues when sold as exports, and would not have wasted time or wool producing coarse cloth with low resale value for local use by the urban poor.[58] This trade in woolen *vaðmál* persisted into the fifteenth to seventeenth centuries, with British customs accounts continuing to list *wodmol* or *wadmol* as a common import product.[59]

Another textile or garment type in the early Middle Ages for which Icelanders were known internationally was *vararfeldir*, or pile-woven cloaks. Pile-woven cloaks are mentioned throughout the law code *Grágás* (1117–1271) as worth far more than *vaðmál*.[60] *Vararfeldir* were woven first as a 2/2 twill, with additional tufts of wool added to the surface of the fabric while still on the loom.[61] Some scholars have interpreted these cloaks as a local adaptation to the lack of furs in Iceland.[62] Others, however, have argued that this was predominantly an Irish tradition and that pile-woven cloaks were among the articles traded by the Frisians from c. 600–900 and were made in, and exported from, Ireland at this time.[63] The Irish connection may be important in the Icelandic context, fitting well into the pattern of textile production described earlier, with strong connections to the British Isles infiltrating local Norwegian production. The pile-woven cloak was said to be so popular that Icelanders could not keep up with Norwegian demand.

Despite frequent mention of this garment type in sagas, they are almost absent archeologically, save one well-known fragment (see Figure 7.8).[64] The shaggy-pile woven fragment from Heynes, of medium-coarse weave with a loosely s-spun weft, was clearly so favored and treasured that most of these cloaks must have been exported to Europe, leaving very few to be discarded and found on archeological sites.

This garment type—unique to Iceland and Ireland, both cultures involved in the settlement of Iceland—can be considered an example of another item of national Icelandic dress that reflects an amalgamation of these two ethnic groups.

FIGURE 7.8: Fragment of pile-weaving from Heynes, Iceland. Photo: M. Hayeur Smith.

EXAMPLES OF MARGINALIZATION
IN NORSE GREENLAND

By far the best evidence of everyday clothing in the North Atlantic comes from the graveyard site of Herjolfnes, near the southern tip of Greenland. These garments were used as burial shrouds, and have been the topic of much scholarly debate.[65] Many of them are intact garments, representing the most complete collection of medieval European secular clothing in existence. Furthermore, many of the twenty-three pieces from this find have been specifically labeled as "gored gowns," garments constructed to provide width from the waist down. The important features are the panels used to add flare to the shape of the garment, which were inserted both in front and back and occasionally on the sides.

Although superficially resembling the "close-bodied" garments worn in the rest of Europe during the fourteenth and fifteenth century, Robin Netherton has convincingly demonstrated that gored gowns are in fact different, as they possess no openings at the back to make them tight-fitted. The Greenlandic gored gowns were too loose, with the waist situated too high, while the European close-bodied garments were fitted for European elites who could afford elaborate tailoring and fine materials.[66] While the insertion of gores and gussets has been interpreted as evidence of skill and sophistication, it is also a relatively simple mechanism to prevent waste, allowing the seamstress to make use of recycled cloth in garments, a widespread practice documented in Icelandic and Greenlandic textile assemblages.[67]

By the thirteenth and fourteenth centuries, Greenlandic contact with the mainland was in rapid decline. The last official trading ship sailed to Greenland in 1368.[68] The possibility that Greenlanders would have seen new fashions from Europe is slim, with any news of innovations probably coming via Iceland, much delayed. Greenlandic gored gowns were therefore either based on antiquated European models, or were hybrid interpretations of European fashions by a marginalized group who created their own version of the garment while still clinging to cultural ideals of northern Europe.

Looking at the social dynamics of Norse Greenland during the periods leading up to the end of the colony, many features suggest that socially things were also out of balance, and that a powerful ecclesiastic elite may have been partially to blame for the society's demise. While this elite certainly looked toward Europe for cultural contact, they also apparently consumed a disproportionate amount of the country's foreign imported goods and were responsible for the building of large manors and churches.[69] Smaller farmers did not fare as well, and this elite may have monopolized most of the colony's resources for themselves while imposing both a cultural conservatism and their "carefully maintained cultural barriers" vis-a-vis the Inuit, who were moving into Norse settlement areas by the late thirteenth or early fourteenth centuries.[70] This may have impacted on the clothing observed at Herjolfnes: the antiquated fashions, as well as Greenlanders' refusal to adopt the efficient skin clothing of the Inuit over European woolen garments that were not well adapted to the cooling climatic conditions of the Little Ice Age.[71]

As a marginalized community at the edge of the western world, they tried to adapt in a different manner, through their textile production, though without radically changing the overall appearance of the cloth. Greenlandic textiles are known as unique thanks to the pioneering research of Else Østergård, who identified subtle changes in weaving techniques that occurred during the fourteenth and fifteenth centuries, when weavers suddenly began incorporating more weft threads than warps in their textiles. This contrasts with earlier Greenlandic textiles, which were identical to contemporary Icelandic ones.[72]

Midden excavations carried out by Konrad Smiarowski between 2009 and 2010 in southwestern Greenland have added to our knowledge of when this shift in weaving practices occurred. The find of ninety-eight fragments of textile from a farm site located on the eastern shore of the Igaliku Fjord has allowed a chronological sequence to be built up. In Phases 1–2 (1000–1200), the site's textiles clearly mirror the Icelandic weaving traditions; yet by late Phase 2 things begin to change with an increasing amount of cloth produced using weft-dominant weaves. Textiles from Phase 3 (1200–1300) have weft-dominant weaves, as did the textiles from Herjolfsnes where this weft-dominance intensified with extremely high weft thread counts (Figure 7.9). Based on carbon dating, this shift happened somewhere between 1308 and 1362, well within the range for the first major cold transition of the Little Ice Age in the North Atlantic.[73] Greenlandic textile data, therefore, suggests some kind of experimentation took place before weft-dominant cloth, requiring more labor and more wool, became the norm.

Through conservatism in garment construction and cloth technology, the Greenlanders therefore appear to have kept cultural and emotional ties to western Europe. While their clothing and cloth remained "European," however, it also reflected the trials and tribulations of the hardship, isolation, and marginalization that these Norse settlers experienced. "Almost like" the cloth and clothing of their ancestors, it had changed, and in the final result, despite desperate attempts at making warmer cloth, it still proved no match for the well-adapted Inuit practices. Dressed in skin clothing, the Inuit moved slowly into Greenlandic territories and provided fierce competition for resources. By the late fifteenth century, dress and marginalization may have lead to the demise of the Greenland Norse.

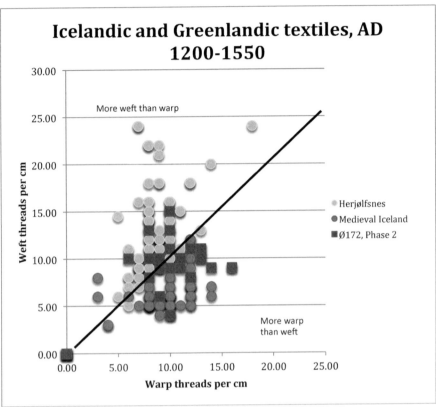

FIGURE 7.9: Weft dominant weaves from Herjolfnes, and Ø172 compared to Medieval Icelandic cloth. M. Hayeur Smith, 2014.

CONCLUSION

The colonies of the North Atlantic provide a useful case study to explore the effects of migration, cultural interaction, colonization, and ethnicity on dress, for it is through cultural contact that the projection of cultural identity becomes more apparent. Scandinavian dress styles made their way to the North Atlantic colonies through the agency of Norwegian colonists who settled these regions and brought with them standard dress practices. However, with streams of colonists coming directly from Norway or via the northern regions of the British Isles, the cultural makeup of the population arriving in Iceland in 873 was anything but homogeneous. Clearly the elite and dominant Scandinavians imposed their cultural mark though visual appearance: clothing, textiles, and jewelry were generally Scandinavian, and yet the impact of the marginalized groups—people of mixed cultural heritage or slaves—within the colonizing population was also felt. Their material culture and dress items were mixed in among Scandinavian ones, so that new styles emerged to the point that the burials of the North Atlantic present a unique cultural mixture within the Viking world because of the inclusion of these Hiberno-Norse elements.

In some cases, the cultural practices of these subaltern groups persisted into the medieval period, changing the nature of society and making it uniquely Icelandic. By modifying how the Norwegians made cloth, the Icelandic settlers created a new product— *vaðmál*—that was used as currency in Iceland and traded to the rest of Europe for the goods Icelanders needed. This cloth, by the sixteenth century, was known as *wadmal* and imported into England and beyond, as testified in customs documents of that period.[74]

In Greenland, the social dynamics were different. Greenlanders were said to have come from western Iceland, a uniquely Christian part of the island and possibly the location and home of many Celtic peoples. No pre-Christian burials have ever been found in Greenland, and therefore, it is not known what people wore in the tenth century in that colony. By the fourteenth and fifteenth centuries, the finds of Herjolfnes represent the most complete collection of European garments known and have mistakenly been used by scholars as examples of contemporary European fashions. Remote, Greenland's contact with mainland Europe was infrequent and declining in the later years of its settlement. The Herjolfnes gowns should therefore not be regarded as mirroring European clothing styles of the same period, but instead as representing the clothing of a marginalized community living at the very edge of the western world, desperately trying to maintain its emotional, cultural, and economic ties with Europe. In an environment where temperatures were plummeting by the decade, people had difficulty feeding themselves and keeping their livestock alive, and so in a desperate attempt to keep warm, around 1306, Greenlandic women began to weave weft dominant cloth as their standard product. This became Greenland's trademark.[75] Despite all attempts, the Greenland colonists were unsuccessful, and ultimately the colony died. The last recorded marriage at the Hvalsey church in the Eastern settlement was in 1408; it was followed by silence.[76] Iceland, too, went through its own hardships—as did the rest of the North Atlantic colonies—and yet survived, in part due to its closer proximity to western Europe and its cloth.

ACKNOWLEDGEMENTS

Much of the research in this chapter was made possible with funds from the National Science Foundation (Arctic Social Sciences, Polar Programs, award nos. 1023167 and 1303898) and with the help from the following institutions: Haffenreffer Museum of Anthropology, Brown University; the National Museum of Iceland; Fornleifastofnun Íslands; the Greenland Museum and Archives; the National Museum of Denmark; and the National Museum of Scotland. I would like to thank the following individuals: Lilja Árnadóttir, Freyja Hliðkvist Ómarsdóttir, Guðmundur Ólafsson, Gavin Lucas, Jette Arnaborg, Georg Nygaard, Guðrún Sveinbjarnardóttir, Mjöll Snæsdóttir, Martin Goldberg, Adolf Friðriksson, Guðrún Alda, Howell M. Robert, Ramona Harrisson, Douglas Bolender, John Steinberg, Thomas McGovern, Konrad Smiarowski, Kevin P. Smith, Steinunn Kristjándóttir, Guðney Zoega, and Hildur Hákonardóttir.

CHAPTER EIGHT

Visual Representations

DÉSIRÉE KOSLIN

The visual material that survives from the European medieval period (for the purpose of this study, c. 1000–1500) and that at times includes representations of fashion is rich and varied. It consists of sculpture in stone, wood, metal, and animal bone such as ivory; monumental painting on walls, glass, and wood panel; imagery woven in flat tapestry, knotted carpets,[1] and embroidered on fabric; and most particularly and in the greatest numbers, as drawn, painted, or printed illustrations in books. Each art medium requires its own set of approaches to interpret the information it contains, and as we are removed by several centuries and incalculable social distance from the medieval context, the multi-disciplinary perspective of Alfred Gell, a cultural anthropologist, seems useful. As we attempt to pinpoint and extract notions of fashion in medieval art, it is especially important to be mindful of the complex, interactive process in the creation of the medieval work of art. With a starting point in the artist's ability, materials, and mindset, the art object was mediated also in the collaborative process between the patron, its first recipient, and other arbitrators, such as clerical/scholarly advisors.[2] While art historians have given serious consideration to context and material culture, there has also been a tendency to deal with art objects outside the social framework, as in "art for art's sake." The developments in the humanities as a whole have also had an impact on art history, and scholars focusing on the medieval period have increasingly sought to broaden their discourse to explore more broadly issues such as social conditions, exercise of power, material specificity, production and use.[3] In particular, ideas regarding "reception" and "reception aesthetics" are productive when applied to expressions of fashion in medieval art; while the subject matter, usually set in a devotional context or a moralistic secular narrative, the patron's aspiration was also to have the artwork reflect the latest in courtly appearance and accoutrements.

An exclusive focus on tracing and teasing out fashion's development from the entirety of medieval works of art has been a preoccupation of many antiquarians and researchers over several centuries. It has often resulted in rather myopic, decontextualized alignments, starting with the rhapsodizing cavalcades in early printed books showing dress and fashions by regions and in timelines.[4] This linear presentation of the fashion material has often been uncritically repeated in standard surveys up to the present, and is usually still gratefully taken in by new generations of students. It is certainly useful to bring a sense of order and evolutionary development to the appearance of fashionable dress in Europe, and to define its conditions, but for this to be a relevant exercise, a deeper and more comprehensive examination of the context for each, un-cropped visual representation needs to be included. Such features concern the composition, architectural components, patronage, intended audience, purpose as well as date and place of the piece. Clearly, historical events, whether of *longue durée* or immediate impact, also inform fashion, but have rarely been given much space in general works. Costume historians have also had a tendency to interpret and take at face value the represented object, often through a contemporary, anachronistic assessment of the appearance, materials, colors, cuts, and construction taken from an art object of the medieval period. This concerns especially the contemporary interpretation of, for instance, the medieval artist's understanding of a garment's construction aspects, or the difference between the painting palette's colors vis-à-vis those used for dyeing fabric. In a recent article, Heather Pulliam brings in useful distinctions regarding early and later medieval concepts of color and use of dyes.[5]

The current generation of scholars is making great strides to mediate and expand our understanding of medieval fashion. By extrapolating the rich fashion content in French literature, Sarah-Grace Heller has proposed a much-needed modification to the generally accepted, and narrowly discipline-based notion of fashion in Europe as having its birth in the fourteenth century.[6] By close readings and nimble translations of the secular and vernacular literature of the twelfth and thirteenth centuries, she has convincingly shown that the authors eagerly engaged in describing fashion in prose and poetry. She has also performed a most useful task in synthesizing the opinions of the theoreticians of the past century on the topic of fashion, many of whom reveal serious presentist notions in their work insofar as they consider the medieval material at all.[7] There is, of course, great value and purpose in establishing specific timelines in closely related and securely dated material if it can be delivered as comprehensively as in Anne van Buren's lavishly illustrated *Illuminating Fashion*.[8] She links events like the Great Plague and the Hundred Years War in the fourteenth century to the pivotal changes in French and English societies and their upper classes in style and luxury fashions in France and the Netherlands. Particularly useful are the discussions on formal, old-fashioned uses vis-à-vis contemporary high style, distinctions in localized practices, the annotated glossary, and a decade-by-decade chronology of fashion features. Odile Blanc also points to the Hundred Years War as a moment when fashion ceased to be primarily a status marker, bubbling up to elite society from the martial context, and affirming the active male participation in instigating the fashion cycle.[9] It is worth re-emphasizing: it was upper class men in society who went abroad for war or studies or trade, and who returned home to their families with new fashion goods and information. And again, it was mostly elite status men who engaged and instructed artists to carry out prestige productions, such as illuminated prayer books, grandiose sculpture projects, and courtly furnishings for their buildings and peripatetic lifestyles. In the images taken up in examples that follow, one ought to regard the depictions (whether they portray women or men) as well-matched and precise expressions of the patron's intent. Of course, exceptional women also gave birth to new, local fashions as they married and settled in their new abodes with cartloads of dowry and retinues of help to begin a new life at a foreign court. In the review of works of art to follow, these and related issues need to be kept in mind.

Ultimately, in order to exist, proliferate, and change, fashion needs to be seen.[10] The reactions that fashionable dress provoked in the medieval responses ranged from outraged condemnation and moralizing rants to participatory delight, or a combination of all three, and it is here that we can begin the search for the evidence for fashion in medieval texts and images. As twenty-first century viewers/readers of these opinions and visual representations of fashion, we need to ask questions to evaluate this material to avoid, if at all possible, anachronistic and decontextualized use. Perhaps the most important aspect is to investigate for whom and for whose eyes the work originally was created—much medieval art today on public display in museums and in publications may not have been intended for anyone but the patron and a select circle.

Jonathan Alexander has mapped the developments in book illustration as having a continued tradition within the monastic communities from the fifth century onwards, the scribe often providing the illustrations as well as copying the text. By the twelfth century, one finds examples of books where monks, secular clergy, and lay-people collaborated in the scriptoria on the writing and images—even nuns were involved as scribes.[11] In the earlier medieval period, the art expression developed seemingly perfunctorily, having didactic and mnemonic purposes and within strong constraints of decorum. When people are depicted, an interest in dress is primarily to denote rank and stature, seen in shorter tunics for lay people, long, and more voluminous for the clergy and upper class women and men. From the later twelfth century onwards, the scope of an artwork's function broadened considerably, but the image's reason for being was still governed by the patron's demands and largesse, dictating the conditions for an artist's sophistication and skills. The limited patronage as well as the scarcity and cost of art materials in the early period must certainly have kept artistic impulse restricted to merely record, follow tradition and instructions issued. In certain cases, the manuscripts contain traces of the instructions in both written and visual form issued to the artist in the margins, sometimes a device to keep a tally of the images as well as to dictate content.[12]

Unlike the scant visual evidence from the early medieval period in regard to fashion, there is a continued tradition in the early medieval texts from the patristic writers of the first centuries onwards. Of course, the mention of fashionable dress occurs in the form of a condemning reaction to perceived frivolity. It is, for instance, through the keenly observing and provoked eye of Bishop Leander of Seville (c. 540–c. 600), that we acquire detailed and early indicators of fashionable dress features. He wrote, seemingly in some personal torment, on the importance of modest dress for the training of nuns in his sister Florentina's foundation,

> Do not wear stunning clothes, anything having a pleat, for the eye is curious before and behind, and do not wear dresses that billow. Be careful of clothes carefully and diligently patterned and bought at a very high price, for that is the care of the flesh, that is the eager desire of the eyes . . . use garments that cover the body, that conceal a maidenly decorum, that keep out the rigors of cold; not those that produce the incentive and capacity to fleshly lust.[13]

A contemporary illustration to the garment described in such detail by Leander is not to be found, but a suitable image can be chosen from the art of a half-millennium later, a Romanesque ivory plaque, once part of a Spanish reliquary with Gospel narrative, c. 1115–20.[14] The low relief's expressive power and dramatic gestures are realized primarily through the lavish garment folds that waft and swirl as if in movement independent of the body, a device ultimately derived from Byzantine models (discussed later) (Figure 8.1).

The lack of expression or differentiation in the facial features of the figures are typical of the earlier medieval mode of representation, explored by Stephen Perkinson in a recent article, who cites St. Augustine saying that, "mimetic representation of an individual's facial features was not a reliable means of representing that person, as the artist could not assume that later audiences would be able to recognize the person in question."[15] Instead, as in the ivory plaque, the animated, layered, and highly ornamented clothing surely intend to convey the emotion and recognition of the dramatic *Noli Me Tangere* moment. Mary Magdalene's head veil, worn over a plain wimple or chest cloth, has elaborate edge

FIGURE 8.1: Plaque with the *Journey to Emmaus* and *Noli Me Tangere* (detail). Ivory, traces of gilding. Spanish, c. 1115–20. The Metropolitan Museum of Art, New York.

decoration, her mantle's excessive volume wraps her outstretched, longing arms, and the tunic's lower border eddies with the decorations above her finely shod feet—all features of fashionable dress. Christ's garments, seeming to swing in opposing directions, express an equally strong emotion, one that He must resist. The knot at the side of Mary Magdalene's head veil is a code frequently seen in medieval art to denote Jewish women— here it is reciprocated by a knot at the left edge of Christ's mantle, and link the couple's dynamic postures. Fashionable *bliaut*-style horizontal pleating at the upper part of Christ's tunic can also be seen here as well as in contemporary monumental sculpture, such as Chartres' famous portal figures.[16]

Visual representations of people in early medieval art are primarily of divine or saintly figures, or of people shown as donors of the artwork, among them a few depicting women. As leaders of their religious communities, abbesses were famous and powerful, came from well-born families where high-status clothing was a prerogative, and they could therefore request, one may propose, to be portrayed as such in their book commissions. There is an early textual reference to monastic dress fashions to illustrate this. Aldhelm of Wessex (639–719) bishop of Malmesbury, wrote a missive to the abbess for the nuns at Barking Abbey, England, in which he complained, interestingly, of excessive fashions of both genders. Like Leander of Seville a century earlier, he wrote in a similar, disapproving vein while describing in extraordinary detail dress features and fashion implements among the religious:

> Contrary to the decrees of canon law and the norm of the regular life, vanity and insolence are adopted for one purpose only; that the bodily figure may be adorned with forbidden ornaments and charming decorations, and that the physical appearance may be glamorized in every part and every limb. This consists for either sex in fine linen shirts, in scarlet or blue tunics, in necklines and sleeves embroidered with silk; their shoes trimmed with red-dyed leather; the hair of their forelocks and the curls at their temples are crimped with curling iron; dark grey veils for the head give way to bright and colored headdresses, which are sewn with interlacings of ribbons and hang down as far as the ankles. Fingernails are sharpened after the manner of falcons or hawks.[17]

As if in an illustration to this early text, the Abbess Hitda of Meschede, Westphalia, founder of a house of canonesses, had herself depicted in just the extravagance St. Aldhelm described (c. 1025–50). She is seen in the dedication page of the full-page illustration of the eleventh-century gospel book she hands, proudly standing, to her patron saint, Walburga (Figure 8.2).

Hitda's impressive, mantle-like head veil is trimmed perhaps with the interlaced ribbons that Aldhelm described, or by the elaborate edge crimping common throughout the medieval period for upper class women, also known as goffered or *nebula* headdress. Layers of exceedingly finely woven, folded linen fabric had its multiple edges shaped into

FIGURE 8.2: Dedication page, Hitda Codex, c. 1025. Scriptorium of Cologne. MS 1640, fol. 6. Universitäts- und Landesbibliothek Darmstadt.

tiny frills in starch while still dampened. It might be done either through the use of a crimping board or by skillful folding and clamping, and then let to dry before dressing. It was in all likelihood the time-consuming work of skilled laundrywomen, and lasted only for the day's wearing. Hitda's amply sleeved tunic and lighter undertunic were worn over a white linen shift, visible only at the tightly fitted sleeves at the wrists, the high-status dress of the upper classes. Both women, attenuated to idealized proportions, wear the red leather fretted shoes the bishop condemned. St. Walburga's archaizing dress of toga-like drape has lavish gold decoration and edgings, showing her ancient status and as object of veneration to the live donor.

The lack of difference between male and female dress before 1300 is another frequently and uncritically accepted notion in the standard works on fashion history. In her extensive work on Anglo-Saxon dress, Gale Owen-Crocker has demonstrated significant differences between male and female dress in this early period.[18] Frequently rendered in the medium of pen and ink drawing, the visual representations of this period display explicit indications of the interest to depict gender differences and dress detail, as in the c.1200 rendition of a female personification, also here strongly attenuated and idealized, of one of the liberal arts, *Geometrica* (Figure 8.3).

FIGURE 8.3: Idealized representation of the Liberal Arts: Geometry, c. 1200, ink drawing, detail. Aldersbacher Sammelhandschrift. Clm. 2599 fol. 106. Munich, Bayerische Staatsbibliothek.

The female personification wears a fur-lined mantle, clasped at the neck in courtly, noble fashion,[19] and the tunic's lower edge puddles at the elegantly shod feet. The slender upper body with its small breasts is accentuated with side-lacings, creating the *bliaut*-style numerous horizontal pleats mentioned earlier, and seen in both men's and women's portrayals. Geometrica's excessively elongated trumpet sleeves that fall to the ground appear to have secondary under-sleeves of even greater fabric excess artfully arranged in fluted ripples, a style effectively precluding any useful work or mobility, and requiring the assistance of maids in dressing. In this period, tightly draped, voluminous clothing was a signifier and prerogative for courtly, ritualized appearance and comportment, stressing self-composure and noble serenity.[20] The luxurious detail, wasteful fabric excess, and erotized allure of the figure carried also the stamp of the unchaste, the tempting expression of *Superbia*, the mortal sin of pride, a parallel, seemingly tortured message of clerical disapprobation conveyed so often in medieval images.

Byzantine art, architecture, and visual culture had a lasting impact on the art of western Europe. In the fashion context, the fabrics and clothing brought by princesses from Constantinople marrying western princes and nobles transmitted styles in silk fabrics and dress that were admired, envied and copied in Europe. Princess Theophano, daughter of Emperor John I Tzimiskes, who married Otto II in 972, is perhaps the best known of these fashion arbiters, another is Maria Argyropoulaina who married the son of the Doge of Venice in 1004. In her book on Byzantine dress, Jennifer Ball deals with imperial as well as court dress, and that of the fashions of the borderlands around the Mediterranean and Eastern Europe.[21] The continuing Byzantinizing aspects on Italian, and especially Venetian art, is strikingly present in the gold-ground mosaic decoration of the central vault of the Basilica of San Marco in Venice, c. 1260 (Fig. 8.4).[22]

Here a collective view of the upper stratum of Venetian society is seen in a procession headed by the patriarch and his clergy, then the Doge and his entourage, followed by

FIGURE 8.4: The miraculous revelation of the relics of St. Mark, c. 1260. Gold-ground mosaic decoration, central vault of the Basilica of San Marco, Venice. Photo: Mondadori Portfolio/ Getty Images.

representatives of the patrician cohorts of men, women, and children, a mid-thirteenth-century cross-section of the city's elite. The procession of brightly-dressed celebrants stands out against the brilliant gold, the occasion is the restitution of the relics of St. Mark. The patriarch and clergy wear processional vestments in timeless styles, copes of dark blue and purple with gold patterns, but woven in the new, Orientalizing lampas style recently introduced to Lucca and Venice through the imports from Central Asia during the *pax mongolica*.[23] The Venetian republic kept up trade relations with the Byzantine Empire through its demise in 1261, and carried on trade thereafter with the new Ottoman rulers of Constantinople—fashion fabrics from Venice and Bursa have been documented in use in either court, exchanged across the Adriatic.[24] The doge's red cloak in the mosaic is lined in squirrel fur, worn over a blue silk tunic with massive gold embroidery at the lower border often also seen in Orthodox dress depictions; a member of his entourage has an ermine-lined mantle. A group of men in soberly colored but jewel-clasped mantles follows, then comes a crowd of matrons, the first in a red, ermine-lined mantle with gold trim over a lavishly draped gown. The women behind her wear brightly-colored cloaks over gowns with embroidered decoration, one has, like the doge and one of the men, a decorated badge at the upper arm, all wear bejeweled headdresses and elaborate hair arrangements. Two children, male and female, accompany the procession in mini-versions of the adult dress styles also with applied decorated panels.

In the standard fashion histories, little attention has been given to the Iberian peninsula, where for centuries a fertile exchange of learning and culture had taken place between the Andalusian Islamic courts and the northern, Christian princedoms.[25] Luxury arts and refined fashions were produced in great quantity at the Umayyad court in Cordoba during the Caliphal period from the tenth century, and dazzled visitors from the Christian north. The thirteenth-century Christian royal burials at the monastery of Santa Maria La Real de Huelgas in Burgos, Spain, include numerous well-preserved garments made of silks and cottons from the Andalusian workshops, and in styles not seen in other parts of Europe, such as the jumper-like sleeveless garment worn by men and women, the *pellote*, found in the burial of Fernando de la Cerda (d. 1275) at Burgos.[26] It is depicted also in the *Book of Chess, Dice and Tables*, now at the Escorial Library near Madrid (Figure 8.5), a compendium on the games of skill and chance introduced into Europe from eastern sources around 1000.

The manuscript was written and illustrated in French Gothic style, and completed in 1283 at the Toledo scriptorium of the Spanish king Alfonso X, called the Wise (1221–84). A game of chess is taking place between two women. They wear the sleeveless *pellote*, showing as an exceedingly narrow version of the northern surcoat, and with a full display of the gown or *cotte* underneath. The lady at right wears a red *pellote* over a *camisa margomada*, a shift embroidered in elaborate Islamic geometric motifs along the sleeves, and across the yoke. This embroidery was of such high cost that it was subject to sumptuary legislation in 1256.[27] The chess playing man wears a variation of the *pellote* with lacing at one side, and with attached sleeves outlined in gold trim under a green mantle lined with white fur. His companion holds a hunting falcon on his gloved left hand, and wears culottes, a patterned sash, and a sleeveless coat fastened at the neck. The fashions in this and other manuscript productions of Alfonso's scriptorium, such as the illustrated cycle of songs to the Virgin Mary, the *Cantigas de Santa Maria*, deserve to be examined for its many depictions of thirteenth-century Spanish and Islamic fashions as well as the rich array of contextual objects of material culture.

FIGURE 8.5: *The Book of Chess, Dice and Tables*, c. 1283, Court of Alfonso El Sabio, Cordoba, Spain. Biblioteca del Monasterio de San Lorenzo de El Escorial, Spain, MS T-1-6, fol. 32r. Photo: Leemage/UIG via Getty Images.

Noble women's devotion, their knowledge of Latin, and roles as educators of their children have been studied in detail recently, and many psalters and books of hours contain information of women's ownership of religious books. They were in use by lay and clergy to recite the daily and nightly rounds of prayers. The books were also fashionable accessories, and the aristocratic French female owner, Comtesse de la Table, is depicted in exquisite fashion detail on the page facing the Hours of the Virgin (Figure 8.6), of her 1280–90 psalter-hours containing a calendar for use in Amiens.

The countess kneels in an elaborately decorated Gothic chapel with turrets, pinnacles, and rosette windows in front of the Virgin Mary. The transparent veil and chin band of silk or finest linen envelop the devotee's hair arrangement of golden netting which covers her head and is arranged in small horns or temples over the ears in a fashion that from this moment will increase in height and width through the late fifteenth century. The reticulated pattern is a miniature version of the armorial design in red on gold seen on shields around the edifice and on her mantle's large-scale diaper pattern, felines passant. The mantle is squirrel fur-lined, and held with a clasp at center front. Her gown is soberly colored, however, although in latest fashion, the ample bell sleeves tightly stitched at the under-arm, while the still narrower sleeves of the under-tunic in matching color have closely set, tiny buttons up to the wrist where the shift's white edge is barely visible. The walls of the chapel keep the menagerie of pets, birds, and human-headed hybrids at bay. Shielded by the dazzling architecture and under the weight of the formidable armorial mantle, the Comtesse de la Table in her humbly-colored gown seems akin to a religious woman, and one might speculate that it was her own wish to be so portrayed. In her

FIGURE 8.6: Comtesse de la Table, dame de Coeuvres, in the Psalter-Hours of Yolande de
Soissons, c. 1280–90. Amiens, France. Pierpont Morgan Library, MS M.729, fol. 232v. © 2016.
Photo Pierpont Morgan Library/Art Resource/Scala, Florence.

progress toward her spiritual goal she begins each day with the recitation of the Matins
of the Office of the Virgin Mary, as she perceives herself in an image of devotion in her
book.[28]

One of the most highly symbolic places in medieval pictorial life was the walled garden,
hortus deliciarum, where lovers could meet for rites of seduction and transgression. It is
the profane counterpart to the *hortus conclusus,* the inviolate, chaste space used in the
Middle Ages as an image for the miracle of the immaculate conception of the Virgin
Mary. In this version, a Middle Rhine tapestry of c. 1400, recalling a *mille-fleurs* courtly
setting, elegant and extravagantly dressed men and women are at play in five scenes in an
unabashed frolic around a central castle (Figure 8.7).

Adjudicated by Lady Love/Frau Minne, enthroned in an enclosed garden to the lower
right, the couples participate in an encyclopedic, high-fashion cavalcade of courtly
pastimes. In pairs of matched dress, they form a frame around a central castle as if in the
margins of a manuscript page. While drably-dressed country folks go about their tasks
outside the enclosed garden, the extravagantly bejeweled and ostentatiously dressed
couples engage in unashamed sexual abandon. It seems unlikely that this tapestry would
ever be on public display, as hands grope, chins are chucked, and limbs twine and thrust.

FIGURE 8.7: Courtly games before a castle, c. 1385–1400. Tapestry, made in Alsace. Nuremberg, Germanisches Nationalmuseum.

The men's fashions of the second half of the fourteenth century consist of short, wasp-waisted jackets that have cinched, ornamented belts, with low-slung hip girdles set with bells, tight-fitting parti-colored hose, and buttons are on erect display along the pigeon-breasted chest contours. The men have crimped, short locks, some with softly draped chaperons on their heads, and pointy *poulaines* or *crackowes* on their feet. Most of the men are *jeunes*, but a few are mature, with beards, evidently elderly as they enjoy a romp with younger statuesque women. The women's deep décolletages are ornamented with embellishments and necklaces, fringes dangle from sleeve borders; like the men, the women wear belled girdles as well as wide baldrics across the chest also set with bells that peal and ring out. Two women at center front are dressed in elaborate versions of parti-colored clothing, one sports a gown made up of pieced vertical fabric sections in alternating red and white, the other shows a back view of diagonally pieced bands of fabric in dramatic neutrals, with a matching, *liripipe* chaperon. Women's headdresses range from simple fillets and flowered head bands to elaborate crowns, and goffered, *nebula*-frilled veils as well as a few unusual examples of broad-brimmed hats seen in back view. A woman in Lady Love's garden ties two men, seated on the ground, with ropes to the enclosure, and at lower left, a couple get help in a thrusting game. Michael Camille describes the action as the war between the sexes, as displayed in the banderoles of the thrusting couple: she: *din stosen gefelt mir wol/lieber stos als es sein sol* (I love thrusting/Rather a thrust than as it should be) and the man responds *Ich stes gern ser/so mag ich leider nicht mer* (I like to thrust/but in this manner I don't want to thrust any more).[29] Collared pet dogs yelp and yap, tresses come undone, eyes espy right and left to miss nothing—the fashions depicted are extreme and of the explicitness that surely would have occasioned clerical censure. Camille appoints the crowned lady in squirrel fur-lined mantle and demure composure and her red-robed suitor with matching chaperon as the matrimonial couple for whom the games unfold. The patron of the tapestry, however, was not a nobleman but a wealthy member of the upper bourgeoisie in Speyer, Middle Rhine, from the prominent Diehl family of fabric merchants. The commission, executed with considerable compositional skill, was clearly an ambitious and enhancing status symbol for its owner. Large armorial devices are applied around the figural composition.

In the Central European region of Bohemia, a local and easily recognizable, "Beautiful Style" emerged in the second half of the fourteenth century in the political and cultural capital of Prague during the fourteenth century under Charles IV, Holy Roman Emperor and King of Bohemia. With strong family ties to France and military and cultural interests in Italy, Charles gathered "International Gothic" artists and art works from France and Italy to his court in Prague, and the new, vernacular style that emerged here became widespread in central Europe. Illuminated books, objects in precious stones and metal, embroidered ornaments in ecclesiastical vestments and panel paintings define the style. It is characterized in figure compositions by elegantly and softly draping garments in brilliant colors; the women's heads are small, doll-like ovals with finely drawn, pursed mouths, the faces framed by tight locks of hair, and head veils that drape in sinuous ripples. The tempera panel painting of the Crucifixion has the Italian and Byzantinizing elements also typical of the International Style in the crowded composition and the gold ground. (Figure 8.8).

The stacked layers of the Roman centurions on horseback dressed in livery of Oriental splendor add depth to the scene. The opulent colors, vivid patterns and the sumptuous, archaized garments are hallmarks of the Beautiful Style, where the deep, jewel-like colors

FIGURE 8.8: *The Kaufmann Crucifixion*, c. 1350. Tempera and gold on panel. Gemäldegalerie, Berlin. Photo: The Print Collector/Print Collector/Getty Images.

are set off effectively against the gold ground. The refined and idealized linearity and surface interest bring intensely felt emotions to the group of mourners in golden halos at the foot of the cross, with its focus on Mary's sorrow. The Virgin Mary, wearing a gown of heavenly blue and sumptuous purple mantle of lustrous silk lined in vivid red, is supported by John, dressed in a green robe lined in gold. Mary Magdalene wears a gown of brilliant red. The strong, contrasting colors may well signal another cultural strain and influence. In her study of signifiers of dress to designate Others in medieval society, Ruth Mellinkoff has identified several features that serve to identify Jews, and in this Crucifixion scene, the color contrasts and the dress splendor of the mourners, and especially the Magdalene, closely correspond to her theory that offers tools to refine and expand fashionable content.[30]

The immodest power display of family pride seems only partially reconciled by the devotional postures of the kneeling Lady Joan Beaufort and her daughters in a book of hours (Figure 8.9) commissioned in France c. 1430–5. Against a barrel-vaulted interior, the walls are hung with a red luxury fabric patterned in gold and blue; a similar fabric is draped softly over a *prie-dieu* with its prayer book covered in green, and puddles on the floor to offer its velvet softness to the countess at prayer. In the matron's demure white

FIGURE 8.9: *Lady Joan Beaufort and her daughters*, Neville Hours, c. 1430–5. French, possibly Rouen. MS Lat. 1158, f. 34v. Bibliothèque nationale de France.

linen head veil, artfully arranged over horns, the countess's chin-band, over which she wears a thick gold neck ornament, emphasizes her proud posture.

Of royal blood herself, she may appropriately wear the ermine-lined mantle, doubtless of black silk velvet, as is her *houppelande,* worn underneath, with a jeweled belt, and lined in gray squirrel fur of modest sleeve proportions. One of England's most powerful families of diplomats and military leaders of the fifteenth century, the Nevilles of Raby, north of Durham, came to prominence with Ralph who became the first Earl of Westmorland. With possessions on both sides of the Channel, Earl Ralph's second wife, Joan, engaged French artists for the family's several manuscripts, one aspect of extensive art and building patronage. Joan had herself portrayed with her six most advantageously married daughters, their coats of arms beside her own in *bas de page.* Depicted here are Elizabeth, Margaret, Katherine, Eleanor, Anne, and Cecily (a seventh, Joan, became a nun). One might make a sport of counting the precious stones set into the sisters' horned headdresses, known as temples or *hennin* and perhaps in this way identify which of them might be of greatest importance, as their facial features are without personal traits. Lady Joan's youngest daughter Cecily, 1415–95, nick-named "Proud Cis", became Duchess of York and thus grandmother of Edward IV of England, as well as Richard III. She would have been more than fifteen years old at the time of the creation of the book, and she may very well therefore be the young woman immediately behind her mother, the immense bombard sleeves of her gold-ground *houppelande*, likely figured silk velvet, lined with squirrel fur, fall trailing to the ground. Her horned headdress, topped with a diaphanous short veil like three of her sisters and possibly denoting matrimonial status, seems indeed to contain the biggest and most plentiful stones and large pearls, and the scale of the gown's pattern is larger than her sisters'. Behind "Proud Cis" kneels the next ranking sister in a red with double collars *houpplande* of the same fabric as the *prie-dieu*; from her waist falls a long belt of fabric or leather to the ground, in blue set with gold-colored ornament. The other, lesser sisters appear in green, blue and dark blue respectively, the one at left wears a simpler, collarless gown in plain green, without the lavish *houpplande* pleats; she is also shorter in stature.

Medieval secular literature's most popular text, the *Roman de la Rose*, is an allegorical dream vision in which the Lover navigates between the typologies of opposites so pervasive in medieval thought in his quest for the Rose of human love and his meeting with its several antitheses in female personifications. The many thousands of lines of the poem were written over the course of the thirteenth century by two different authors, the first Guillaume de Lorris, in the 1230s, and the other Jean de Meun from 1275. Over the next 200 years, the *Roman de la Rose* was copied in hundreds of manuscripts, some exquisitely illustrated. The epitome of courtly love, the poem's enchantment takes place in the walled garden, *hortus deliciarum,* where beautiful people summoned by the Angel of Love move in a stately dance, the *carolle,* to divine music as they tread over the ground perfumed by scents of mint and fennel. The *Roman de la Rose* in the British Library, c. 1490–1500, was composed in the manuscript tradition after the introduction of the printing press, and commissioned by Count Engelbert II of Nassau, in the august service of the Duke of Burgundy; it was illuminated by the Master of the Prayer Books (Fig. 8.10).

This particular manuscript production exhibits a paradoxical exercise in nostalgia, a circumstance that seems replicated in the image of the stately dance in the garden. The Lover, in a short *houppelande* with bagpipe sleeves and the pointy *poulaines* of the early fifteenth century, regards the dancers perform the *carolle* in the future fashions of the end of the century, observing the men in their newly fashionable, broad-shouldered doublets,

FIGURE 8.10: The lovers meet, *Roman de la Rose*, c. 1490–1500, Bruges. Harley MS 4425, f. 14v. © British Library.

codpieces, duck-billed shoes and extraordinary plumed headdresses; the women similarly in new styles having square décolletages, gabled headdresses, and the long trains rucked up to the waistband, revealing the skirt's fur lining. The musicians, denoted as Others, have clothing in extravagant slashing and dagging in garish, complementary colors.

In medieval art, archaizing visual components are frequently included to signal a historical past, such as the toga-like draping of Christ and his disciples, or as the presence of early fabric patterns to indicate an ancient setting.[31] The illustrated accounts of saints' lives in altar panels frequently feature pictorial information in dress and textiles of past centuries. Shifts in chronological time can also provide evidence of intended and purposeful conservatism. A particularly thorough investigation of a tomb effigy of Margaret Fitzgerald, Countess of Ormond, and her husband Piers Butler in St. Canice's Cathedral, Kilkenny, Ireland, revealed such old-fashioned bent certainly intended by the patrons of the tomb who died in 1539 and 1542 respectively (Figure 8.11).[32]

The Countess, who died after her husband and was a strong-willed person, was likely to have been the one to decide the manner of dress on the sixteenth-century tomb effigy. Margaret wears, to eternity, a horned temple headdress, and a full, pleated broadcloth *houppelande* gown with falling double collar, ample bagpipe sleeves, and a long decorative belt, all in the style of the previous century. The suit of armor of her husband, the eighth Earl of Ormond, is also in archaic style, and with significance specific to Ireland. According

FIGURE 8.11: Double tomb effigy of Piers Butler and Margaret Fitzgerald, c. 1515–27. Stone sculpture, St. Canice's Cathedral, Kilkenny, Ireland. Photo: RDImages/Epics/Getty Images.

to Elizabeth Wincott Heckett, "wearing the dress of your own land showed your loyalty, and adopting other styles could be dangerous."[33] Thus, the Fitzgerald *retartadaire* form of dress is a conscious choice of both personal conservatism and an expression of Margaret Fitzgerald's independence of thought and place in society, and not, as one may at first sight assume, to be an example of country styles lagging behind the developments of "true" fashion in the urban centers.

Perhaps the most troubling component of medieval art in the context of fashion, as noted in several instances earlier, is its pervasive attitude of misogyny that takes its beginnings in the patristic literature and survives into the present. A number of medievalists in various disciplines have addressed this problem in medieval society in general during the past half-century.[34] In the discipline of art history, outstanding research in addition to those already mentioned, has also been done.[35] Martha Easton has dealt with the absence and presence of fashionable dress in medieval art in an important recent article.[36] She has examined in particular the cycle of eleven images of Saint Catherine's Life that follow directly after the calendar pages in the book of hours, the *Belles Heures*, now in the collection of the Cloisters Museum of the Metropolitan Museum of Art, one of the famous prayer books that the brothers Herman, Paul, and Jean de Limbourg illustrated for their patron, Jean, Duke of Berry in the first decade of the fifteenth century (Figure 8.12).

Art historians have noted with much interest the extremely close relationship of remuneration and *étrennes*, gift giving, between the duke and the brothers that was listed in the ducal accounts, and clearly indicate the unusually personal relationship between patron and artists. This would have included detailed discussions on the subject matter to be used in the illuminations, a collaboration, one must presume, far removed from the

FIGURE 8.12: St. Catherine stripped naked and tortured in the *Belles Heures* of Jean de France, duc de Berry, by the Limbourg brothers. Paris, c. 1405–9. 54.1.1a, fol. 17v. The Metropolitan Museum of Art, New York.

perfunctory marginal instructions to the illuminator noted in some earlier manuscripts that merely indicated color and generic posture. Generations of art historians have speculated on the duke's engagement in the artistic process, and no doubt wished themselves to have been flies on the wall during the planning sessions.[37] In the *Belles Heures* Saint Catherine cycle, the eleven full-page images portray the saint in various states of dress and undress, from lines of view that are unabashedly voyeuristic and climax-building to the blind-folded beheadings of both the saint and the pagan Empress Faustina that Catherine converts to Christianity. In fol. 17v, Catherine is seen, semi-nude after her torture, through the prison window, her naked upper body massaged with healing salves by angels. Facing Catherine in a mirroring posture through the prison cell's doorway, Faustina is dressed in a blue, gold-trimmed, sleeveless surcoat with the large side cutouts, called "windows of hell" by contemporary fashion critics. As interchangeable objects of the male gaze, as if through multiple keyholes, Catherine and Faustina are seen in the image cycle wearing the same colors, mantles rendered in luxurious cobalt blue pigment over springtime green gowns, with indistinguishable facial features and hairstyles. Easton concludes that "Overt sexual activity or sexual temptation are conveyed through the vehicle of clothing, the bodies of the women, naked or clothed."[38]

CONCLUSION

As has already been noted, fashion in general, and medieval fashion in particular, ought not to be studied in isolated examples or out of its context, and we need to expand our knowledge by getting access to the many images in different art media that remain in many cases little-known or still unpublished. We must also continue to ask why was the art made, and for whom. The medieval visual material is primarily a sumptuous display for the very privileged, disproportionately portrayed in a severely undemocratic hierarchy. As we have seen, some works, like the tapestry commissioned by the wealthy merchant from Speyer (Figure 8.7) were even made to provide a vicarious experience in upper-class style for ambitious status seekers. Certain objects, types of physiognomies, colors, and patterns depicted may never have existed, might have been highly idealized, or were made to depict a heroic, mythical or historical past. We must be mindful, too, of the drab, everyday urban landscape as it existed, where except for a few moments of spendthrift pageantry, most medieval men and women experienced an altogether different reality from the one depicted in the visual arts.[39]

CHAPTER NINE

Literary Representations

MONICA L. WRIGHT

Medieval authors, influenced by Classical rhetorical practices, created highly structured literature and economical narratives in European vernacular languages, combining Classical formulas and tropes with contemporary themes, motifs, and cultural preoccupations to relate stories often borrowed from local oral tradition.[1] Selecting their stories from prior sources, often from other languages, authors might choose tales that prominently feature clothing and textiles and amplify those instances to please the taste of their contemporary audience, or if the source material contained few instances of attire, they might integrate sartorial imagery.[2] The medieval practice of translation and adaptation is less a matter of rendering a text faithfully into a new language than using a source tale, perhaps even melding several sources together, and taking liberties with how that material is interpreted, all in light of its new audience.[3] A tendency arises, beginning in the twelfth century, to integrate fashion imagery into texts and to use such imagery in a number of interesting ways.[4] Clothing in literature always serves a narrative function in the text.[5] Here, my goal is to examine the narrative functions of clothing in selected medieval texts to illustrate how clothing in medieval literature materially expresses the major themes that preoccupy the culture. In France, for example, these themes include class tensions due to societal changes,[6] while in Iceland, we can discern a discourse of power emerging along with a nascent society.[7]

Clothing provides authors with a means to incorporate a rich site of cultural meaning into a text. In contrast with visual artists, it is not necessary for authors to provide information about their characters' dress, and when authors chose to describe clothing, it is to accomplish particular narrative functions. Descriptions of clothing in literature appear precisely to tell us something beyond what the rest of the character presentation does. Whether used to depict attire itself or to relate actions involving clothing, the use of sartorial images provides both visual and tactile information to the reader, evoking a multi-sensory response. Authors invite their readers' imagination to see the garment and feel the fabric, quickly infusing their text with greater sensory impact and giving their readers a fuller experience, often in few words. Alice M. Colby in her study of descriptive portraits in medieval French literature affirms that a major function of these passages is to provide readers with a "clear idea of a person"[8] and that often these descriptions use formulas as a basis to achieve such elaboration of character.[9]

The medieval Irish tale *Thochmarc Becfhola* ("The Wooing of Becfhola"), written in early Middle Irish and probably dating to the late ninth or early tenth century, is the earliest work I will consider here.[10] The work uses elaborate sartorial imagery to establish the high social status of the two main characters, Becfhola and Flann, by portraying them in the finest of clothes. Becfhola arrives in a chariot:

She wore rounded sandals of white bronze, inset with two jewels of precious stone; a tunic covered with red-gold embroidery about her; a crimson mantle on her; a brooch in fully-wrought gold with shimmering gems of many hues fastening the mantle over her breast; necklets of refined gold around her neck; a golden circlet upon her head.[11]

Niamh Whitfield analyzes in detail Becfhola's attire and shows how all the elements indicate high status, claiming that she is wearing "the costume of kings, queens, and nobles in early medieval Ireland."[12] Shortly later, we encounter Flann, Becfhola's love interest. He, too, is dressed splendidly, and from this description, we see not only his high status but also his vocation as a warrior:

He was clad in a silken tunic with a bright border, embroidered with circular designs of gold and silver. A helmet of gold, silver, and crystal was on his head, clusters and loops of gold around every lock of his hair, which hung down to his shoulder blades. Two golden balls were at the parting of his braids, each one of them the size of a man's fist. His golden-hilted sword on his belt [. . .] A cloak of many hues lay beside him. His two arms were laden to the elbows with gold and silver bracelets.[13]

These portraits indicate that Becfhola and Flann are of the highest status and possess great wealth, as well as providing insight into the material culture of medieval Ireland. Whitfield attests that most items in these two descriptions indeed appear in archeological finds from roughly the period of the tale's composition.[14] It is nevertheless worth remembering that the written story may contain anachronistic elements as well as fabric or other materials not normally present during the time period represented, for the narrative function of such a description—both the illustration and celebration of wealth and status—necessitates a degree of hyperbole in the representation of the material world; we must never assume accurate historicity in literary clothing.

Indeed, the majority of sartorial portraits in medieval literature describe exceptional garments worn by the upper nobility and therefore are replete with an exaggerated vision of luxury and splendor. Courtly attire is produced from the finest materials: brilliantly dyed silks, ornamented with gems, gold, and silver, and lined with the rarest furs. The conventional formulas used to create a discourse of fashionability arises first and foremost from hard-to-obtain materials, lending exoticism and high monetary value to literary portraits, materials nearly inaccessible in the real world. As Anna Zanchi explains in her discussion of scarlet in Icelandic saga, it is most probable that most Icelanders knew of scarlet but did not possess it despite its appearance in the tales.[15] The function of hyperbolic clothing in literature relates less to realistic depiction than to delectation, as Sarah-Grace Heller remarks.[16] These descriptions are entirely fabulous, and authors seem to know few limits as they parade an array of courtly ladies wearing bejeweled luscious silks vividly dyed in exotic pigments down the runways of their narratives.

The fourteenth-century Middle English poem *Pearl* offers us a counterexample to the courtly lady in multicolored finery. When the Dreamer perceives the Maiden, she is attired all in white, her dress decorated with pearls instead of brilliant jewels of many colors: "In linen robe of glistening white / With open sides that seams enlaced / With merriest margery pearls (. . .) With no gem but the pearl all white / And burnished white her garments were."[17] Because her attire formally resembles that of a courtly lady, the Dreamer initially mistakes her for a romance heroine instead of recognizing her as a heavenly being.[18] As Schotter indicates, the poet's use of clothing formulas is ambiguous, simultaneously evoking courtly elegance in the gown's components but also rejecting convention: "The reason clothing formulas are able to create the ambiguity that they do in *Pearl* is that they echo description of clothing in other alliterative poems, descriptions whose meaning varies so greatly according to context that the precise meaning of the formulas used by the dreamer is difficult for the reader to infer."[19] This use of clothing that both adheres to a courtly model and yet modifies it to convey an allegorical meaning—supreme purity, in this case—demonstrates the vast signifying power that clothing provides an author, who here juxtaposes material luxury with celestial perfection to create a new reading of the garments portrayed.

The Pearl Maiden shows how an author can subvert normal convention to make assertions about his character, but sartorial portraits can also contain contrasting elements which integrate satire, irony, or ambivalence into our understanding of the character portrayed. The resulting portraits are dynamic and invite the reader to interpret the character rather than simply receive a static list of characteristics. Chaucer's depiction of the Wife of Bath in his *General Prologue* contains extraordinary ambivalence, and she jumps from the page through the expertly rendered contrast between her bourgeois respectability and her vivid sartorial frivolity (Figure 9.1).

FIGURE 9.1: *The Wife of Bath*, drawing of a depiction in the Ellesmere Manuscript of the Canterbury Tales, early fifteenth century. Photo: Getty Images.

Chaucer describes her appearance, to be sure, but within the vestimentary information he provides, a complex personality emerges as well. Chaucer depicts the Wife in two separate outfits, beginning with her Sunday attire for church: "Hir coverchiefs ful fyne weren of ground; / I dorste swere they weyenden ten pound / That on a Sonday weren upon hir heed. / Hir hosen weren of fyn scarlet reed, / Ful steite yteyd, and shoes ful moyste and newe" (ll, 453–7). Next, he describes her pilgrim attire: "Ywympled wel, and on hir heed an hat / As brood as is a bokeler or a targe; / A foot-mantel aboute hir hipes large, / And on hir feet a paire of spores sharpe" (ll, 470–3). Fitting these two images together gives readers a more complex and complete idea of the Wife: we know from the rest of Chaucer's portrait that she is skilled at her profession, cloth-making, so we conclude that she is wealthy, which her clothing confirms.[20] We have a sense of her economic success not just from the depiction of her Sunday finery but also from the portrayal of her traveling outfit, which includes several specialized items useful to guarantee her comfort during a long journey: a broad hat for shade, a foot mantle to keep her clean and warm on horseback, and sharp spurs to manage her horse. We thus have a clear image of a woman with the means to obtain everything she needs in any situation; she is a consumer of specialized goods, and her vanity enjoys putting them on display. Her skill at her craft has made her prosperous, and she possesses the trappings of that success; her respectability extends to her participation in a pilgrimage, expressing spiritual aspirations that align with her station, while also proving her competence materially through her traveling outfit. All of these factors point to a level of social respectability, but there is more to consider in her clothing.

The Sunday outfit reads of excess, style, and means. She wears new shoes with scarlet red hose and a headdress of such exuberance as to make Chaucer wonder at its weight. Married women were required to cover their heads, and perhaps the ten pounds Chaucer swears by refers not simply to its heft or high monetary value—though it clearly has weight and worth!—but also to the weight of many weddings, for Alisoun has been married five times. The Wife is a woman who has already borne much and can certainly bear the many-layered sumptuary excess of her frilly headdress, as well as any criticism she may receive for it.[21] As Carolyn Dinshaw asserts, the Wife is not afraid to live fully and make a scene; she talks, her clothes talk, and "her body [. . .] can speak for itself."[22] Much has been made of her scarlet hose,[23] with many ascribing an overt sexuality to them,[24] but there can be no doubt about the high quality of their materials, for scarlet is the color obtained from the expensive dye kermes, and no one would waste scarlet on lesser fabrics.[25] To understand the Wife's clothing requires a sensitivity to the particular dynamism of her personality, caught between her craftswoman's respectability and her exuberant, vain frivolity, as well as the ambivalence of her social position in Chaucer's time.

Chaucer's use of clothing here provides evidence of a crisis of legibility in the fashion system in England, a period during which class distinctions, once thought to have been easily readable through a person's clothing, were becoming blurry. Andrea Denny-Brown argues that in England at the time, members of the mercantile class—to which the Wife belongs—employed their wealth and new power to "purchase social status, to use their new goods as a conduit to the social performance of the aristocracy" and that "the typical complaint about this new kind of spending was that it confused social hierarchy."[26] Concurrently, satire appeared to poke fun at such presumption on the part of the merchant class; Laura F. Hodges has asserted that on Sunday, the Wife wears "three items of expensive dress commonplace in estates satire," her headdress, her hose, and her shoes.[27]

Chaucers depicts the Wife in a nuanced portrait of contrasts, one that demands attention. As Cindy Carlson suggests,

> Chaucer's regular supply of fashion information for his readers in addition to status information indicates to his readers that more than one legible system of the bodies of his pilgrims may be readable at once and those systems may communicate the same—or different—meanings to various audience members.[28]

For characters like the Wife of Bath, readers must engage with their attire both deeply and subtly to read the rich layers of meaning inscribed therein, but our efforts are rewarded with characters that spring from the page and show off their finery in living color before our eyes.

Portraits that infuse interpretive dynamism into the text—and even more conventional portraits—also serve the text in a variety of ways, including not only the establishment of the socio-economic status and political identities of characters,[29] but also to indicate personal identity, such as the blazons on knights' armor and shields, which was critically important on the battlefield (Figure 9.2).

Yet, face-obscuring armor also provided authors with a ready and effective means to conceal a knight's identity by donning him in unfamiliar armor, as when Chrétien de Troyes' Lancelot borrows armor to participate incognito in a tournament at Arthur's court.[30] Disguise is an essential trope in medieval literature, allowing events to occur that

FIGURE 9.2: Knights' identities were often declared by their arms, but obscured by their helmets. Illustration of a tournament in the time of Charles V in the *Grandes Chroniques de France*, fourteenth century. Photo: Leemage/Getty Images.

otherwise could not, specifically because attire conceals in the same measure that it reveals. In Béroul's *Tristan*, the hero disguises himself as a leper not only to attend Yseut's oath but also to re-establish their status at court through both the clandestine acquisition of courtly clothing—the outer trappings of courtliness—and Yseut's ambivalent oath itself—in which his disguise is instrumental.[31]

Disguise extends beyond obscuring personal identity temporarily: Cross-dressing and gender ambivalence are important features of medieval literature.[32] As E. Jane Burns attests, gender in these literary texts is fabricated by attire, that is, read through the clothed body rather than the body itself; see her discussion of *Le Roman de Silence* in Chapter 5.[33] A range of possibilities exists, including temporary states of cross-dressing that function primarily as disguise, such as when Nicolette dresses as a man to escape her family[34] or when Thor dresses as a woman to recover his hammer.[35]

Clothing often communicates temporary states of being for characters: grief, as seen through the destruction of apparel, as when Yvain sees Laudine for the first time, grieving her slain knight and expressing her grief in part by destroying her clothing.[36] Defeat becomes apparent through damaged armor. Authors use clothing to make material transformations in characters, changing their attire to indicate and track characters' changing situations or personal evolution. Perceval begins his journey dressed in Welsh homespun and is mocked for believing in its superiority to courtly clothes, but while learning both chivalric skills and courtly manners, he acquires fine armor and attire appropriate to his station.[37] Just as clothing can serve as evidence of a transitory state, it can also provide a remedy to a temporary situation; the use of a textile or other adornment item as a recognition device between two people who have spent a great deal of time separated is common, such as the ring that identifies the long lost son to his father in Marie de France's *Milun*.[38] Magical clothing also abounds in medieval works: sartorial items that cannot be removed except by one person,[39] cloaks that confer special abilities on the wearer,[40] and items that fit only if the wearer possesses a certain quality.[41] Such sartorial wonders provide protection, succor, or proof of worthiness to their wearers, intensifying the common function of clothing as protection from the elements and extending it into a social realm.

In keeping with clothing's social importance, medieval authors closely associate attire with civilization and humanity, using its inverse, nudity, to denote a variety of reduced states: the abjection of Yvain as he slips into madness and removes his clothing to become a social outcast, or later as Lunete is taken to be burnt at the stake "nue en sa chemise."[42] Nowhere is the dehumanizing effect of nudity clearer than in the figure of the werewolf, whose descent into his beast phase comes with a stripping of the clothes that defined him as a man.[43] Moreover, forcibly undressing a vanquished opponent humiliates him beyond his defeat; a naked knight is vulnerable, stripped of the trappings of his vocation. Interestingly, Beowulf as he prepares to fight Grendel, removes his armor, thereby eliminating a crucial part of his human identity—the warrior—in order to meet his opponent on the monster's terms.[44] Elizabeth Howard argues that Beowulf has previously conducted himself as an exemplary civilized human, employing reason and strategy, using tools, telling tales, and wearing clothes, but when he meets the monster, he temporarily rejects the trappings of his humanity to descend into a monstrous state.[45] Nudity for Dante Alighieri appears in stark contrast to the celestial attire of the inhabitants of Paradise; nakedness is not simply the absence of clothing but also the vulnerability of mankind after the Fall, and the souls trapped in Purgatory suffer this kind of awareness of their unclothed state.[46] In his *Inferno*, Dante takes the dehumanizing effect of undressing to its most abject conclusion, stripping some damned souls not just of their clothing but also their skin.[47] Those without clothes, without a socially-constructed identity, have no place in medieval society (Figure 9.3).

Providing clothing to others, then, takes on special meaning and can be understood as a sign of acceptance and inclusion. Gifts of clothing are particularly important for medieval society because they solidified personal bonds and relationships.[48] A typical scene of royal largesse involves the king distributing clothes, armor, and other valuable gifts to those present at his court. Feudal obligations included not only the equipping of knights so that they can perform their military service but also the distribution of goods to members of the court to express the esteem and affection of the lord. Love tokens constitute a different order of gift but whose effect is the same: acceptance of a gift materializes the bond between the giver and receiver.

The case of Griselda is far more complicated. The story first appears in Italy in the thirteenth century and is translated into English and French over the course of the next two centuries.[49] The basic story remains stable. A young nobleman, Walter, will only agree to marry a woman of his choosing. He assembles his people and proposes to a low-born maiden at her father's home and, upon her consent, has his servants strip her publicly so

FIGURE 9.3: Nudity in Dante's *Divine Comedy*: "Dante's notion of nakedness in the Comedy as not only the absence of clothing, but the vulnerability of humankind after the Fall." Photo: DEA/G. NIMATALLAH/Getty Images.

that they can dress her in a fine set of new clothes. The clothes are a wedding gift that also confers a new status on Griselda. She proves herself a worthy wife, bears him two children, and manages their household well. Nonetheless, he tests her loyalty by twice convincing her to surrender a child for him to kill. After gaining her consent both times, he hides the child nearby. Finally, he explains his wish to divorce her and remarry, and demands that she remove the clothes he gave her and return to her father's home naked (Figure 9.4). She convinces him to allow her to wear her shift to cover her nudity slightly. After she agrees to prepare his wedding bed for his new wife, he reveals their children alive, explains it was all a ruse, and provides her a new set of fine clothes.

In terms of the gift economy and the convention of love tokens, Walter's gift fails. Rather than create a mutual bond between the two spouses, his gift covers and uncovers his wife's vulnerability in ways that reflect badly on him. He reduces her and their children to pawns in a game and objects of exchange. Roberta Krueger argues that Griselda is "translated" between poverty and wealth, low and high status, and father and husband, much as the tale moved through time, culture, and language.[50] She and Carlson consider Griselda's initial acceptance of Walter's clothing a contract in which the heroine agrees to obey him and allow him to humiliate her however he chooses.[51] Yet, his behavior is shameful, not only to his wife but also to him. As Carlson explains, Griselda's second public stripping transfers her shame to the witnesses, relieving Griselda of it and providing a measure of pleasure in the transfer as she reveals to the world her status as cast-off wife. She finds herself at the intersection of clothing's dual capacity for revelation and concealment, and at the intersection of status and caprice, but she has cast off her shame.

FIGURE 9.4: Griselda removing her clothing, in Laurent de Premierfait's translation of Boccacio's *Decameron*, second quarter of the fifteenth century. Français 239, fol. 295. Bibliothèque nationale de France.

Making textiles, usually a female endeavor, carries special meaning because it allowed women to express themselves and provided financial means for women to gain some independence.[52] The Wife of Bath owes her fortune to her skill as a cloth-maker, exhibiting such skill in her craft that Chaucer tells us her wares are superior to those produced in the great cloth centers of Ypres and Ghent: "Of clooth-makyng she hadde swich an haunt / She passed hem of Ypres and of Gaunt."[53] The Wife enjoys financial independence due to the wealth earned from her commercial enterprise. In the Old Norse tradition, there are numerous depictions of women spinning, weaving, and sewing;[54] D'Ettore provides a number of examples in her discussion of the production of textile items by female characters in the Icelandic sagas.[55] The benefit of their labor is not explicitly economic but instead allows them to enter into the discourse of power, facilitating outcomes they desire through their production. The Old French *Philomena* also uses a textile to provoke a resolution for herself; after she is raped, rendered mute by removal of her tongue, and imprisoned by her brother-in-law, she seeks the aid of her guardian, a weaver, to procure the materials to begin a tapestry.[56] Philomena's tapestry relates her story to her sister, who frees her sister and, once reunited with her, plots revenge on her husband. Philomena's skill at weaving gives her freedom and vengeance, all in the context of a narrative of exchange.

The fourteenth-century English lay *Emaré* depicts the eponymous heroine as the daughter of a widowed emperor and insists multiple times upon her great skills at needlework.[57] Her father takes an incestuous interest in her, has a wedding dress made for her from a precious and splendid cloth of gold, and banishes her when she refuses to marry him. She leaves by boat with nothing but her beautiful dress, which, as Amanda Hopkins argues, becomes the emblem of her vulnerability and the wrongdoings she suffers.[58] She marries a Welsh knight against his mother's will and, through his mother's contriving, finds herself again banished in a boat with only her dress and her newborn son. A merchant in Rome takes her in, and eventually she is reunited with her husband and her father, who no longer blames her for her refusal. Not only does Emaré have great textile skills entirely appropriate to her station, but she also teaches others, empowering them during her own period of powerlessness. Crucially, she did not make the fine gown she wears and that symbolizes her abuse; as Hopkins attests, the dress is imposed upon her.[59] What defines Emaré is not the external trappings she is forced to wear but rather what she does: her generosity, her nobility, and her clothwork. The gown may be the mark of her oppression, but her ability to make textiles gives her agency.

The relationship between making textiles and creating text was apparent to medieval writers, who undertook great projects of weaving new works from old tales. Jean Renart, in his thirteenth-century romance *Le Roman de la Rose, ou de Guillaume de Dole*, stresses the similarities between the process of literary creation and cloth production, describing his own process of embellishing his text through the addition of songs to the process of dyeing fabric with the expensive red derived from kermes to increase its worth and to the process of embroidery.[60] Sartorial images strengthen the narrative cohesion of works by developing their themes and providing structuring devices.

One of the most innovative uses of clothing and textiles in medieval literature involves the opening and closing of narrative threads.[61] A remarkable example of clothing opening a narrative thread also involves a clothing gift and appears in the *Laxdœla Saga*, when the sister of the king of Norway gives a beautiful white headdress to the Icelander Kjartan to take with him on his journey home and give to his beloved for their wedding. Upon his return, however, Kjartan learns that Guðrún has married his friend in his absence. The headdress not only becomes a symbol of the strife that follows, which entails a multi-generational deadly revenge cycle that occupies the rest of the saga, but also occasions it.[62] Icelandic authors use clothing to open narrative threads by announcing conflict, or the possibility of conflict, to follow. As D'Ettore makes clear, this device is a convention inscribed in a discourse of power in the emerging Icelandic society where clans were struggling to exert dominance over others.[63]

The Middle High German epic *Das Nibelungenlied*, composed around 1200,[64] in which a more established society attempts to assert its courtliness despite deep power struggles and an ineffective king, presents an elaborate series of interrelated, formally similar instances involving attire that open and also close a crucial narrative sequence through sartorial thefts and gifts, disguise with a magical cloak, and undressing. The garments occasion deception, come to symbolize it, provoke dramatic conflict, and precipitate the death of a major character. Moreover, the sequence through its ingenious use of clothing renders material the causal relationship that links the different episodes, strengthening the structure while elaborating the central theme of the epic: the conflict that arises from deception. The melding of Germanic convention—clothing that announces conflict—and French literary innovations—employing sartorial devices to structure narrative—facilitates the development of the crisis, brings it to its murderous climax, and symbolizes its fragile dénouement.

The narrative sequence begins in Chapter Seven with Siegfried's use of a magical cloak, or *Tarnkappe*, which renders him invisible and as strong as twelve men, to deceive Brünhild as Gunther fights with her to win her hand in marriage. Gunther, who cannot defeat the warrior queen alone, solicits Siegfried's assistance, and Siegfried, wearing the *Tarnkappe*, holds Gunther's shield so that Brünhild believes Gunther is holding it while they fight. As a result, Gunther and Siegfried are able to overpower her, and she agrees to marry Gunther. This deception, coupled with the fact that Gunther has led Brünhild to believe that Siegfried is his vassal instead of his friend and a fellow king, opens a narrative thread that continues through the rest of the first half of the epic and culminates in Siegfried's funeral. Once married, Brünhild refuses to consummate their union and instead uses her girdle to bind him and render him powerless the whole night. Again, Siegfried assists Gunther by wearing *Tarnkappe*. He enters their bedroom and impersonates Brünhild's husband, again overpowering her. She finally relents, and he steals her ring (Figure 9.5) and girdle, which he subsequently gives to his own wife, Gunther's sister, Kriemhild:

> Siegfried left the maiden lying there and stepped aside as though to remove his clothes and without the noble Queen's noticing it, he drew a golden ring from her finger and then took her girdle, a splendid orphrey. I do not know whether it was his pride which made him do it. Later he gave them to his wife, and well did he rue it. And now Gunther and the lovely girl lay together.[65]

Brünhild, however, is suspicious of Siegfried and upset that Gunther would allow his sister to marry whom she mistakenly believes to be his vassal. Later, Kriemhild reveals to Brünhild that she has the items Siegfried stole that night, using the ring and girdle to prove that Siegfried and not Gunther took her maidenhood.

Brünhild is understandably enraged to learn this. Her husband's kinsman and court strongman, Hagen, hears of her anguish and decides to kill Siegfried. He knows that Siegfried is invincible for having bathed in the blood of a dragon he vanquished but also that he has a single spot of vulnerability where a leaf fell on him while he was bathing.

FIGURE 9.5: An example of an inscribed gold ring, English, c. 1300. © Victoria and Albert Museum, London.

Hagen convinces Kriemhild that he wishes to take special care in protecting her husband from harm to that vulnerable point, but he claims that to do so, she must sew an indicator—"ein kleinez zeichen"—on his clothes. She agrees to embroider a small cross in silk—"mit kleinen sîden næ ich ûf sîn gewant / ein tougenlîchez kriuze"—on the back of his tunic to indicate the point on his body where he can be injured.[66] Siegfried's clothes will get him killed. The scene of Siegfried's killing and its aftermath is rich in sartorial imagery. We see Siegfried and Hagen remove their protective outer garments and race to a stream wearing only their white tunics.[67] When Siegfried extends his body over the stream to drink, Hagen spies the embroidered cross and spears him through his back, striking his heart directly. Blood spills from Siegfried's body and drenches his clothing. Word of his death reaches his family at court, and his father's people, awakened and still nude from their night's sleep, forget to put on clothes immediately and stand naked in their grief:

> Hearing the women lament so dolefully it occurred to some that they ought to have their clothes on. So great was the suffering embedded in their hearts that they had quite forgotten themselves.[68]

Their nudity is quickly reflected in the removal of Siegfried's clothes so that they may wash his body to prepare it for burial.[69]

The first use of the *Tarnkappe* begins a series of events involving attire that end in tragedy. One act opens the way for the following act, which reflects the previous one and in turn prepares the next, forming a thread of interrelated actions involving clothing that thrust the narrative forward. Siegfried's second use of the *Tarnkappe* to deceive Brünhild reflects his first use but also incorporates the theft of her ring and girdle. The theft occasions Kriemhild's revelation to Brünhild, provoking her rage that leads to Hagen asking Kriemhild to mark Siegfried's tunic. In order to see the mark on his tunic, Hagen contrives a situation necessitating Siegfried's removal of his outer clothing, which itself prefigures the removal of his clothing after his death for preparation of his body for burial (Figure 9.6).

In addition to this complex string of actions, there are instances of clothing formally linked to others that show extreme states of pathos, adding both imagery and emotional impact to the narrative. That Siegfried's family members are so distraught to learn of his demise that they forget to cover their nudity conveys their grief materially but also connects the event formally to the act they will soon perform on their loved one's body. Clearly, they need to remove Siegfried's clothes to prepare his body before his funeral, but they must also remove them because they are soaked with blood. This image shows the gravity of the wound inflicted on his body by Hagen and constitutes a strong visual and

FIGURE 9.6: The death of Siegfried in the Nibelungen (Nibelung), fifteenth century, illustration from manuscript K 1480/1490, National Library Vienna. Image: INTERFOTO/Alamy.

tactile image of suffering. Moreover, the tunic soaked with blood is directly responsible for that blood through the deceptive words of Hagen and the misguided hands of Kriemhild that embroidered the cross. His tunic is simultaneously the cause of Siegfried's death and the emblem of it in the same way that Brünhild's stolen girdle is both the reason Siegfried deceived her the second time and, along with the stolen ring, the emblem of that deception. All of these actions involving clothing create a sense of inevitability in the story and develop the theme of betrayal. Joachim Bumke argues that although Gunther's court appears to be a model of courtliness and order, it is only a façade: Gunther is a weak king who cannot win his lady without Siegfried's help, and in eliminating the threat to order that Siegfried poses, Hagen becomes a murderer because Gunther cannot maintain the façade.[70] Accordingly, "the story culminates in the downfall of an entire society which had concealed its corruption behind a courtly mask."[71] Indeed, we can clearly perceive the courtly mask in Siegfried's *Tarnkappe*, which initiates the thread of deception and betrayal that ends with its wearer's funeral. He concealed himself when he should not have in the same way that Kriemhild revealed clothing items she should not have, and in the end, they are both laid bare, he as a corpse and she in her grief. Their nudity closes the complex narrative thread begun by Siegfried's donning of the *Tarnkappe*.

Clothing is often more pervasively employed than for initiating and developing specific sequences of events. Chrétien de Troyes' use of fashion, especially in *Erec et Enide*,[72] to structure the narrative and express and reinforce thematic unity is among the most highly developed in medieval literature. It is possible to read the plot through the clothing of the two protagonists, who must grow into their clothes.[73] When we meet each of them, Erec and Enide are dressed inappropriately for the task they are about to face: the unarmed Erec cannot fight the knight whose dwarf affronts the queen, and Enide, dressed in tatters, is not attired properly to go to court. Chrétien uses their clothing to indicate their insufficiency at the beginning of the romance but also to establish and elaborate the thematic unity of the work. Erec will spend the remainder of the romance atoning first for his initial lack of armor and his post-nuptial *recreanz*[74] through feats of arms, while Enide, once dressed by the queen, overcomes her vestimentary lack but must still prove to Erec that she loves and trusts in his prowess.

The relationship between *Gereint uab Erbin*,[75] the Welsh version of the tale, remains unclear, but although initially the Welsh version presents the Erec figure as unarmed and Enide as poorly dressed and that these deficiencies must be rectified, the author does not continue to use clothing in the innovative ways that Chrétien does. The Welsh lacks a number of sartorial episodes and themes that Chrétien relies upon to develop his characters and plot. Chrétien's romances were translated from Old French into Middle High German[76] and Old Norse,[77] but the German and Norse versions of *Erec et Enide* also do not include the wealth of vestimentary imagery and devices that Chrétien crafted. Though adaptations of Chrétien's work, they are without the complex web of sartorial meaning that Chrétien wove into his narrative. Clothing may begin as important for establishing that Erec and Enide need to evolve personally and socially, but it does not continue to be so for the duration of the other versions.

Chrétien focuses the narrative in a very precise way on the interconnected themes related to clothing: the insufficiency that the two protagonists must overcome initially, Erec's *recreanz* and Enide's inability to prove her devotion to her husband, particularly in light of his rejection of his chivalric duties. This narrow focus is not present in the other versions, as we can see in the fact that they not only describe Enide's tattered dress but also the poor garments of her father in the German and Norse and those of her father and mother in the Welsh. Because Chrétien limits his view to Erec's lack of armor and Enide's threadbare attire, these narrative threads converge and put the lovers in relief. Moreover, in Chrétien's version, we learn that Enide's father has rejected previous attempts to dress his daughter better, and Erec agrees with this attitude and insists that only the queen should dress Enide, showing to what extent the two families share the same courtly values. In the other versions, different reasons govern the decision to bring Enide to Arthur's court dressed as she was when Erec met her. Chrétien's careful weaving leads to the first scene of sartorial splendor with the elaborate refashioning of Enide in Guenevere's own new *bliaut*[78] and mantle, to which the poet devotes ninety verses of description. This scene is given short shrift in the other versions, with Hartmann providing only forty-one lines devoted to Enide's remaking, immediately overshadowed by the arrival of finely dressed kings whose apparel receives fifty verses of description and Erec's three sets of armor, accorded an additional thirty-four lines of verse. The Norse version grants only two and a half prose lines of description to Enide's new dress, while the Welsh provides no description at all.

In Chrétien Enide's dressing scene punctuates the first partition of the romance, closing it with the image of the queen she will soon become and formally announcing Erec's coronation and Arthur's gift of the fabulous coronation robe and mantle, to whose description Chrétien devotes seventy-six verses. The mantle in particular is an extraordinary object: made of fine silk, embroidered by four fairies to depict four of the liberal arts, and lined with the fur of a magical and exotic beast. Chrétien incorporates imagery and motifs that evoke the classical world, Celtic folklore, Eastern fabrics, imaginary beasts, scientific knowledge, and French medieval fashion, and he knits it all into a single garment, given to Erec by the highest king. It is a description to end all descriptions, and it punctuates the romance in the same way that Enide's refashioning punctuates the end of the first section. The two scenes reflect each other and reflect the perfection that the two protagonists have attained; their clothes fit them marvelously.

The Norse adaptation is unique in echoing Chrétien's coronation scene, only Erec does not receive the gown; Evida does:

> But to Evida he gave a precious robe; on it were depicted the liberal arts. It glittered all over and was so precious that no merchant could estimate its value. It was woven by four elfwomen in an underground dwelling nine leagues under the earth where no daylight ever reached.[79]

In Hartmann's German adaptation, Erec is crowned but there is no description. In the Welsh version, Erec became king after his marriage, so the story ends with him and his wife simply going home. Although all of the versions of the story begin by depicting the insufficiencies of Erec and Enide through their inappropriate dress, none but Chrétien's text exploits the full range of possibilities for the narrative use of clothing throughout. Chrétien proves himself a master weaver in incorporating fashion in his works to perform a wide range of narrative functions and to create structure and thematic cohesion.

Heller has argued that we can find evidence of a fashion system in the literature of twelfth-century France.[80] Certainly, there are plenty of passages in the French literature of the period to make a strong case for pervasive and varied narrative use of clothing in the texts. The French influence in both fashion and literature is clear throughout the rest of western Europe, and I would argue for a close, structural relationship between them. The great merchant fairs of the county of Champagne brought exotic textiles and furs into the region nearly year round, supplying the necessary components of the most desirable attire to the aristocratic set. Eleanor of Aquitaine's eldest daughter, Marie, whose tastes in literature, courtly diversion, and luxury were indubitably influenced by her illustrious and well-traveled mother, presided over a highly cultured, prosperous court. Finally, Chrétien, who enjoyed the patronage of the countess of Champagne, plied his skill with a quill in such a milieu and created a masterful discourse around the fashions in evidence at court, whetting the appetite of his noble audience through descriptions of marvelous garments and scenes that expertly employ sartorial imagery to construct narratives in which clothing plays a central role. The adaptations of his works into other languages show us that Europe was watching, ready to alter his designs to create a better fit for the new audience to admire.

NOTES

Introduction

1. G. Lipovetsky, *The Empire of Fashion: Dressing Modern Democracy* (Princeton: Princeton University Press, 2002).
2. P. Post, "Die französisch-niederländische Männertracht einschliesslich der Ritterrüstung im Zeitalter der Spätgotik, 1350–1475. Ein Rekonstruktionsversuch auf Gründ der zeitgenössichen Darstellungen" (Halle a. d. Saale, Dissertation, 1910).
3. E.g. C. Breward, *The Culture of Fashion. A New History of Fashionable Dress* (Manchester: Manchester University Press, 1995), 8; F. Davis, *Fashion, Culture, and Identity* (Chicago: University of Chicago Press, 1994), 17; S. Kaiser, *The Social Psychology of Clothing: Symbolic Appearances in Context*, 2nd ed., revised (New York: Fairchild Publications, 1998), 389; A. Hunt, *Governance of the Consuming Passions: A History of Sumptuary Law* (New York: St. Martin's Press, 1996), 149–50.
4. O. Blanc, *Parades et parures: L'invention du corps de mode à la fin du Moyen Age.* (Paris: Gallimard, 1997); F. Piponnier, "Une révolution dans le costume masculin au XIVe siècle," in *Le Vêtement: Histoire, archéologie et symboliques vestimentaires au Moyen Âge*, ed. M. Pastoureau (Paris: Léopard d'Or, 1989), 225–42.
5. L. Wilson, "'De Novo Modo': The Birth of Fashion in the Middle Ages," PhD diss., Fordham University, 2011.
6. E. Salin, *La civilisation mérovingienne d'après les sépultures, les textes et le laboratoire* (Paris: Picard, 1949).
7. C. Lelong, *La Vie quotidienne en Gaule à l'époque mérovingienne* (Paris: Hachette, 1963), 124.
8. V. Garver, *Women and Aristocratic Culture in the Carolingian World* (Ithaca: Cornell University Press, 2009), 189; J. Ball, *Byzantine Dress: Representations of Secular Dress in Eighth- to Twelfth-century Painting* (New York: Palgrave Macmillan, 2005), 112–15.
9. M. Miller, *Clothing the Clergy: Virtue and Power in Medieval Europe, c. 800–1200* (Ithaca, NY: Cornell University Press, 2014); C.S. Jaeger, *The Origins of Courtliness: Civilizing Trends and the Formation of Courtly Ideals, 939–1210* (Philadelphia: University of Pennsylvania Press, 1985), 116–21, 188–9.
10. S.-G. Heller, *Fashion in Medieval France* (Woodbridge: Boydell and Brewer, 2007).

1 Textiles

1. R. Woodward Wendelken, "Silk," in *Encyclopedia of Medieval Dress and Textiles of the British Isles*, eds G.R. Owen-Crocker, E. Coatsworth, and M. Hayward (Leiden: Brill, 2012), 515–22.
2. J. Munro, "Three Centuries of Luxury Textile Consumption in the Low Countries and England, 1330–1570: Trends and Comparisons of Real Values of Woollen Broadcloths (Then and Now)," in *The Medieval Broadcloth: Changing Trends in Fashions, Manufacturing and Consumption*, eds K. Vestergård Pedersen and M.-L.B. Nosch, Ancient Textiles Series Vol. 6 (Oxford: Oxbow, 2009), 1–73.
3. D. Leed, "Laundry," in *Encyclopedia*, Owen-Crocker et al., 314–16.

4. A.R. Bell, C. Brooks, P.R. Dryburgh, "Wool trade: England c. 1250–1330," in *Encyclopedia*, Owen-Crocker et al., 642–6.

5. M. Tangl (ed.), *S. Bonifatii et Lulli Epistolae*, Monumenta Germaniae Historica, Epistolae 4, Epistolae Selectae, 1 (Berlin: Weidmannschen Verlagsbuchhandlung, 1916), 159 l. 18; 131, ll. 18–20.

6. P. Walton Rogers, *Tyttels Halh: The Anglo-Saxon Cemetery at Tittleshall, Norfolk, the Bacton to King's Lynn Gas Pipeline,* East Anglian Archaeology 150, Vol. 2 (2013): 26, 44–5, 98.

7. H.M. Sherman, "From Flax to Linen in the Medieval Rus Lands," *Medieval Clothing and Textiles* 4 (2004): 1–20; M. FitzGerald, "Linen," in *Encyclopedia*, Owen-Crocker et al., 325–9.

8. Leed, "Laundry," in *Encyclopedia*, Owen-Crocker, et al.; "Lye" and "Soap," ibid., 351, 525.

9. T. Izbicki, "*Linteamenta altaria*: The Care of Altar Linens in the Medieval Church," *Medieval Clothing and Textiles* 12 (2016).

10. J. Arnold, "The jupon or coat-armour of the Black Prince in Canterbury cathedral," *Journal of the Church Monuments Society* 8 (1993): 12–24.

11. M.F. Mazzaoui, *The Italian Cotton Industry in the Later Middle Ages, 1100–1600* (Cambridge: Cambridge University Press, 1981).

12. D. Bamford, M. Chambers, and E. Coatsworth, "Cotton," in *Encyclopedia*, G. Owen-Crocker et al., 153.

13. Wendelken, "Silk," in *Encyclopedia*, G. Owen-Crocker et al., 67–71.

14. Ibid.

15. B. Haas-Gebhard and B. Nowak-Böck, "The Unterhaching Grave Finds: Richly Dressed Burials from Sixth-Century Bavaria," *Medieval Clothing and Textiles* 8 (2012): 1–23, esp. 14–16.

16. E. Wincott Heckett, *Viking Headcoverings from Dublin*, National Museum of Ireland, Medieval Dublin Excavations 1962–81, Ser. B, Vol. 6 (Dublin: Royal Irish Academy, 2003); P. Walton, *Textiles, Cordage and Raw Fibre from 16–22 Coppergate*, The Archaeology of York 17.5 (London: Published for the York Archaeological Trust by the Council for British Archaeology, 1989), 360–77; A. Muthesius, "The silk fragment from 5 Coppergate," in *Anglo-Scandinavian finds from Lloyd's Bank, Pavement and other sites*, ed. A. MacGregor, The Archaeology of York, 17.3 (London: for the York Archaeological Trust by the Council for British Archaeology, 1982), 132–6.

17. The coffin contained a silver gilt crown, sceptre, and orb, as well as the (boiled) head of the king. The rest of his body was cremated. Personal communications to Gale R. Owen-Crocker from Rossella Lorenzi, Senior Correspondent, *Discovery News*, 28 and 29 May 2014 and http://news.discovery.com/history/archaeology/unique-silk-cloth-found-in-emperor-henry-viis-coffin-140530.htm. The tomb had been opened previously in 1727 and 1921.

18. R. Fleming, "Acquiring, flaunting and destroying silk in late Anglo-Saxon England," *Early Medieval Europe* 15.2 (2007): 127–58.

19. E.B. Andersson, "Textile Tools and Production in the Viking Age," in *Ancient Textiles: production, craft, and society: proceedings of the First International Conference on Ancient Textiles, held at Lund, Sweden, and Copenhagen, Denmark, on March 19–23, 2003,* eds C. Gillis and M.-L.B. Nosch (Oxford: Oxbow Books, 2007), 17–25.

20. K. Buckland "Spinning Wheels," in *Encyclopedia*, Owen-Crocker et al., 539–40.

21. See Karen Nicholson's experiments with whorls of different shapes and sizes, and spindles of different shapes, all factors which could affect the type of thread produced by hand spinning: K. Nicholson, "The Effect of Spindle Whorl Design on Wool Thread Production: A Practical Experiment Based on Examples from Eighth-Century Denmark," *Medieval Clothing and Textiles* 11 (2015): 29–48.

22. E. Coatsworth, "Broadcloth," in *Encyclopedia*, Owen-Crocker et al., 97; Gale R. Owen-Crocker 2012. "Looms," in *Encyclopedia*, Owen-Crocker et al., 346.

23. T. Anderlini, "The Shirt Attributed to St Louis," *Medieval Clothing and Textiles* 11 (2015): 49–78.

24. See "Raines" in the Lexis of Cloth and Clothing database, http://lexissearch.arts.manchester. ac.uk/entry.aspx?id=3961

25. The thread count from Anderlini, 77. The heart was placed in a sealed lead box inscribed HIC IACET COR RICARDI REGIS ANGLORUM, and deposited in the church of Notre Dame in Rouen; P. Charlier, J. Poupon, G.-F. Jeannel, D. Favier, S.-M. Popescu, R. Weil, "The embalmed heart of Richard the Lionheart (1199 A.D.): a biological and anthropological analysis," in *Scientific Reports*, Nature Publishing Group (February 28, 2013), http://www. nature.com/srep/2013/130228/srep01296/full/srep01296.html There is a detail of the linen at Figure 2A.

26. J. Munro, G.R. Owen-Crocker, and H. Uzzell "Kermes," in *Encyclopedia*, Owen-Crocker et al., 301–2.

27. E. Coatsworth, "Opus anglicanum," in *Encyclopedia*, Owen-Crocker et al., 392–7.

28. L. Monnas, "Cloth of Gold," and M. Chambers and E. Coatsworth, "Baudekin," in *Encyclopedia*, Owen-Crocker et al., 132–3 and 56–7, respectively.

29. P. Walton, "Textiles," in *English Medieval Industries: craftsmen, techniques, products*, eds J. Blair and N. Ramsay (London and Rio Grande: Hambledon, 1991), 323–4.

30. E. Crowfoot, F. Pritchard, and K. Staniland, *Textiles and Clothing c. 1150–c. 1450*, Medieval Finds from Excavations in London 4 (London: HMSO 1992), 19; the authors are grateful to Emily Field for this reference.

31. C. Given-Wilson (gen. ed.), *The Parliament Rolls of Medieval England, 1275–1504*, 16 vols. (Woodbridge: Boydell, 2005); E. Coatworth, "Cloth: dimensions and weights," in *Encyclopedia*, Owen-Crocker et al., 130–2.

32. P. Merrick, "Alnage or Ulnage" and "Alnagers and Ulnagers," in *Encyclopedia*, Owen-Crocker et al., 34–6; P. Merrick, "The administration of the ulnage and subsidy on woollen cloth between 1394 and 1485, with a case study in Hampshire," Unpublished MPhil thesis, University of Southampton (1997); M. Riu, "The Woollen Industry in Catalonia in the Later Middle Ages," in *Cloth and Clothing in Medieval Europe: Essays in Memory of Prof. E.M. Carus-Wilson*, N. Harte and K.G. Ponting, Pasold Studies in Textile History 2 (London: Heinemann Educational, 1983), 205–29.

33. E.M. Carus-Wilson and O. Coleman, *England's Export Trade 1275–1547* (Oxford: Clarendon Press, 1963).

34. See for example, D. Hill and R. Cowie (eds), *Wics: the Early Medieval Trading Centres of Northern Europe*, Sheffield Archaeological Monographs 14 (Sheffield: Sheffield Academic Press, 2001).

35. A.R. Bell, C. Brooks, P.R. Dryburgh, "Wool Trade: England c. 1250—Dress and Textiles of the British Isles," in *Encyclopedia*, Owen-Crocker et al., 642–6. For a fuller account see A.R. Bell, C. Brooks and P.R. Dryburgh *The English Wool Market c. 1230–1327* (Cambridge: University Press, 2007).

36. E. Coatsworth, "Cloth: dimension and weights," in *Encyclopedia*, Owen-Crocker et al., 130–2; Merrick, "Alnage or Ulnage" and "Alnagers or Ulnagers," ibid., 34–5, 35–6.

37. See http://focus.library.utoronto.ca/people/567-John_Munro, for a complete list of publications.

38. For the full text in Latin, see T. Hunt, *Teaching and Learning Latin in the Thirteenth Century*, 3 vols. (Cambridge: D.S. Brewer, 1991), Vol. I, 184–5. For a translation of the section on weaving, see U.T. Holmes Jr., *Daily Living in the Twelfth Century, Based on the Observations of Alexander Neckam in London and Paris* (Madison, WI: University of Wisconsin Press, 1952), 146–50.

39. Hunt, *Teaching and Learning* vol. I, 196–203, esp. paragraphs 10, 26, 50, 66, 68, 69. See also Martha Carlin, "Shops and shopping in the early thirteenth century," in *Money, Markets and Trade in Late Medieval Europe: essays in honour of John H.A. Munro*, eds Lawrin Armstrong, Ivana Elbl, and Martin M. Elbl (Leiden: Brill, 2007), 497–8.

40. P. Ménard (ed.), "Le 'Dit de Mercier'," in *Mélanges de Langue et de Littérature du Moyen Age et de la Renaissance Offerts à Jean Frappier*, Publications romanes et françaises 112 (Geneva:

Droz, 1970), 797–810; R.A. Ladd, "The London Mercer's Company, London Textual Culture," and John Gower's *Mirour de l'Omme, Medieval Clothing and Textiles* 6 (2010): 127–50.

41. E.W. Stockton (ed. and trans.), *The Major Latin Works of John Gower* (Seattle, WA: University of Washington Press, 1962); W.B. Wilson (ed. and trans.), *Mirour de l'Omme/The Mirror of Mankind, John Gower* (East Lansing: Colleagues Press, 1992).

42. Ladd, *Medieval Clothing and Textiles* 6: 139–44.

43. See for example M. Clegg Hyer, "Recycle, reduce, reuse: imagined and re-imagined textiles in Anglo-Saxon England," *Medieval Clothing and Textiles* 8 (2012): 49–62; E. Crowfoot, F. Pritchard, and K. Staniland, *Textiles and Clothing c. 1150–c. 1450*, Medieval Finds from Excavations in London 4 (London: HMSO, 1992), *passim* but see especially, 107–22, 150–98.

2 Production and Distribution

1. S. Lebecq, "Routes of change: Production and distribution in the West (5th–8th century)," in *The Transformation of the Roman World AD 400–900*, eds L. Webster and M. Brown (Berkeley: University of California Press, 1997), 67–78.

2. T. Calligaro and P. Périn, "D'or et des grenats," *Histoire et images médiévales* 25 (2009): 24–5.

3. A. Mastykova, C. Pilet, and A. Egorkov, "Les perles multicolores d'origine méditerranéenne provenant de la nécropole mérovingienne de Saint-Martin de Fontenay (Calvados)," in *Bulletin Archéologique de Provence* supp. 3 (2005): 299–311.

4. R. Lopez, "Silk Industry in the Byzantine Empire," *Speculum* 20.1 (1945), 4–9.

5. R. Forbes, *Studies in Ancient Technology* 8 (Leiden: Brill, 1971), 56.

6. P. Périn et al., "Enquête sur les Mérovingiens," *Histoire et images médiévales* 25 (2009): 14–27.

7. M. Schulze, "Einflusse byzantinischer Prunkgewander auf die frankische Frauentracht," *Archeologhische Korrespondanzblatt* 6.2 (1976): 149–161.

8. C. Fell et al., *Women in Anglo-Saxon England* (London: British Museum, 1984); P. Henry, "Who produced Textiles? Changing Gender Roles," in eds F. Pritchard and J.P. Wild, *Northern Archaeological Textiles NESAT VII* (Oxford: Oxbow, 2005), 51–7; D. Herlihy and A. Molho, *Women, Family, and Society in Medieval Europe: historical essays, 1978–1991* (Providence, RI: Berghahn Books, 1995).

9. P. Walton Rogers, *Textiles, Cordage and Raw Fibres from 16–22 Coppergate*, The Archaeology of York Vol. 17, fasc. 5 (London: Published for the York Archaeological Trust by the Council for British Archaeology, 1989), 412.

10. E. Andersson, *Tools for Textile Production from Birka and Hedeby*, Birka Studies 8 (Stockholm: Birka Project for Riksantikvarieämbetet, 2003).

11. C. Fell et al., *Women in Anglo-Saxon England* (London: British Museum, 1984), 40; P. Henry. "Who produced Textiles? Changing Gender Roles," in eds F. Pritchard and J.P. Wild, *Northern Archaeological Textiles* NESAT VII (Oxford: Oxbow, 2005), 52; P. Walton Rogers, *Textile Production at 16–22 Coppergate*, The Archaeology of York Vol. 17, fasc. 11 (York: Council for British Archeology, 1997), 1821.

12. V. Garver, *Women and Aristocratic Culture in the Carolingian World* (Ithaca: Cornell University Press, 2009), 178–215.

13. Fell, *Women in Anglo-Saxon England*, 40–2. My translation (ESA).

14. Walton Rogers, *Textile Production at 16–22 Coppergate*, 1823.

15. D. Herlihy, *Opera muliebria: women and work in medieval Europe* (Philadelphia: Temple University Press, 1990), 33; Garver, *Women and Aristocratic Culture*, 224–68.

16. Garver, *Aristocratic Women*, 259–67; F. and J. Gies, *Cathedral, Forge and Waterwheel: technology and invention in the Middle Ages* (New York: Harper Collins, 1994), 49–50.

17. Walton Rogers, *Textile Production at 16–22 Coppergate*, 1821.

18. Herlihy, *Opera muliebria*, 88.

19. Ibid., 36–7; Henry, "Who produced Textiles?" 54.
20. J. Oldland, "Cistercian Clothing and Its Production at Beaulieu Abbey, 1269–70," *Medieval Clothing and Textiles* 9 (2013): 73–96.
21. Fell, *Women in Anglo-Saxon England*, 41.
22. E. Andersson Strand and U. Mannering, "Textile production in the late Roman Iron Age—a case study of textile production in Vorbasse, Denmark," in *Arkæologi I Slesvig Archäologie in Schleswig 61st International Sachsen symposium publication 2010 Haderslev, Danmark*, eds L. Boye, P Ethelberg, L. Heidemann Lutz, P. Kruse and A.B. Sørensen (Neumünster: Wachholtz, 2011), 77–84.
23. K.-E. Behre, "Pflanzliche Nahrung in Haithabu," in *Archäologische und Naturwissenschaftliche Untersuchungen an ländlichen und frühstädtischen Siedlungen im deutschen Küstengebiet*, eds H. Jankuhn et al. (Weinheim: Acta Humaniora, 1984), 208–15; A.-M. Hansson and J. Dickson, "Plant Remains in Sediment from the Björkö Strait Outside the Black Earth at the Viking Age Town of Birka, Eastern Central Sweden," in *Environment and Vikings with Special Reference to Birka*, PACT 52 = Birka Studies 4, eds U. Miller, et al. (Rixensart: PACT, 1997), 205–16; A. Pedersen, et al., *Jordbrukets första femtusen år, 4000 f. Kr.–1000 e. Kr.* (Stockholm: NOK-LTs förlag, 1998).
24. L. Bender Jørgensen, "The introduction of sails to Scandinavia: Raw materials, labour and land," in *N-TAG TEN: Proceedings of the 10th Nordic TAG conference at Stiklestad, Norway 2009* (Oxford: Archeopress, 2012), 173–82; E. Andersson Strand, *Textilproduktion i Löddeköpinge endast för husbehov?* in *Porten till Skåne, Löddeköpinge under järnålder och medeltid*, eds F. Svanberg and B. Söderberg, Arkeologiska undersökningar 32 (Lund: Riksantikvarieämbetet, 2000).
25. F. Svanberg et al., *Porten till Skåne, Löddeköpinge under järnålder och medeltid* (Lund: Riksantikvarieämbetet, 2000); H. Kirjavainen, "A Finnish Archaeological Perspective on Medieval Broadcloth," in *The Medieval Broadcloth*, eds K. Vestergård Pedersen and M.-L.B. Nosch, 90–8; F.M. Laforce, "Woolsorters' disease in England," *Bulletin of the New York Academy of Medicine* 54.10 (1978): 956–63.
26. Andersson, *The Common Thread*; *Tools for Textile Production*.
27. O. Vésteinsson, "The North Expansion Across the North Atlantic," in *The Archaeology of Medieval Europe*, Vol. 1, eds J. Graham-Campbell and M. Valor (Aarhus: Aarhus University Press, 2007), 53; M. Hermanns-Auðardóttir, *Islands tidiga bosättning*, dissertation (Umeå: Universitet Arkeologiska institutionen, 1989), 125; B.F. Einarsson, *The settlement of Iceland; a critical approach*, dissertation, Gothenburg University, Dept. of Archaeology (Gothenburg: 1994), 101, 129–30.
28. Marta Hoffmann, *The Warp-weighted Loom: studies in the history and technology of an ancient implement*, Studia Norvegica 14 (Oslo: Universitetsforlaget, 1964), 212; M. Nockert, "Vid Sidenvägens ände. Textilier från Palmyra till Birka," in *Palmyra. Öknens drottning* (Stockholm: Medelhavsmuseet, 1989), 77–105; A. Geijer, et al., *Drottning Margaretas gyllene kjortel i Uppsala Domkyrka* (Stockholm: KVHAA, 1994); J. Jochens, *Women in Old Norse Society* (Ithaca: Cornell University Press, 1995), 125, 134, 141–60.
29. H. Þorláksson, "Arbeidskvinnens, särlig veverskens, økonomiske stilling på Island i middelalder," in *Kvinnans ekonomiska ställning under nordisk medeltid* (Gothenberg: Strand, 1981), 61.
30. E. østergård, *Som syet til jorden: tekstilfund fra det norrøne Grønland* (Aarhus: Aarhus universitatsforlag, 2003), 58.
31. Þorláksson, "Arbeidskvinnens," 55, 59; Jochens, *Women in Old Norse Society*, 139.
32. Hoffmann, *The Warp-weighted Loom*, 216.
33. Þorláksson, "Arbeidskvinnens," 60-61.
34. Hoffmann, *The Warp-weighted Loom*, 219.
35. Jochens, *Women in Old Norse Society*, 139.
36. Historians still largely support the outlines of Henri Pirenne's theses, *Medieval Cities: Their Origins and the Revival of Trade* (1925; repr. Princeton University Press, 1976).

37. Walton Rogers, *Textile Production at 16–22 Coppergate*, 1753–5.

38. P. Baker, *Islamic Textiles* (London: British Museum Press, 1995), 36–63; R. Serjeant, *Islamic Textiles; Material for a History Up to the Mongol Conquest* (Beirut: Librairie du Liban, 1972), 7–27.

39. See E.J. Burns, *Sea of Silk* (Philadelphia: University of Pennsylvania Press, 2009), 37–69.

40. A. Guillou, "La soie sicilienne au Xe-XIe siècles," in *Byzantino-sicula* II: *miscellanea di scritti in memoria di Giuseppe Rossi Taibbi* (Palermo: Istituto Siciliano di Studi Bizantini e Neoellenici, 1975), 285–8.

41. S. Kinoshita, "Almería Silk and the French Feudal Imaginary: Toward a 'Material' History of the Medieval Mediterranean," in *Medieval Fabrications*, ed. E.J. Burns (New York: Palgrave, 2004), 165–76.

42. D. Abulafia, "The Role of Trade in Muslim-Christian Contact during the Middle Ages," in *The Arab Influence in Medieval Europe*, eds D. Agius and R. Hitchcock, (Reading: Ithaca Press, 1994), 1–24.

43. E. Lévi-Provençal, *Histoire de l'Espagne musulmane*, vol. 3 (Leiden: Brill, 1953), 299–313.

44. Abulafia, "The Role of Trade," 8–9.

45. T. Madden, *Venice: A New History* (New York: Viking, 2012); D. Jacoby, *Trade, Commodities and Shipping in the Medieval Mediterranean* (Aldershot: Variorum, 1997).

46. F. Edler de Roover, "Lucchese Silks," *Ciba Review* 80 (1950): 2902–30.

47. K. Reyerson, "Medieval Silks in Montpellier: The Silk Market c. 1250–1350," *Journal of Economic History* 11 (1992): 117–40.

48. R. Berlow, "The Development of Business Techniques used at the Fairs of Champagne from the end of the twelfth century to the middle of the thirteenth century," *Studies in Medieval and Renaissance History* 8 (1971): 3–31.

49. J. Richard, *Mahaut, comtesse d'Artois et de Bourgogne, 1302–1329. Une petite-nièce de Saint-Louis: étude sur la vie privée, les arts et l'industrie, en Artois et à Paris au commencement du XIVe siècle* (Paris: Champion, 1887; repr. Cressé: Editions des Régionalismes, 2010/2013).

50. S. Farmer, "*Biffes, Tiretaines*, and *Aumonières*: The Role of Paris in the International Textile Markets of the Thirteenth and Fourteenth Centuries," *Medieval Clothing and Textiles* 2 (2006): 72–89.

51. G. Fagniez, *Études sur l'industrie et la classe industrielle à Paris au XIIIe et au XIVe siècle* (Paris: Vieweg, 1877), 4–5.

52. J. Archer, "Working Women in Thirteenth-Century Paris," PhD Thesis, University of Arizona, 1995.

53. S. Heller, "Obscured Lands and Obscured Hands: Fairy Embroidery and Ambiguous Vocabulary of Medieval Textile Decoration," *Medieval Clothing and Textiles* 5 (2009): 15–35.

54. C. Dyer, *Making a Living in the Middle Ages: The People of Britain 850–1520* (New Haven: Yale University Press, 2002), 187–96.

55. M. Davies, and A. Saunders, *The History of the Merchant Taylors' Company* (Leeds: Maney, 2004).

56. A. Sutton, *The Mercery of London: Trade, Goods and People, 1130–1578* (Aldershot: Ashgate, 2005).

57. K. Staples, "Fripperers and the Used Clothing Trade in Late Medieval London," *Medieval Clothing and Textiles* 6 (2010): 151–171.

58. G. Brereton and J. Ferrier (eds), *Le Menagier de Paris*, trans. K. Uelschi (Paris: Librairie générale française, 1994).

3 The Body

1. J. Le Goff, *Medieval Civilization 400–1500*, trans. J. Barrow (Oxford: Basil Blackwell, 1988), 357–8.

2. Ibid., 355.

3. M.H. Green, "Introduction," in *A Cultural History of the Human Body in the Medieval Age*, ed. L. Kalof (Oxford and New York: Berg, 2010), 2.

4. On the different extant manuscripts of the *Tacuinum Sanitatis*, see C. Hoeniger, "The Illuminated *Tacuinum sanitatis* Manuscripts from Northern Italy ca. 1380–1400: Sources, Patrons, and the Creation of a New Pictorial Genre," in *Visualizing Medieval Medicine and Natural History, 1200–1550*, eds J.A. Givens, K.M. Reeds, A. Touwaide (Aldershot and Burlington: Ashgate, 2006), 51–81.

5. L.C. Arano, *The Medieval Health Handbook*: Tacuinum Sanitatis (New York: George Braziller, 1976).

6. Ibid., § 93.

7. D. Poirion and C. Thomasset, *L'art de vivre au Moyen Âge: Codex vindobonensis series nova 2644, conserve à la Bibliothèque nationale d'Autriche* (Paris: Editions du Félin, 1995), 326.

8. Aldebrant: Aldebrandino da Siena, *Le Régime du corps*, eds, L. Landouzy and R. Pépin (Geneva: Slatkine, 1978).

9. Ibid., 28–30.

10. Ibid., 26, ll. 11–15, *"si se gart qu'il ne demort mie trop, fors tant qu'il puist sen cors laver et soi netiier de l'ordure que li nature cache fors par les pertruis de le char."* On the issue of bathing, see A.-L. Lallouette, "Bains et soins du corps dans les textes médicaux (XIIe–XIVe)," in *Laver, monder, blanchir: Discours et usages de la toilette dans l'occident médiéval*, ed. S. Albert (Paris: Presses de l'Université Paris-Sorbonne, 2006), 33–49.

11. Aldebrant, *Le Régime du corps*, 72.

12. Ibid., 74, *"Mais il est plus seür cose de prendre. i. fil de lainne retors et loier sor le boutine, et apriès metre desus drapiaus mollies en oile, et laissier jusques à. iiij. jors, et lors cara . . ."*

13. M.H. Green (ed. and trans.), *The Trotula: An English Translation of the Medieval Compendium of Women's Medicine* (Philadelphia: University of Pennsylvania Press, 2001), 51.

14. Ibid., 65, §2. On the question of the *Trotula*'s authorship, see Green's introduction.

15. Ibid., 93, §149.

16. Ibid., 122, §302.

17. Ibid., 85, §129.

18. Ibid., 87, §131.

19. Ibid., 1.

20. Poirion and Thomasset, *L'art de vivre au Moyen Âge*, 49–64.

21. Guillaume de Lorris and Jean de Meun, *Le Roman de la Rose*, ed. and trans. A. Strubel (Paris: Librairie générale française, 1992), 794, vv. 13535–48.

22. Guillaume de Lorris and Jean de Meun, *The Romance of the Rose*, trans. C. Dahlberg (Princeton, New Jersey: Princeton University Press, 1971), 233.

23. For more on fashion and clothing in the *Romance of the Rose*, see S.-G. Heller, *Fashion in Medieval France* (Cambridge: D.S. Brewer, 2007).

24. O. Blanc, *Parades et parures: L'invention du corps de mode à la fin du Moyen Age* (Paris: Gallimard, 1997), 73–9, 89–95, 109–12.

25. O. Blanc, "From Battlefield to Court: The Invention of Fashion in the Fourteenth Century," in *Encountering Medieval Textiles and Dress: Objects, Texts, Images*, eds D.G. Koslin and J.E. Snyder (New York: Palgrave Macmillan, 2002), 165. See also Blanc, "L'orthopédie des apparences ou la mode comme invention du corps," in *Le Corps et sa parure/The Body and its Adornment*, ed. Agostino Paravicini Bagliani, *Micrologus* 15 (Florence: Sismel, Edizioni del Galluzzo, 2007), 107–19.

26. Blanc, "From Battlefield to Court," 169–70.

27. On dagged clothes, see A. Denny-Brown, "Rips and Slits: The Torn Garment and the Medieval Self," in *Clothing Culture, 1350–1650*, ed. Catherine Richardson (Aldershot and Burlington: Ashgate, 2004), 223–37.

28. C. Franklin et al., *Fashion: The Ultimate Book of Costume and Style* (New York: Dorling Kindersley, 2012), 74–5, 80–1.

29. Heller, *Fashion in Medieval France*, 133.

30. F. Garnier, *Le Langage de l'image au Moyen Âge,* II: *Grammaire des gestes* (Paris: Le Léopard d'or, 1982), 118–20.

31. Cf. Heller, *Fashion in Medieval France*, ch. 3: "Desire for Novelty and Unique Expression," 61–94.

32. *The Holy Bible*, Douay version, R. Challoner, ed. and trans. (London: Catholic Truth Society, 1963), 689.

33. For more on kinesis, see G. Bolens, *The Style of Gestures: Embodiment and Cognition in Literary Narrative* (Baltimore: Johns Hopkins University Press, 2012).

34. H. Martin, *Mentalités médiévales II: Représentations collectives du XIe au XVe siècle* (Paris: PUF, 2001), 61; J.-C. Schmitt, *La Raison de gestes dans l'Occident médiéval* (Paris: Gallimard, 1990).

35. A. Denny-Brown, *Fashioning Change: The Trope of Clothing in High- and Late-Medieval England* (Columbus: The Ohio State University Press, 2012), 32.

36. Ibid., 61.

37. *The Life of Christina of Markyate, a Twelfth Century Recluse*, ed. and trans. C.H. Talbot (Oxford: Clarendon, 1959), 100 §38, trans. 101.

38. Ibid., 76 §25, trans. 77–9.

39. Ibid., 76 §24, trans. 77.

40. K. Allen Smith, *War and the Making of Medieval Monastic Culture* (Woodbridge: Boydell Press, 2011), 90.

41. For an explanation of the origins of association between the girdle and monasticism, see R. Deshman, *The Benedictional of St Aethelwold* (Princeton: Princeton University Press, 1995), 197.

42. G.J. Botterweck, H. Ringgren (eds), *Theological Dictionary of the Old Testament,* Vol. 4 (Stuttgart: William B. Eerdman, 1980), 442–3.

43. G. Owen-Crocker, *Encyclopedia of Medieval Dress and Textiles* (Brill: Leiden, 2012), 193–6.

44. "The Twelve books of John Cassian. Institutes of the Coenobia and the Remedies for the Eight Principal Faults," in *Nicene and Post-Nicene Fathers: Second Series*, ed. Philip Schaff, Vol. XI (New York: Cosimo, 2007), 201–2.

45. Smaragdus of Saint-Mihiel, *Commentary on the Rule of Saint Benedict*, trans. D. Barry OSB (Kalamazoo: Cistercian Publications, 2007), 88.

46. Ibid., 89; Smaragdus, Sancti Michaelis, *Smaragdi Abbatis Expositio In Regulam S. Benedicti*, eds A. Spannagel, P. Engelbert (Siegburg: Apud F. Schmitt Success, 1974), 35.

47. C.M. Woolgar, *The Senses in Late Medieval England* (New Haven and London: Yale University Press, 2006), 38.

48. C. Marshall, "The Politics of Self-Mutilation: Forms of Female Devotion in the Late Middle Ages," in *The Body in Late Medieval and Early Modern Culture*, eds D. Grantley and N. Taunton (Aldershot and Burlington: Ashgate, 2000), 11.

49. Ibid., 12.

50. B. Millet and J. Wogan-Browne (eds and trans.), *Medieval English Prose for Women: From the Katherine Group and* Ancrene Wisse (Oxford: Clarendon Press, 1990), 137.

51. J. McNamara and J.E. Halborg (eds and trans.), *Sainted Women of the Dark Ages* (Durham and London: Duke University Press, 1992), 81.

52. Ibid., 81.

53. Ibid., 81.

54. Ibid., 82.

55. On "Bodily Relics and Contact Relics," see C.W. Bynum, *Christian Materiality: An Essay on Religion in Late Medieval Europe* (New York: Zone Books, 2011), 131–9.

56. McNamara and Halborg, *Sainted Women of the Dark Ages*, 84.

57. Hildegard of Bingen, *Two Hagiographies: Vita sancti Rupperti confessoris; Vita sancti Dysbodi episcopi*. H. Feiss (intro and trans.) and C. P. Evans (Latin ed.) (Paris, Leuven, Walpole, MA: Peeters, 2010), 48–9 §3 ll. 44–9.

58. Ibid., 50–1 §4 ll. 67–8.

59. Ibid., 58–9 §6 ll. 144–5.

60. Ibid., 58–9 §6 ll. 157–9.

61. For more on the loss of an original garment in Christian theology, see S. Brazil, *The Corporeality of Clothing in Medieval Literature* (Kalamazoo: Medieval Institute Publications, 2017, forthcoming).

62. Ibid., 49.

63. J. Swann, "English and European Shoes from 1200 to 1520," in *Fashion and clothing in late medieval Europe. Mode und Kleidung im Europa des späten Mittelalters*, ed. R.C. Schwinges (Riggisberg: Abeg-Stiftung, 2010), 16. "If you have wondered why the Virgin Mary is so often depicted (from at least 1000) in red shoes, which have less pure connotations since at least the nineteenth century, they were simply considered the best."

64. M. Rubin, *Mother of God: A History of the Virgin Mary* (London: Allen Lane, 2009), 63.

65. Bynum, *Christian Materiality*, 58.

66. L. Hodne, *The Virginity of the Virgin: A Study in Marian Iconography* (Roma: Scienze E Lettere, 2012).

67. C. Leyser, "From Maternal Kin to Jesus as Mother" in *Motherhood, Religion and Society in Medieval Europe, 400–1400* (Aldershot and Burlington: Ashgate, 2011), 26.

68. For more on Mary as Second Eve see Rubin, *Mother of God*, 311–2.

69. A. De Marchi, *Autour de Lorenzo Veneziano: Fragments de polyptyques vénitiens du XIVe siècle* (Tours: Musée des beaux-arts: Silvano, 2005), 114.

70. R. Woolf, *The English Religious Lyric in the Middle Ages* (Oxford: Clarendon Press, 1968), 287.

71. A. Winston-Allen, *Stories of the Rose: The Making of the Rosary in the Middle Ages* (Pennsylvania: Pennsylvania State University Press, 1997), 92.

72. On the idea of medieval art as persuasive, see M. Carruthers, *The Experience of Beauty in the Middle Ages* (Oxford: Oxford University Press, 2013), 14.

73. For detail on attendance of Marian shrines by women, especially before or after giving birth, see G. Waller, *The Virgin Mary in Late Medieval and Early Modern English Literature and Popular Culture* (Cambridge: Cambridge University Press, 2011), 94.

74. T.D. Jones, et. al., *The Oxford Dictionary of Christian Art and Architecture Second Edition* (Oxford: Oxford University Press, 2013), 602.

75. E.J. Burns, "Saracen Silk and the Virgin's 'Chemise': Cultural Crossing in Cloth," *Speculum* 81.2 (2006): 365–6. Burns notes that "The duchess of Orléans was said to possess four 'chemises de Chartres' in 1409," 368. Cf. K.M. Ash, *Conflicting Femininities in Medieval German Literature* (Aldershot and Burlington: Ashgate, 2013).

76. Jean le Marchant, *Miracles de Notre-Dame de Chartres*, ed. P. Kunstman (Ottawa: Université d'Ottawa, 1973), 69, ll. 111–24. A canon of Chartres Cathedral wrote an earlier Latin version of this in 1210, and Jean le Marchant wrote his French version around 1262.

77. Ibid., 163, l.36.

78. B. Nilson, *Cathedral Shrines of Medieval England* (Woodbridge: Boydell Press, 1998), 3.

79. D. Cressy, *Birth, Marriage and Death: Ritual, religion and the life-cycle in Tudor and Stuart England* (Oxford: Oxford University Press, 1999), 22. "In some places, it was believed, a woman's own girdle would serve to ease labour if it had been wrapped around sanctified bells."

80. M.E. Fissell, *Vernacular Bodies: The Politics of Reproduction in Early Modern Britain* (Oxford: Oxford University Press, 2004), 14–15.

81. Cressy, *Birth, Marriage and Death*, 22. See also E. Duffy, *The Stripping of the Altars: Traditional Religions in England 1400–1580* (New Haven: Yale University Press, 1992), 384. Duffy lists other relics used for aiding women in pregnancy, including four other girdles.

82. R. Gilchrist, *Medieval Life: Archaeology and the Life Course* (Woodbridge: Boydell, 2013), 138.

83. J.M. Bennett and R. M. Karras (eds), *The Oxford Handbook of Women and Gender in Medieval Europe* (Oxford: Oxford University Press, 2013), 517. "Childbirth prayers were

addressed to the Virgin or to St. Margaret were sometimes written on a parchment roll by a priest and lent out as a birth-girdle for a pregnant woman, the manuscript thus functioning doubly as both devotional reading and apotropaic protection."

84. *Paston Letters and Papers of the Fifteenth Century Part 1*, Early English Text Society S.S.20, ed. N. Davis (Oxford: Oxford University Press, 2004), 216. "[P]reyng yow to wete þat my modyr sent to my fadyr to London for a govne cloth of mvstyrddevyllers to make of a govne for me . . . I pre yow, yf it be not bowt, þat ye wyl wechesaf to by it and send yt hom as sone as ye may, for I haue no govne þis wyntyr but my blake and my grene a Lyere, and þat ys so comerus þat I ham wery to wer yt."

85. n. Muster-de-vilers (a). *Middle English Dictionary*, 2001, the Regents of the University of Michigan. 15.01.2014. http://quod.lib.umich.edu/m/med/. n. Lire (n.4)(a). *Middle English Dictionary*.

86. *Paston Letters*, 217. "As for þe gyrdyl þat my fadyr be-hestyt me . . . I pre yow, yf ye dor tak it vppe-on yow, þat ye wyl weche-safe to do mak yt a-yens ye come hom; for I hadde neuer more need þer-of þan I haue now, for I ham waxse so fetys þat I may not be gyrte in no barre of no gyrdyl þat I haue but of on."

87. Gilchrist, *Medieval Life*, 96.

4 Belief

1. J. Jacobs, *Cities and the Wealth of Nations: Principles of Economic Life* (New York: Vintage, 1995), 221–2.

2. *The Holy Bible, Translated from the Latin Vulgate . . . at Douay A.D. 1609 . . . at Rheims, A.D. 1582*, ed. Richard Challoner (Rockford, IL: Tan Books and Publishers, 1989).

3. Early Rabbinical writers and exegetes—Philo in particular—were fascinated by the role of God as tailor or cloth-maker in Genesis 3:21. See S.N. Lambden, "From Fig Leaves to Fingernails: Some Notes on the Garments of Adam and Eve in the Hebrew Bible and Select Early Postbiblical Jewish Writings," in *A Walk in the Garden: Biblical, Iconographical and Literary Images of Eden*, eds P. Morris and D. Sawyer, *Journal for the Study of the Old Testament*, Supplement Series 136 (1992): 74–90.

4. In my overview of early Bible interpretations in the following pages, I have found several scholarly works especially helpful. As these studies show, interpretations of the garments of skin varied greatly in ways that I do not address; for instance, some rabbinical literature describes these garments as "garments of light," or garments made from fingernails, or snake skin, rather than of human or animal skin. Others interpret God as covering Adam with a priestly cloth, rather than a rough, common cloth. Please see the following works for more in depth analysis of these complex traditions: Lambden, "From Fig Leaves to Fingernails"; H. Reuling, *After Eden: Church Fathers and Rabbis on Genesis 3:16–21* (Leiden: Brill, 2006); G. Anderson, "The Garments of Skin in Apocryphal Narrative and Biblical Commentary," in *Studies in Ancient Midrash*, ed. J.L. Kugel (Cambridge: Harvard University Press, 2001), 101–43; and S.D. Ricks, "The Garment of Adam in Jewish, Muslim, and Christian Tradition," in *Judaism and Islam: Boundaries, Communication and Interaction. Essays in Honor of William M. Brinner* (Leiden: Brill, 2000), 203–25.

5. Anderson, "The Garments of Skin," 133, 143.

6. Ibid., 132. Alternate spellings of the author are Ephram, Ephraem, and Ephraim.

7. The *Cave of Treasures* is especially interesting in terms of clothing symbolism because it links the entire episode of the Fall to Satan's jealousy of Adam's special "garments of glory," which he acquires when he enters the garden, and which are replaced by the garments of skin when he is exiled from it. Quoted and discussed in ibid., 135–36.

8. Ibid., 140.

9. Reuling, *After Eden*, 108–9.

10. *Saint Augustine on Genesis: Two Books on Genesis Against the Manichees and On the Literal Interpretations of Genesis*, trans. Roland J. Teske (Washington, DC: Catholic University of America Press, 1991), 2.21.32, 127–8. On Augustine's allegorizing of the garments of skin as scriptural parchment, see Erik Jager, *The Tempter's Voice: Language and the Fall in Medieval Literature* (Ithaca, NY: Cornell University Press, 1993), esp. 69–72, 93.

11. On Augustine's interest in lying and his connection between the garments of skin and verbal lies, see Jager, *The Tempter's Voice*, 69–72, 93.

12. D. Miller, *Stuff* (Cambridge: Polity, 2009), 12–41; quotation 16.

13. London, British Library, MS Harley 4894, fol. 176v, quoted and modernized in G.R. Owst, *Literature and Pulpit in Medieval England* (Cambridge: Cambridge University Press, 1933; repr. Oxford: Basil Blackwell, 1961), 404. See also the discussion of Rypon's work in S. Wenzel, *Latin Sermon Collections from Later Medieval England* (Cambridge: Cambridge University Press, 2005), 66–73.

14. *William Durand on the Clergy and Their Vestments: A New Translation of Books 2–3 of the Rationale divinorum officiorum*, trans. Timothy M. Thibodeau (Chicago: University of Scranton Press, 2010),149. For a more thorough discussion of the complex rhetorical strategies involved in distinguishing sacred from secular attire in Durand's work, see A. Denny-Brown, *Fashioning Change: The Trope of Clothing in High- and Late-Medieval England* (Columbus: Ohio State University Press, 2012), 82–96.

15. As quoted and discussed in Owst, *Literature and Pulpit*, 405.

16. *Mirk's Festial: A Collection of Homilies by Johannes Mirkus (John Mirk)*, ed. T. Erbe. Early English Text Society e.s. 96 (London: Kegan Paul, Trench, and Trübner, 1905; reprint 1987), 291, l. 23.

17. *Middle English Dictionary*, eds Hans Kurath and Sherman M. Kuhn (Ann Arbor: University of Michigan Press, 1952), s.v. "pilch(e)." (n.) 1c.

18. *Aelred of Rievaulx's De Institutione Inclusarum: Two English Versions*, eds J. Ayton and A. Barratt, Early English Text Society o.s. 287 (London: Oxford University Press, 1984), 9.

19. *The Book of Margery Kempe,* eds S.B. Meech and H.E. Allen, Early English Text Series o.s. 212 (London: Oxford University Press, 1940; reprint 1963), 106, l. 7.

20. This moment is especially ripe for vestimentary symbolism because Merlin is about to be caught by the cross-dressing knight Grisandole. *Merlin,* ed. H.B. Wheatley, et al. 4 vols., Early English Text Series o.s. 10, 21, 36, 112 (London: Kegan Paul, Trench, and Trübner, 1865, 1866, 1869, 1899; reprint as two vols. 1987), 424.

21. *Riverside Chaucer*, gen. ed. L.D. Benson (Boston: Houghton Mifflin, 1987), 657. On regulation of wearing furs in the summer, see Edward III: 8–14 (1363), in *The Statutes of the Realm* (London: Dawsons, 1963), I. 381. For other contemporary complaints about the use of fur worn in the summer months for fashion's sake, see F. Baldwin, *Sumptuary Legislation and Personal Regulation in England* (Baltimore, MD: Johns Hopkins University Press, 1926), 68.

22. See my discussion of this poem in *Fashioning Change*, 6–7.

23. See for example the well-dressed torturers in the Towneley *Play of the Dice*, in *The Towneley Plays*, Vol. 1, eds M. Stevens and A.C. Cawley, EETS, s.s., 13–14 (Oxford: Oxford University Press, 1994), 309–22. For excellent examples of these costumes in visual art, see R. Mellinkoff, *Outcasts: Signs of Otherness in the Northern European Art of the Middle Ages*, 2 vols. (Berkeley: University of California Press, 1993); discussion at Vol. 1, 21.

24. *Miller's Tale, Riverside Chaucer*, l. 3384.

25. John of Reading, *Chronica Johannis de Reading et Anonymi Cantuariensis 1346–1367,* ed. J. Tait (Manchester: Manchester University Press, 1914), 89.

26. On the tradition of Adam and Eve being "aparlet in whytt lether," see C. Davidson, "Nudity, the Body and Early English Drama," *The Journal of English and Germanic Philology* 98.4 (Oct. 1999), 499–522. For the likelihood that the Chester cycle Adam and Eve wore whiteleather costumes, see P. Happé, *English Mystery Plays* (New York: Penguin, 1975), 62. Curriers, or those who dressed and colored tanned leather, were also associated with

whittawers; see A.D. Justice, "Trade Symbolism in the York Cycle," *Theatre Journal* 31.1 (March 1979): 47–58.

27. *The Creation, and Adam and Eve*, in Happé, 76, ll. 361–76. R.M. Lumiansky and D. Mills preserve an example of the Middle English stage directions in their edition of the play: "Then God, puttynge garmentes of skynnes upon them." *The Chester Mystery Cycle*, eds Lumiansky and Mills (Oxford: Oxford University Press for the Early English Text Society, 1974), 28.

28. Happé states that this play was originally joined with the Tanners' *Fall of Lucifer*, the previous (and first) play in the cycle and speculates on the interest the Tanners may have had in producing it (Happé, *English Mystery Plays*, 62).

29. There are many studies of sumptuary laws in Europe during this time period, only a few of which I will cite here. For sumptuary laws in France and elsewhere, see S.-G. Heller, "Limiting Yardage and Changes of Clothes: Sumptuary Legislation in Thirteenth-Century France, Languedoc, and Italy," in *Medieval Fabrications: Dress, Textiles, Clothwork, and Other Cultural Imaginings*, ed. E. J. Burns (NY: Palgrave Macmillan, 2004), 121–36; and "Anxiety, Hierarchy, and Appearance in Thirteenth-Century Sumptuary Laws and the *Romance of the Rose*," *French Historical Studies* 27. 2 (Spring 2004): 311–48. On Italy, see D.O. Hughes, "Sumptuary Law and Social Relations in Renaissance Italy," *Disputes and Settlements: Law and Human Relations in the West*, ed. J. Bossy (Cambridge: Cambridge University Press, 1983), 69–100; and C. K. Killerby, *Sumptuary Law in Italy 1200–1500* (Oxford: Oxford University Press, 2002). On Germanic sumptuary laws, see N. Bulst, "Kleidung als sozialer Konfliktstoff: Probleme kleidergesetzlicher Normierung im sozialen Gefüge" (Clothing as Social Conflict: On the Problems of Sumptuary Law Standardization within the Social Fabric), *Saeculum: Jahrbuch für Universalgeschichte* 44 (1993): 32–46. For an overview of the history of sumptuary law more generally, see A. Hunt, *Governance of the Consuming Passions: A History of Sumptuary Law* (New York: St. Martin's Press, 1996). For a more recent overview of sumptuary concerns, see M.C. Howell, *Commerce Before Capitalism in Europe, 1300–1600* (Cambridge: Cambridge University Press, 2010), 208–60. For studies dealing more particularly with English sumptuary laws, see footnote 34 below.

30. *The Statutes of the Realm* (London: Dawsons, 1963), Vol. I, 378–83, quotation 370.

31. 3 Edward IV, *Statutes of the Realm* II.392–402, quotation 399; 24 Henry VIII, *Statutes of the Realm* III.430–32, quotation 430; 30 Elizabeth I, *Tudor Royal Proclamations* (3 vols.), eds P.L. Hughes and J.F. Larkin (New Haven: Yale University Press, 1969), Vol. III quotation 3.

32. These and associated laws specifically targeted cloth-making and cloth-selling practices, citing groups of craftspeople by name and holding them legally responsible for providing regulation-approved wares to their customers. Near the end of the archetypal 1363 sumptuary law upon which subsequent English regulations were based, for example, drapers and other cloth-makers are directed to make ample materials according to the prices outlined in the accompanying legislation; this is presented as a crucial element of the law, necessary to ensure that each customer can purchase the types of garments legally required by his or her status and income bracket. By comparison, in the 1463 law this legislative focus had shifted to tailors and shoemakers (*Statutes of the Realm* I.382 and II.402).

33. Elsewhere I make the argument that fashion is inherently connected to free will in England in this period. See *Fashioning Change*, esp. chapter two.

34. *The Middle English Genesis and Exodus*, ed. O. Arngart, Lund Studies in English 36 (Lund: Lund University, 1968), l. 377.

35. *MED*, s.v. 11a, b, e. *OED* 3a, b.

36. *Statutes of the Realm* II.396–97; quotation 396. The 1460s were an especially active period for English legislation of cloth-making materials, which included laws to ensure new standards for locally-made cloth. See for example 4 Edward IV (1464–65), 7 Edward IV (1467), and 8 Edward IV (1468), *Statutes of the Realm* II. 403–30.

37. *Fall of Man*, in Bevington, *Medieval Drama*, 272, l. 141.

38. *Creation of the World; Fall of Man*, ed. Douglas Sugano, *The N-Town Plays* (Kalamazoo, Michigan: Medieval Institute Publications, 2007), l. 247.

39. Ibid., ll. 322–34; emphasis mine.

40. The phrase was used in a sermon by the radical priest John Ball: "When Adam delved and Eve span, / Who was then a gentleman?" R.B. Dobson, *The Peasant's Revolt of 1381* (London: Macmillan, 1983), 374.

41. See also the related tradition of associating clothing with biers or tombs; Owst, *Literature and Pulpit*, 411.

42. For the specific use of the verb "senden" to indicate God's dispatch of Christ to mankind, see *MED*, s.v. "senden," v(2), 3b.

43. *Julian of Norwich's Revelations of Divine Love: The Shorter Version, Ed. from B.L.* MS 37790, ed. F. Beer, *Middle English Texts* 8 (1978): 39–79; 43.

44. *Parson's Tale, Riverside Chaucer*, l. 933.

45. "Jhesus doth him bymene," *Medieval English Lyrics 1200–1400*, ed. Thomas G. Duncan (New York and London: Penguin, 1995), 136, ll. 1–10.

46. "Jhesus doth him bymene," ll. 18–26. For a similar passage attributed to Saint Bernard, see *The Golden Legend; or, Lives of the Saints, as Englished by William Caxton* (New York: AMS Press, 1973), 1.72–3.

47. "O Vernicle: A Critical Edition," ed. Ann Eljenholm Nichols, in *The Arma Christi in Medieval and Early Modern Material Culture: With a Critical Edition of "O Vernicle,"* eds Lisa H. Cooper and Andrea Denny-Brown (Farnham: Ashgate, 2014), 360–1.

48. London, British Library MS Harley 45, f. 163v; quoted in Owst, *Literature and Pulpit*, 411.

49. Gilles Lipovetsky, *The Empire of Fashion: Dressing Modern Democracy*, trans. Catherine Porter (Princeton, NJ: Princeton University Press, 1994), 24.

5 Gender and Sexuality

1. Christine de Pisan, *Book of the City of Ladies*, ed. K. Brownlee and trans. R. Blumenfeld-Kosinski (New York: W.W. Norton, 1997), 121.

2. Kate Bornstein, *My Gender Workbook* (New York: Routledge, 1998), 35.

3. *Le Roman de Silence: A Thirteenth-Century Arthurian Verse Romance by Heldris de Cornuaille*, L. Thorpe, ed. (Cambridge: W. Heffer and Sons, 1972).

4. E.J. Burns, *Bodytalk: When Women Speak in Old French Literature* (Philadelphia: University of Pennsylvania Press, 1993), 243–5.

5. M. Garber, *Vested Interests: Crossdressing and Cultural Anxiety* (New York: Routledge, 1992), 216–17.

6. W.P. Barrett, trans., *The Trial of Jeanne d'Arc* (New York: Gotham House Inc., 1932), 160, 163. For the original Latin text and modern French translation see *Procès de condamnation de Jeanne d'Arc*, ed. Pierre Champion (Paris: Champion, 1921), Vol. 2.

7. M. Warner, *Joan of Arc: The Image of Female Heroism* (New York: Vintage Books, 1982), 146.

8. Ibid., 14. The imagined portrait of Joan of Arc by Clément de Fauquembergue, found in a register of the Parlement of Paris dated 1429, is reproduced at https://commons.wikimedia. org/wiki/File:Joan_parliament_of_paris.jpg

9. D. Riley, *Am I that Name? Feminism and the Category of "Women" in History* (Minneapolis: University of Minnesota Press, 1988), 98–114.

10. C. Delphy, "Rethinking Sex and Gender," *Women's Studies International Forum* 16.1: 1–9.

11. *Robert de Blois's Floris et Lyriope*, ed. P. Barrette (Berkeley: University of California Press, 1968); see discussion in E.J. Burns, *Courtly Love Undressed: Reading through Clothes in Medieval French Culture* (Philadelphia: University of Pennsylvania Press, 2002), 126–9.

12. E. Doss Quinby et al., eds and trans., *Songs of the Women Trouvères* (New Haven: Yale University Press, 2001), #37, l. 44.

13. *Le Roman de la Rose ou de Guillaume de Dole*, ed. F. Lecoy (Paris: Champion, 1962), vv. 3236–40.
14. Burns, *Courtly Love Undressed*, 88–118.
15. Chrétien de Troyes, *Cliges*, ed. A. Micha (Paris: Champion, 1957), vv. 1145–54; 1607–14, 1618.
16. Burns, *Courtly Love Undressed*, 129–30.
17. J. Butler, *Gender Trouble* (New York: Routledge, 1990), 25.
18. J. Butler, *Bodies That Matter* (New York: Routledge, 1993), 30.
19. *La Mort Le Roi Artu*, ed. J. Frappier (Paris: Champion, 1964).
20. Burns, *Courtly Love Undressed*, 3–11.
21. Guillaume de Lorris, *Le Roman de la Rose*, ed. F. Lecoy, 3 vols. (Paris: Champion, 1965-66, 1970), Vol. 1, vv. 2153–4.
22. E.J. Burns, *Sea of Silk: A Textile Geography of Women's Work in Medieval French Literature* (Philadelphia: University of Pennsylvania Press, 2009), 70–80.
23. D. Alexandre-Bidon and M.-T. Lorcin, *Le Quotidien aux temps des fabliaux* (Paris: Picard, 2003), 278.
24. Burns, *Sea of Silk*, 88–98.
25. Chrétien de Troyes, *Erec et Enide*, ed. M. Roques (Paris: Champion, 1976).
26. E.J. Burns, "Ladies Don't Wear Braies: Underwear and Outerwear in the French *Prose Lancelot*," in *The Lancelot-Grail Cycle*, ed. W. Kibler (Austin: University of Texas Press, 1994), 152–74.
27. *Lancelot: Roman en prose du XIIIe siècle*, Vol. 1, ed. A. Micha, 9 vols. (Geneva: Droz, 1978–83), vol. 9, 322; Burns, "Ladies Don't Wear Braies."
28. *Lancelot: Roman en prose*, Vol. 1, ed, Micha, 181; Burns, *Courtly Love Undressed*, 141–2.
29. Burns, *Courtly Love Undressed,* 137.
30. L. Finke and M. Shichtman, *Cinematic Illuminations: The Middle Ages on Film* (Baltimore: Johns Hopkins University Press, 2010), 264–9.
31. K. Busby, ed., *Le Roman des eles and the Anonymous Ordene de Chevalerie* (Philadelphia: J. Benjamins, 1983).

6 *Status*

1. S.H. Rigby, "Introduction: Social Structure as Social Closure," in *English Society in the Later Middle Ages: Class, Status and Gender* (London: Macmillan Press, 1995), 1–16 (status as social difference, 12).
2. See J. Dumolyn, "Later Medieval and Early Modern Urban Elites: Social Categories and Social Dynamics," in *Urban Elites and Aristocratic Behaviour in the Spanish Kingdoms at the End of the Middle Ages*, ed. M. Asenjo-González (Studies in European Urban History (1100–1800), Book 27), (Turnhout: Brépols, 2013), 3–18.
3. J. Crawford, "Clothing Distributions and Social Relations c. 1350–1500," in *Clothing Culture, 1350–1650*, ed. C. Richardson (Aldershot: Ashgate, 2004), 153, refers to "a profound increase in the complexity of clothing practices" in the later fourteenth century.
4. The beginning of fashion in the West is a contentious subject. For summaries of debates, see S. Heller, *Fashion in Medieval France* (Cambridge: D.S. Brewer, 2007); L.A. Wilson, "'De Novo Modo': The Birth of Fashion in the Middle Ages" (PhD diss., Fordham University, 2011), esp. 11–13.
5. J. Friedman, *Breughel's Heavy Dancers: Transgressive Clothing, Class and Culture in the Late Middle Ages* (Syracuse: Syracuse University Press, 2010), xiii–xiv.
6. A. Hollander, *Sex and Suits: The Evolution of Modern Dress* (New York: Kodansha International, 1995), 6; O. Blanc, "From Battlefield to Court: The Invention of Fashion in the Fourteenth Century," in *Encountering Medieval Textiles and Dress: Objects, Texts, Images*, eds D. Koslin and J. Snyder (New York: Palgrave Macmillan, 2002), 170.

7. See S. Gordon (ed.), *Robes of Honor: The Medieval World of Investiture* (New York: Palgrave, 2001), "Introduction," 1–19 and "Robes, Kings, and Semiotic Ambiguity," 379–86.

8. M. Miller, *Clothing the Clergy: Virtue and Power in Medieval Europe c. 800–1200* (Ithaca, NY: Cornell University Press, 2014); B. Effros, "Appearance and Ideology: Creating Distinctions Between Clerics and Lay Persons in Early Medieval Gaul," in Koslin and Snyder, *Encountering Medieval Textiles*, 7–24.

9. See L. Bonfante, *Etruscan Dress* (Baltimore: Johns Hopkins University Press, 1975), 283, on "heroized" clothing; also A. Hollander, *Fabric of Vision: Dress and Drapery in Painting* (London: National Gallery, 2002).

10. For early depictions of the tunic ensemble, see the late sixth-century manuscript known as the Tours or Ashburnham Pentateuch (Bibliothèque nationale Française ms. nouv. acq. lat. 2334), for example fol. 18; the eleventh-century Bayeux Tapestry contains many examples of the tunic ensemble.

11. Einhard, "The Life of Charlemagne," in *Two Lives of Charlemagne*, ed. L. Thorpe (New York: Penguin Books, 1969), 77, §23. See also Notker's description, written roughly fifty years later, which includes more detail of the mantle. (Notker the Stammerer, "Charlemagne," ibid., 132–3, §34.)

12. Paris, BnF, ms. lat. 1, fol. 423r., "Présentation du livre"; Paris, BnF, ms. lat. 1146, fol. 2v, "Allegorie: Royauté de droit divin."

13. Examples of the tunic ensemble as ceremonial and/or royal dress: Heinrich der Zänker, Regensburg, 985 (Bamberg, Cod. Lit. 142, *Regelbuch von Niedemünster*, fol. 4v); King Cnut, England, 1031 (London, British Library, MS Stowe 944, New Minster *Liber Vitae*, fol. 6); King David surrounded by musicians, Italy, late eleventh century (Mantua, Lib. Bibl. Commune, ms. 340, Polirone Psalter, fol. 1).

14. "*Reges terrae, principes, et mercatores*": Béatus of Saint-Sever (Paris, Bibliothèque Nationale Française, ms. lat. 8878), fol. 195. On widespread aristocratic use of the tunic ensemble, F. Piponnier and P. Mane, *Se vêtir au Moyen Âge* (Paris: Adam Biro, 1995), 71–2.

15. See J. Harris, "'Estroit Vestu Et Menu Cosu': Evidence for the Construction of Twelfth-Century Dress," in *Medieval Art: Recent Perspectives: A Memorial Tribute to C. R. Dodwell*, eds G. Owen-Crocker and T. Graham (Manchester: Manchester University Press, 1998), 89–108; and C. Frieder Waugh, "'Well-Cut through the Body': Fitted Clothing in Twelfth-Century Europe," *Dress* 26 (1999): 3–16.

16. H. Platelle, "Le problème du scandale: Les nouvelles modes masculines aux XIe et XIIe siècles," *Revue belge de philologie et d'histoire* 53, no. 4 (1975): 1071–96.

17. *The Ecclesiastical History of Orderic Vitalis*, ed. and trans. M. Chibnall, Vol. 4 (Oxford: Clarendon Press, 1973), VIII, iii, 327, p. 193.

18. E.g., Glasgow, Glasgow University Library, MS Hunter 229 (Hunterian Psalter), fol. 3r.; London, British Library, ms. Lansdowne 383, fol. 5r.

19. Cambridge, Trinity College, R. 17.1 (Eadwine Psalter), fol. 5v.

20. Cf. Camille's robe in *Enéas*, made by three fairies, and Blonde Esmerée's mantle in *Bel Inconnu* with its fairy-made clasps. M. Wright, *Weaving Narrative: Clothing in Twelfth-Century French Romance* (University Park, PA: Penn State University Press, 2010).

21. See Piponnier and Mane, *Se vêtir au Moyen Âge*, 83–4; S. Newton, *Fashion in the Age of the Black Prince: A Study of the Years 1340–1365* (1980; repr., Woodbridge: Boydell Press, 1999), 3–4.

22. Heller, *Fashion in Medieval France*, 3.

23. This image of Machaut reading his manuscript, BnF MS français 1586 fol. 28v (Paris, c. 1350), may be viewed at http://gallica.bnf.fr/ark:/12148/btv1b8449043q/f63.highres

24. J. Friedman, "The Iconography of Dagged Clothing and Its Reception by Moralist Writers," *Medieval Clothing and Textiles* 9 (2013): 121–38; A. Denny-Brown, "Rips and Slits: The Torn Garment and the Medieval Self," in Richardson, *Clothing Culture*, 223–37; Elisabeth Crowfoot, Frances Pritchard, and Kay Staniland, *Textiles and Clothing c. 1150–c. 1450*.

Medieval Finds from Excavations in London (London: HMSO, 1992), 194–8. See also S. Heller, "Limiting Yardage and Changes of Clothes: Sumptuary Legislation in Thirteenth-Century France, Languedoc, and Italy," in *Medieval Fabrications: Dress, Textiles, Clothwork, and Other Cultural Imaginings*, ed. E.J. Burns (New York: Palgrave Macmillan, 2004), 23–4.

25. London, British Library, Decretals of Gregory IX (the "Smithfield Decretals"), Royal MS 10 E IV.

26. Apparently the clothing is equally confusing to modern scholars, as the British Library website identifies this illumination as a king being led away by *three* men; the figure on the right is a woman.

27. Crawford, "Clothing Distributions," 153.

28. A. Hunt, *Governance of the Consuming Passions* (New York: St. Martin's Press, 1996); C. Lansing, *Passion and Order: Restraint of Grief in the Medieval Italian Communes* (Ithaca: Cornell University Press, 2008); M.-G. Muzzarelli, "Reconciling the Privilege of a Few with the Common Good: Sumptuary Laws in Medieval and Early Modern Europe," *Journal of Medieval and Early Modern Studies* 39, no. 3 (2009): 597–617; L.A. Wilson, "Common Threads: A Reappraisal of Medieval European Sumptuary Law," *The Medieval Globe* 2.2, article 6 (2016). Available at: https://arc-humanities.org/series/arc/tmg/

29. There is one surviving twelfth-century sumptuary law, a regulation of furs issued in Genoa in 1157, but not repeated in the next compilation of Genoese laws. It is possible that there were others, but it is also possible that this is simply an outlier. C. Killerby, *Sumptuary Law in Italy, 1200–1500* (Oxford: Clarendon, 2002), 24; S. Stuard, *Gilding the Market: Luxury and Fashion in Fourteenth-Century Italy* (Philadelphia: University of Pennsylvania Press, 2006), 4; Heller, "Limiting Yardage," 123.

30. On southern French laws, Heller, "Limiting Yardage." On southern Italy, Killerby, *Sumptuary Law in Italy*, 24–5; Heller, "Angevin-Sicilian Sumptuary Statutes of the 1290s: Fashion in the Thirteenth-century Mediterranean," *Medieval Clothing and Textiles* 11 (2015): 79–97. On German laws, Neithard Bulst, "Zum Problem städtischer und territorialer Luxusgesetzgebung in Deutschland (13. bis Mitte 16. Jahrhundert)," in *Renaissance du pouvoir législatif et genèse de l'état*, eds A. Gouron and A. Rigaudière (Publications de la Société d'Histoire du Droit et des Institutions des Anciens Pays de Droit Ecrit, Montpellier 1988), 29–57; and Bulst, "Les ordonnances somptuaires en Allemagne: expression de l'ordre urbain (XIVe–XVIe siècle), in *Comptes rendus des séances de l'année* (Paris: Académie des Inscriptions & Belles-Lettres, 1993), 771–84.

31. "In Italia," in M. Muzzarelli and A. Campanini, eds, *Disciplinare il lusso: la legislazione suntuaria in Italia e in Europa tra medioevo e età moderna* (Rome: Carocci, 2003), 17–108. For Florence: R. Rainey, "Sumptuary Legislation in Renaissance Florence" (PhD diss., Columbia University, 1985); for Venice, M. Newett, "The Sumptuary Laws of Venice in the Fourteenth and Fifteenth Centuries," in *Historical Essays by Members of the Owens College, Manchester*, eds T.F. Tout and J. Tait (Manchester: Manchester University Press, 1907), 245–78; for Orvieto: Lansing, *Passion and Order*.

32. Killerby lists more than 250 sumptuary laws enacted in Italian cities between the late thirteenth century and 1500, *Sumptuary Law in Italy*, Table 2.1. Florence produced the most: sixty-one laws, 25 percent of the total, of which thirty-three, more than half, were enacted in the fourteenth century. The sumptuary laws from other northern Italian cities are similar.

33. Rainey, "Sumptuary Legislation in Renaissance Florence," 218.

34. See Muzzarelli, "Una società nello specchio della legislazione suntuaria: Il caso dell'Emilia-Romagna," in Muzzarelli and Campanini, *Disciplinare il lusso*, 17.

35. Rainey, "Sumptuary Legislation," 206.

36. L. Gérard-Marchant, "Compter et nommer l'étoffe à Florence au Trecento (1343)," *Médiévales* 29 (automne 1995): 87–104, presents a register of licensed clothing from the mid-fourteenth century.

37. Spanish sumptuary law remains somewhat neglected. See Mercè Aventin, "Le legge suntuarie in spagna: Stato della questione," in Muzzarelli and Campanine, *Disciplinare il lusso*, 109–20, for a recent summary of the historiography; J González Arce, *Apariencia y poder: La legislación suntuaria castellana en los siglos XIII–XV* (Jaén: Universidad de Jaén, 1998).

38. Cortes De Valladolid, 1258, XIII.23; translation from "A Thirteenth-Century Castilian Sumptuary Law," *The Business History Review* 37.1/2:99–100.

39. On the duty of knights to wear bright colors: *Las Siete Partidas*, Partida 2, Title 21, Law 18. In Reggio-Emilia, a mid-thirteenth century law required nobles to wear bright colors "to increase the prestige of the Commune" (Muzzarelli, "Emilia-Romagna," 26); there were numerous similar laws in Venice because "it is more useful to the state to remove . . . sorrow and put in its place mirth and rejoicing" (Newett, "Sumptuary Laws of Venice," 267.)

40. Several clauses in the sumptuary law of Jaime I of Aragon, for example, begin their prohibitions with the words "neither we, nor anyone under us shall . . ." (*nos, nec aliquis subditus noster . . .*) P. de Marca and É. Baluze, *Marca Hispanica* (Paris, 1688), Appendix 1428–30. So far as I know, regulations which restrict the king are unique to Spain, though minor restrictions on other members of the royal family do appear elsewhere.

41. González Arce, *Apariencia y poder*, 135–60.

42. See Y. Guerrero-Navarrete, "Gentlemen-Merchant in Fifteenth-Century Urban Castile: Forms of Life and Social Aspiration," in *Urban Elites*, ed. Asenjo-González, 49–60.

43. On English sumptuary law, C. Sponsler, "Narrating the Social-Order: Medieval Clothing Laws," *CLIO* 21, no. 3 (1992): 265–83; Susan Crane, *Performance of Self: Ritual, Clothing, and Identity During the Hundred Years War* (Philadelphia: University of Pennsylvania Press, 2002); K. Phillips, "Masculinities and the Medieval English Sumptuary Laws," *Gender and History* 19, no. 1 (2007): 22–42.

44. See Phillips, "Masculinities," Appendix, 33–7, for summaries of all English sumptuary legislation.

45. W.M. Ormrod said of the rapid repeal of the English sumptuary law of 1363, the legislators "would not remain insistent on the outward trappings of social hierarchy if this proved incompatible with their own economic interest." "Introduction, Parliament of 1363," in *Edward III, 1351–1377*, ed. W.M. Ormrod, Vol. 5 of *The Parliament Rolls of Medieval England, 1275–1504*, ed. C. Given-Wilson (Woodbridge, Boydell Press: 2005), 155–7.

46. He was to add three more dukes in 1362, and the additional rank of marquess in 1385. A. Brown, *The Governance of Late Medieval England, 1272–1461* (Stanford: Stanford University Press, 1989), 137.

47. Phillips, "Masculinities," 24.

48. From 1295 on, the lower House of Parliament consisted of two knights from each shire and two citizens or burgesses from each city or borough (ibid., 180). In the Parliament of 1363, the commons included at least 112 burgesses and seventy-four knights. Ormrod, "Introduction."

49. P. Coss, "Knights, Esquires and the Origins of Social Gradation in England, *Transactions of the Royal Historical Society*, 6th ser., 5 (December 1995): 155. On social gradation among the middle ranks more generally, see also Coss, *The Origins of the English Gentry* (Cambridge: Cambridge University Press, 2003).

50. There was thought to have been a royal sumptuary law in 1229, but Heller argues compellingly that it never existed, "Anxiety, Hierarchy, and Appearance in Thirteenth-century Sumptuary Laws and the *Roman De La Rose*," *French Historical Studies* 27, no. 2 (2004): 317, n. 23.

51. For current work on French sumptuary laws, see especially Heller, "Anxiety," and Heller, "Limiting Yardage"; also Bulst, "La legislazione suntuaria in francia (secoli XIII-XVIII)," in *Disciplinare il lusso*, Muzzarelli and Campanini, 121–36.

52. Heller, "Anxiety," 319–20.

53. For regulations indicating fear of contamination by Jews in Italian cities, Diane Owen Hughes, "Distinguishing Signs: Ear-Rings, Jews and Franciscan Rhetoric in the Italian Renaissance City," *Past & Present* 112 (August, 1986), 34.

54. Canon 68. See R.I. Moore, *The Formation of a Persecuting Society: Power and Deviance in Western Europe, 950–1250*, 2nd ed. (Malden MA: Blackwell Publishing, 2007).

55. Hughes, "Distinguishing Signs," 21, 25; see also J. Brundage, "Sumptuary Laws and Prostitution in Medieval Italy," *Journal of Medieval History* 13, no. 4 (1987): 343–55.

56. Hughes, "Distinguishing Signs"; E. Silverman, *A Cultural History of Jewish Dress* (London: Bloomsbury, 2013), ch. 3.

57. A. Toaff, "La prammatica degli ebrei e per gli ebrei," in *Disciplinare il lusso*, Muzzarelli and Campanini, 91–108; see also Hughes, "Distinguishing Signs."

58. H. Riley, ed. *Memorials of London and London Life: In the 13th, 14th, and 15th Centuries* (London: Longmans, Green and Co., 1868), 266–9, in British History Online, http://www.british-history.ac.uk/report.aspx?compid=57692 [accessed 26 August 2014].

59. Hughes, "Distinguishing Signs"; Brundage, "Sumptuary Laws and Prostitution."

60. Miller, *Clothing the Clergy*, 4.

61. Ibid., p. 12. See also Effros, "Appearance and Ideology," 8.

62. F. Lachaud, "Textiles, Furs, and Liveries: A Study of the Material Culture of the Court of Edward I (1272–1307)" (PhD diss., Oxford University, 1992), and "Liveries of Robes in England, c. 1200–c. 1330," *The English Historical Review* 111, no. 441 (April 1996): 279–98; R. Delort, "Notes sur les livrées en milieu de cour au XIVe" in *Commerce, finances et société (XIe–XVIe siècles)*, eds P. Contamine, T. Dutour, and B. Schnerb (Paris: Presses de l'Université de Paris-Sorbonne, 1995), 361–8; C. de Mérindol, "Signes de hiérarchie sociale à la fin du Moyen Âge d'après les vêtements: méthodes et recherches," in *Le Vêtement: Histoire, archéologie et symboliques vestimentaires au Moyen Âge*. Cahiers du Léopard d'Or 1 (Paris: Léopard d'Or, 1989), ed. M. Pastoureau, 181–224; M. Vale, *The Princely Court: Medieval Courts and Culture in North-West Europe, 1270–1380* (Oxford: Oxford University Press, 2005), especially ch. 3.3, 93–125.

63. "Lanval," in *Lais de Marie de France*, ed. K. Warnke and trans. L. Harf-Lancner (Paris: Librairie générale française, 1990), ll. 201–14.

64. Lachaud, "Liveries of Robes," 282.

65. Ibid., 280.

66. Ibid., 286–7.

67. Delort, "Notes sur les livrées," 363.

68. E. 101/366/12/97, quoted in Lachaud, "Textiles, Furs, and Liveries," 231–2; and in Lachaud, "Liveries of Robes," 285.

69. On William Marshal's deathbed (c. 1219), he insisted on distributing liveries for the last time, because his knights had a right to them. Paul Meyer (ed. and trans.), *L'histoire de Guillaume le Maréchal, Comte de Striguil et de Pembroke, Régent d'Angleterre de 1216 à 1219: poème Français*, 3 vols., vol. 2–3 (Paris: H. Laurens for la Société de l'Histoire de France). Modern French translation: 3:263; original, 2:312–13, ll. 18, 679–716.

70. Cited by the hereditary seneschal of Valenciennes in 1184 as his reason for refusing to perform service on two separate occasions. Vale, *Princely Court*, 37.

71. Ibid., 95, 99.

72. See Mérindol, "Signes de hiérarchie sociale" 204–6; Vale, *Princely Court*, 112–13; Lachaud, "Textiles, Furs, and Liveries," 220–40.

73. Mérindol, "Signes de hiérarchie sociale," 204–6; Vale, *Princely Court*, 111–14; Lachaud, "Liveries of Robes," 289–93; Piponnier and Mane, *Se vêtir au Moyen Âge*, 161.

74. Term coined by R. de Roover in "The Commercial Revolution of the Thirteenth Century," *Bulletin of the Business Historical Society*, 1942 (repr. *Social and Economic Foundations of the Italian Renaissance*, ed. A. Molho [New York: Wiley, 1969]) and popularized by R. Lopez, *The Commercial Revolution of the Middle Ages, 950–1350* (Englewood Cliffs, NJ: Prentice-Hall, 1971). See Peter Spufford, *Power and Profit: The Merchant in Medieval Europe*

(New York: Thames & Hudson, 2003); and Martha C. Howell, *Commerce before Capitalism in Europe, 1300–1600* (Cambridge: Cambridge University Press, 2010).

7 Ethnicity

1. "The World in Dress: Anthropological Perspective on Clothing, Fashion, and Culture," *Annual Review of Anthropology* 33 (2004): 370; A. Cannon, "The Cultural and Historical Contexts of Fashion," in *Consuming Fashion, Adorning the Transnational Body*, eds A. Brydon and S. Niessen (Oxford, Berg, 1998), 24; T. Polhemus and L. Procter, *Fashion and Anti-Fashion: Anthropology of Clothing and Adornment* (London: Thames & Hudson, 1978), 11.

2. H.R. Isaacs, "Basic Group Identity: The Idols of the Tribe," in *Ethnicity, Theory, and Experience*, eds N. Glazer et al. (Cambridge: Harvard University Press, 1975), 35.

3. M. Hayeur Smith, *Draupnir's Sweat and Mardöll's Tears: An Archaeology of Jewellery, Gender and Identity in Viking Age Iceland* (Oxford: John and Erica Hedges, 2004), 10–11.

4. T. Turner, "The Social Skin," in *Reading the Social Body*, eds, C.B. Burroughs and J.D. Ehrenreich (Iowa City: University of Iowa Press, 1993), 15–16; J. Schneider and A.B. Weiner, *Cloth and the Human Experience* (Washington, Smithsonian Institution Press, 1989), 1.

5. C. Gosden and C. Knowles, *Collecting Colonialism, Material Culture and Colonial Change* (Oxford: Berg, 2001), 5.

6. J. Graham-Campbell, *Cultural Atlas of the Viking World* (Oxford: Andromeda, 1994), 38.

7. J. V. Sigurðsson, "Iceland," in *The Viking World*, eds S. Brink and N. Price (London, Routledge, 2008), 572.

8. B. Crawford, *Scandinavian Scotland* (Leicester: Leicester University Press, 1987), 210.

9. A. Helgason et al., "mtDNA and the Origin of the Icelanders: Deciphering Signals of Recent Population History," *American Journal of Human Genetics* 66.3 (2000): 999–1016.

10. T.D. Price and H. Gestsdottir, "The First Settlers of Iceland: an isotopic approach to colonization," *Antiquity* 80 (2006): 142.

11. I. Hägg, *Kvinnodräkten i Birka* (Uppsala: Institutionen för arkeologi Gustavianum, 1974), 108.

12. Hägg, *Kvinnodräkten*; see also *Textilfunde aus der Siedlung und aus den Gräbern von Haithabu* (Neumünster: Wachholtz Verlag, 1991); J.Jesch, *Women in the Viking Age* (Woodbridge: Boydell, 1991), 17.

13. A. Larsson, "Viking Age Textiles," in *The Viking World*, eds S. Brink and N. Price (London: Routledge, 2008), 182.

14. Jesch, *Women in the Viking Age*, 17.

15. L.H. Dommasnes, "Late Iron Age in Western Norway. Female Roles and Ranks as Deduced from an Analysis of Burial Customs," *Norwegian Archaeological Review* 15.1–2 (1982): 73; O. Owen and M. Dalland, *Scar: A Viking Boat Burial on Sanday, Orkney* (East Linton: Tuckwell, 1999), 147.

16. Dommasnes, "Late Iron Age," 73.

17. Hayeur Smith, *Draupnir's Sweat*, 72–4; "Dressing the Dead, Gender Identity and Adornment in Viking Age Iceland," in *Vinland Revisited: The Norse World at the Turn of the First Millennium*, ed. S. Lewis-Simpson (St: John's NL: Historic Sites Ass. of Newfoundland and Labrador, 2003), 230.

18. H.M. Wobst discussed the visibly of artifacts for deciphering social messages: the higher on the body an object is placed, the more rapidly the social message is transmitted. "Stylistic Behavior and Information Exchange," *Anthropological Papers, University of Michigan, Museum of Anthropology* 61 (1977): 328, 332.

19. Hayeur Smith, *Draupnir's Sweat*, 72–3.

20. Larsson, "Viking Age Textiles," 182.

21. J. Graham-Campbell, *Viking Artefacts: A Select Catalogue* (London: British Museum, 1980), 113.

22. Larsson, "Viking Age Textiles," 182.
23. B. Solberg, "Social Status in the Merovingian and Viking Periods in Norway from Archaeological and Historical Sources," *Norwegian Archaeological Review* 18.1–2 (1985): 246.
24. Hayeur Smith, *Draupnir's Sweat*, 5–11.
25. D.M. Wilson and O. Klindt Jensen, *Viking Art* (London: Allen & Unwin, 1966).
26. C. Arcini, "The Vikings Bare their Filed Teeth," *American Journal of Physical Anthropology* 128.4 (2005): 727–33.
27. A. Ibn Fadlan, *Voyage chez les Bulgares de la Volga*, ed. M. Canard (Paris: Sindbad, 1989), 72. My translation.
28. Ibid., 73.
29. K. Wolf, "The Colour Blue in Old Norse—Icelandic Literature," *Scripta Islandica: Isländska Sällskapets Årsbok* 57 (2006), 68–71.
30. Hayeur Smith, "Viking Age Textiles in Iceland."
31. M. Pastoureau, *Blue: The History of a Color*, trans. M. Cruse (Princeton: Princeton University Press, 2001), 13–83.
32. For a critical assessment of ethnic interpretations of early medieval continental fibulae, see B. Effros, "Dressing conservatively: women's brooches as markers of ethnic identity?" in *Gender in the Early Medieval World: East and West 300–900*, eds L. Brubaker and J. Smith (Cambridge: Cambridge University Press, 2004), 165–84.
33. Hayeur Smith, *Draupnir's Sweat*, 78; "Dressing the Dead," 235.
34. Hayeur Smith, *Draupnir's Sweat*, 79; "Dressing the Dead," 236.
35. I. Jansson, *Ovala spännbucklor: en studie av vikingatida standardsmycken med utgangspunkt fran Björköfynden = Oval brooches : a study of Viking period standard jewellery based on the finds from Björkö Sweden* (Uppsala: Institute of Northern European Archaeology, 1985), 228; Owen and Dalland, *Scar*, 147.
36. K. Eldjárn, *Kuml og Haugfé úr Heiðnum sið á Islandi* (Reykjavik: Fornleifastofnun Íslands, 1956), 74–5.
37. Ibid., 74–5.
38. Hayeur Smith, *Draupnir's Sweat*, 38; C. Paterson, "The Viking Age Trefoil Mounts from Jarlshof: a Reappraisal in the Light of Two New Discoveries," in *Proceedings of the Society of Antiquaries of Scotland* 127 (1997): 649.
39. Paterson, personal communication, 2000; Hayeur Smith, *Draupnir's Sweat*, 42–3. Additionally see R.D.E. Welander et al., "A Viking Burial from Kneep, Uig, Isle of Lewis," *Proceedings of the Society of Antiquaries of Scotland* 117 (1987): 149–74.
40. Hayeur Smith, *Draupnir's Sweat*, 42.
41. See burial from Kornsá in C. Batey, "A Viking Age Bell from Freswick Links," *Medieval Archaeology* 32 (1988): 215.
42. Batey, "A Viking Age Bell from Freswick Links," 215.
43. C.J. Minar, "Motor Skills and the Learning Process: The Conservation of Cordage Final Twist Direction in Communities of Practice," *Journal of Anthropological Research, Learning, and Craft Production* 57.4 (2001): 384.
44. L. Bender Jørgensen, *North European Textiles Until AD 1000* (Aarhus: Aarhus Universitetsforlag, 1992), 126.
45. Ibid., 39; also "Scandinavia, AD 400–1000," in *The Cambridge History of Western Textiles* 1 (Cambridge: Cambridge University Press, 2003), 137.
46. M. Hayeur Smith, "Weaving Wealth: Cloth and Trade in Viking Age and Medieval Iceland," in *Textiles and the Medieval Economy, Production, Trade and Consumption of Textiles, 8th–16th Centuries*, eds A.L. Huang and C. Jahnke (Oxford, Oxbow Books, 2015), 23–40. Iceland was unique in that it maintained the archaic warp-weighted loom for over 800 years and only adopted the flat loom during the Danish trade embargo, when the Danish crown took over textile production and introduced industrialization to Iceland.
47. Bender Jørgensen, *North European Textiles*, 122.

48. P. Walton Rogers, *Textiles, Cordage and Raw Fibre from 16–22 Coppergate*, (London: York Trust, 1989), 334; Bender Jørgensen, *Northern European Textiles*, 40.

49. J.R. Hjalmarsson, *History of Iceland, From the Settlement to the Present Day* (Reykjavik: Iceland Review, 1993): 23–4.

50. More evidence about dress emerges for the seventeenth century onwards. See K. Aspelund, *Who Controls Culture? Power Craft and Gender in the Creation of Icelandic Women's National Dress*, PhD diss., Boston University (2011).

51. The textile collections have been the focus of two NSF funded research grants, from 2010 to 2013 and 2013 to 2016. "Rags to Riches, an Archaeological Study of Textiles and Gender from Iceland, from 874–1800"; "Weaving Islands of Cloth: Gender, Textiles, and Trade across the North Atlantic from the Viking Age to the Early Modern Period."

52. M. Hayeur Smith, "Rumpelstiltskin's Feat: Cloth and Hanseatic Trade with Iceland," forthcoming.

53. M. Hayeur Smith, "Thorir's Bargain, Gender, Vaðmál and the Law," *World Archaeology* 45.5 (2013): 732–4.

54. M. Hoffman, *The Warp-weighted Loom: Studies in the History and Technology of an Ancient Implement* (Oslo: Hestholms Boltrykkeri, 1974), 226; P. Meulengracht Sørensen, *The Unmanly Man: Concepts of Sexual Defamation in Early Northern Society*, trans. J. Turvile Petre (Odense: Odense University Press, 1983), 20; H. Robertsdottir, *Wool and Society* (Göteborg: Makadma, 2008), 26; K. Bek-Pedersen, "Are the Spinning Nornir just a Yarn?" *Viking and Medieval Scandinavia* 3.1 (2008): 4 and "Weaving Swords and Rolling Heads: A Peculiar Space in Old Norse Tradition," *Viking and Medieval Scandinavia* 5 (2009): 174; M. Hayeur Smith, "Some in Rags, Some in Jags and Some in Silken Gowns: Textiles from Iceland's Early Modern Period," *International Journal of Historic Archaeology* 16.3 (2012): 2.

55. Hayeur Smith, "Thorir's Bargain," 732.

56. A. Dennis, P. Foote, and R. Perkins, *Laws of Early Iceland=Grágás I* (Winnepeg: University of Manitoba Press, 1980); *Laws of Early Iceland=Grágás II* (2002); Hoffman, *The Warp-weighted Loom*, 213.

57. B. Gelsinger, *Icelandic Enterprise, Commerce an Economy in the Middle Ages* (Columbia, SC: University of South Carolina Press, 1981), 69.

58. Gelsinger, *Icelandic Enterprise*, 69–70.

59. H. Þórlaksson, *Vaðmál og Veðlag, Vaðmál í Útanlandsviðskiptum og Búskap Íslendiga á 13 og 14 Öld* (Reykjavik: Háskóli Íslands, 1991).

60. Andrew Dennis, Peter Foote, and Richard Perkins (eds and trans.), *Laws of Early Iceland: Grágás, the Codex Regius of Grágás, with material from other manuscripts* 5 vols. (Winnipeg, Canada: University of Manitoba Press, 1980), Vol. 1.

61. E. Guðjónsson, *Forn Röggvarvefnaður* (Reykjavik: Árbók hins Íslenzka Fornleifafélags, 1962), 20–1; "Note on Medieval Icelandic Shaggy Pile Weaving," *Bulletin de Liaison du Centre International d'Études des Textiles Anciens* (Lyon: CIETA, 1980).

62. J. Jochens, *Women in Old Norse Society* (Ithaca: Cornell Univeristy Press, 1995), 144.

63. G. Owen-Crocker, *Dress in Anglo-Saxon England* (Woodbridge: Boydell, 2010), 182–3.

64. Guðjónsson, *Forn Röggvarvefnaður*.

65. For comparison of the Herjolfnes gown and similar European gored gowns and a summary of the debates, R. Netherton, "The View from Herjolfnes: Greenland's Translation of the European Fitted Fashion," *Medieval Clothing and Textiles* 4 (2008): 144–53.

66. Netherton, "The View from Herjolfsnes," 158.

67. Hayeur Smith, "Thorir's Bargain," 734.

68. Netherton, "The View from Herjolfsnes," 156.

69. Ibid., 272. See T. McGovern, "The Demise of Norse Greenland," in *Vikings, The North Atlantic Saga*, eds W.W. Fitzhugh and E.I. Ward (Washington: Smithsonian Institution Press, 2000), 338.

70. T. McGovern, "Cows, Harp Seals, and Churchbells: Adaptation and Extinction in Norse Greenland," *Human Ecology* 8.3 (1980): 266.

71. McGovern, "Cows, Harp Seals, and Churchbells," 265.

72. E. Østergård, "The Greenlandic Vaðmál," in *Northern Archaeological Textiles: NESAT VII, textile symposium in Edinburgh, 5th–7th May 1999*, eds F. Pritchard and P. Wilds (Oxford: Oxbow Books, 2005), 80–3; *Woven into the Earth: Textiles from Norse Greenland* (Aarhus: Aarhus University Press, 2004), 63; "The Textile—a Preliminary Report," in *Man Culture and Environment in Ancient Greenland, Report on a Research Programme*, eds J. Arneborg and H.C. Gulløv (Copenhagen: Dansk Polar Center, 1998), 58–65.

73. M. Hayeur Smith, "Dress, Cloth and the Farmer's Wife: Textile from Ø172, Tatsipataakilleq, Greenland with Comparative Data from Iceland," *Journal of the North Atlantic* 6 (sp. 6) (2014): 64–81.

74. H. Þórlaksson, *Sjórán og Siglingar, Ensk Íslensk Samskipti 1580–1630* (Reykjavik: Mál og Menning, 1999), 288.

75. Hayeur Smith, "Dress, Cloth and the Farmer's Wife."

76. On the demise of the Greenland colony see T. McGovern, "The Demise of Norse Greenland," 338, 339.

8 *Visual Representations*

1. The extraordinary and large knotted carpets made c. 1200 with Classical figural themes survive today in fragmentary form in Halberstadt Cathedral and Quedlinburg Convent Church, Germany.

2. A. Gell, *Art and Agency: An Anthropological Theory* (Oxford: Clarendon Press, 1990), proposed a new, anthropologically based theory of visual art, seen as a form of instrumental action: the making of things as a means of influencing the thoughts and actions of others. This is particularly useful as a tool when reviewing the role of fashion in medieval art. I am not yet aware of a work specifically for the medieval fashion context that points to fetishistic elements in visual representations, but a present-day study is available by V. Steele, *Fetish: Fashion, Sex and Power* (New York: Oxford University Press, 1996).

3. See, among many new works, the special issue of *Studies in Iconography: Medieval Art History Today—Critical Terms* 33 (2012), N. Rowe, guest editor. Several of the participants in this volume are, like myself, past students of Professor Jonathan Alexander at New York University's Institute of Fine Arts, who encouraged us to read broadly, work collaboratively, and "listen with our eyes." The recent catalog by A. van Buren and R. Wieck, *Illuminating Fashion: Dress in Medieval France and the Netherlands, 1325–1515* (New York: The Morgan Library and Museum, 2011) is another fine example and rigorously researched work of contextualizing fashion.

4. Well-known and still consulted, see *Vecellio's Renaissance Costume Book* (*De gli Habiti antichi et moderni de Diversi Parte del Mundo*, 1590; reprint New York: 1977); Auguste Racinet, *Le Costume Historique* (Paris, 1888); J. Quicherat, *Histoire du costume en France depuis le temps les plus reculés jusqu'à la fin du XVIIIe siècle* (Paris, 1875); and J. Strutt, *A Complete View of the Dress and Habits of the People of England*, 2 vols. (London, 1842; reprint The Tabard Press, 1970).

5. H. Pulliam, "Color," in *Studies in Iconography* 33 (2012): 3–14.

6. S.-G. Heller, *Fashion in Medieval France* (Woodbridge: D.S. Brewer, 2007).

7. The expression "presentist" views of history is associated with C.W. Bynum and her ideas in several works that seek to go beyond and under the flat, unilinear, and generalizing interpretation of history and into an "intensely cognitive response" to the medieval sources— her inspiring address to the American Historical Association is published online and also in *American Historical Review* 102.1 (1997): 1–26.

8. Van Buren and Wieck, ibid. Among earlier, fine scholarly investigations are S.M. Newton, *Fashion in the Age of the Black Prince: A Study of the Years 1340–1365* (Woodbridge: The Boydell Press, 1980); A. Page, *Vêtir le Prince: Tissus et couleurs à la cour de Savoie (1427–1447)* (Lausanne: Université de Lausanne, 1993); and the careful work of F. Piponnier in her many articles of dress and textile-based sociological research.

9. O. Blanc, "From Battlefield to Court: The Invention of Fashion in the Fourteenth Century," in *Encountering Medieval Textiles and Dress: Objects, Texts, Images*, eds D. Koslin and J. Snyder (New York: Palgrave Macmillan, 2002), 157–72.

10. Still useful is J. Berger, *Ways of Seeing* (London: British Broadcasting Corporation, 1972), reminding us of the primacy of vision and our predilection to then describe/depict according to our proclivities and norms; the work of M. Camille and L. Mulvey, among many important contributors, should be mentioned.

11. J. Alexander, *Medieval Illuminators and their Methods of Work* (New Haven: Yale University Press, 1992), 6–16.

12. See several subject index references in Alexander, *Medieval Illuminators*, 209.

13. Leander's "Training of Nuns," in *Iberian Fathers I: Martin of Braga, Paschasius of Dumium, Leander of Seville*, trans. C. Barrow (Washington DC: Catholic University of America Press, 1969), 195. The Latin version is available in part in P. Migne, *Patrologia Latina* 72 (1878): 873–94, and in its entirety in A.C. Vega, *El "De institutione virginum" de San Leandro de Seville* (Madrid: Escorial, 1948).

14. Three plaques from the reliquary survive, dispersed, in the Masaveu Collection, Oviedo; the State Hermitage Museum, Saint Petersburg; and The Metropolitan Museum, New York.

15. S. Perkinson, "Likeness" in *Studies in Iconography* 33 (2012): 21.

16. See J. Snyder, "From Content to Form: Court Clothing in Mid-Twelfth-Century Northern French Sculpture," in *Encountering Medieval Textiles and Dress: Objects, Texts, Images*, eds D. Koslin and J. Snyder (New York: Palgrave MacMillan, 2002), 85–102.

17. Aldhelm, *The Prose Works*, ed. and trans. M. Lapidge and M. Herren (Ipswich and Cambridge: D.S. Brewer, 1979), 127–8.

18. Among her many publications on the topic, see G. Owen-Crocker, *Dress in Anglo-Saxon England* (Woodbridge: Boydell, 2004).

19. The clasp is situated on the right shoulder, allowing the right opening of the mantle to keep the sword arm free to move—a feature adopted also by the knights' wives. The heavy mantle may also be kept in check in courtly demeanor by a light touch of the finger on the mantle's neck cord.

20. G. Wolter, *Teufelshörner und Lustäpfel: Modekritik in Wort und Bild 1150–1620* (Marburg: Jonas Verlag, 2002), 116–18. Wolter's review of polemics regarding fashion elements is rigorous and entertaining, as are her earlier *Die Verpackung des Männlichen Geschlechtes: Eine Illustrierte Kulturgeschichte der Hose* (Marburg: Jonas, 1988); and *Hosen, weiblich: Kulturgeschichte der Frauenhose* (Marburg: Jonas, 1994).

21. J. Ball, *Byzantine Dress: Representations of Secular Dress in Eighth- to Twelfth-Century Painting* (New York: Palgrave Macmillan, 2005).

22. See articles by M. Georgopoulou, R. Nelson, and M. Ainsworth in *Byzantium: Faith and Power (1261–1557)*, ed. H. Evans (New York: The Metropolitan Museum of Art, 2004), 489–94, each describing the impact of Greek artists on Italy and Northern Europe.

23. A. Wardwell, "Panni Tartarici: Eastern Islamic Silks woven with gold and silver," in *Islamic Art* 3 (1998–9): 95–173.

24. L. Monnas, *Merchants, Princes and Painters: Silk Fabrics in Italian and Northern Paintings 1300–1550* (New Haven: Yale University Press, 2008).

25. See J. Dodds (ed.), *Al-Andalus: The Art of Islamic Spain* (New York: The Metropolitan Museum of Art, 1992).

26. See Concha Herrero-Carretero, *Museo de telas medievales: Monasterio de Santa Maria la Real de Huelgas* (Madrid: Patrimonio Nacional, 1988).

27. A.D. Lorenzo, "Les vêtements royaux du monastère Santa Maria la Real de Huelgas," in *Fashion and Clothing in Late Medieval Europe*, eds Rainer C. Schwinges and Regula Schorta (Riggisberg and Basel: Abegg-Stiftung, 2010), 97–106.

28. A. Sand, "Vision, Devotion and Difficulty in the Psalter-Hours of 'Yolande of Soissons'," in *Art Bulletin* 87.1 (2005): 6–23. Based on research of the heraldry depicted (as noted on the website of the Morgan Library and Museum), the lady is no longer thought to be Yolande of Soissons, since the arms of her husband, Bernard de Moreuil (azure flory or a lion issant argent) are not present. Instead, she is Comtesse de la Table, dame de Coeuvres, who died in 1300 and whose arms (or fretty gules charged with lions passant) appear on her mantle and on four heraldic shields. She was the third wife and widow of Raoul de Soissons who died in 1270. She would have been the stepmother of Yolande de Soissons who was the daughter of Comtesse de Hangest, the second wife of Raoul de Soissons.

29. M. Camille, *The Medieval Art of Love: Objects and Subjects of Desire* (New York, Harry N. Abrams, 1998), pp. 124–9.

30. R. Mellinkoff, *Outcasts: Signs of Otherness in Northern European Art of the Late Middle Ages*, 2 vols. (Berkeley: University of California Press, 1993), vol. 1, 35–9 and in the volume of illustrations.

31. See examples in D. Koslin, "Value-added Stuffs and Shifts in Meaning: An Overview and Case Study of Medieval Textile Paradigms," in *Encountering Medieval Textiles and Dress*, 233–49.

32. E. Heckett, "The Margaret Fitzgerald Tomb Effigy: A Late Medieval Headdress and Gown in St. Canice's Cathedral, Kilkenny" in *Encountering Medieval Textiles and Dress*, 209–31. The article also includes a full account of the materials and techniques used in the reconstruction of a horned temple headdress for exhibition purposes.

33. Ibid., 211, and a reference to the Tudor rule in England at the time that tried to suppress Irish indigenous styles.

34. Among the many works, see J. McNamara, *Sisters in Arms: Catholic Nuns Through Two Millennia* (Cambridge, MA: Harvard University Press, 1996); D. Hafter (ed.), *European Women and Preindustrial Craft* (Bloomington: Indiana University Press, 1995); B. Newman, *From Virile Woman to Womanchrist: Studies in Medieval Religion and Literature* (Philadelphia: University of Pennsylvania Press, 1995); M. Warner, *Alone of All Her Sex: The Myth and the Cult of the Virgin Mary* (New York: Knopf, 1976); *Women in the Middle Ages: An Encyclopedia*, eds K. Wilson and N. Margolis, 2 vols. (Westport, CT: Greenwood Press, 2004).

35. See J. Oliver, *Singing with Angels: Liturgy, Music, and Art in the Gradual of Gisela von Kerssenbrock* (Leiden: Brepols, 2007); M. Caviness, *Visualizing Women in the Middle Ages: Sight, Spectacle, and Scopic Economy* (Philadelphia: University of Philadelphia Press, 2001); K. Smith, *Art, Identity, and Devotion in Fourteenth-Century England: Three Women and Their Books of Hours* (Toronto, University of Toronto Press, 2003), S. Marti, ed. *Krone und Schleier: Kunst aus Mittelalterlichen Frauenklöstern* (Bonn: Ruhrlandmuseum, 2005).

36. M. Easton, "Uncovering the Meanings of Nudity in the Belles Heures of Jean, Duke of Berry," in *The Meanings of Nudity in Medieval Art*, ed. S. Lindquist (Farnham: Ashgate, 2012), 149–82. The manuscript is published in its entirety and in full color in Timothy B. Husband, *The Art of Illumination: The Limbourg Brothers and the Belles Heures of Jean de France, Duc de Berry* (New York: The Metropolitan Museum of Art, 2008).

37. See, for instance, M. Camille, "'For Our Devotion and Pleasure': The Sexual Objects of Jean, Duc de Berry," in *Art History* 24.2 (2001): 1–69.

38. Easton, "Uncovering the Meanings of Nudity," 182.

39. See, among the many studies on the topic, D. Hafter, *European Women and Pre-Industrial Craft*; and S. Shahar, *Fourth Estate: A History of Women in the Middle Ages* (London: Routledge, 2003).

9 Literary Representations

1. See D. Kelly's chapter on *conjointure* in *The Art of Medieval French Romance* (Madison, WI: University of Wisconsin Press, 1992), 15–31, for a complete discussion of this process.

2. Clothing as a narrative device becomes more important in the twelfth century precisely because social interest in the acquisition of exotic clothing and fabrics was increasing in Western Europe. For a discussion of this social interest, see S.-G. Heller, *Fashion in Medieval France* (Woodbridge: Brewer, 2007).

3. For example, when Chrétien de Troyes translated Ovid's tale of *Philomena* into Old French, he amplified the heroine's skill at weaving, adding extensive passages praising her skills and further developing the scene in which she produces her textile message to her sister, *Philomena: Conte raconté d'après Ovide*, ed. C. de Boer (Paris: Paul Geuthner, 1909).

4. For a discussion of this phenomenon in French literature, see M. Wright, *Weaving Narrative: Clothing in Medieval French Romance* (University Park, PA: Penn State Press, 2010).

5. As Roland Barthes reminds us, written clothing always has a view to signification, *Système de la mode* (Paris: Seuil, 1967), 23.

6. Wright, *Weaving Narrative*, 7–9.

7. K. D'Ettore, "Clothing and Conflict in the Icelandic Family Sagas: Literary Convention and Discourse of Power," in *Medieval Clothing and Textiles 5* (2009): 1–14.

8. A. Colby, *The Portrait in Twelfth-Century French Literature* (Geneva: Droz, 1965), 99.

9. Portraits, though never identical, proceed in a predicable order, depicting a nearly standard set of features; see Colby for more detail. The emphasis is often on the fineness of the fabric, the luxuriousness of the decorative elements, and the impression of perfection obtained from fit and overall beauty of the character, which is itself enhanced by the attire.

10. N. Whitfield, "Dress and Accessories in the Early Irish Tale 'The Wooing of Becfhola'," *Medieval Clothing and Textiles* 2 (2006): 2.

11. M. Bhreathnach, "A New Edition of *Tachmarc Becfhola*," *Ériu* 35 (1984): 72, §1. Translation by Bhreathnach, 77, §1.

12. Whitfield, "Dress and Accessories," 5.

13. Bhreathnach, "A New Edition of *Tachmarc Becfhola*," 73, § 6, trans. 78, § 6.

14. Whitfield, "Dress and Accessories," 34.

15. A. Zanchi, "'Melius Abundare Quam Deficere': Scarlet Clothing in Laxdœla Saga and Njáls Saga," *Medieval Clothing and Textiles* 4 (2008): 21–37.

16. Heller, *Fashion in Medieval France*, 6–8.

17. *Pearl*, in *The Complete Works of the Pearl Poet*, eds M. Andrew et al., trans. C. Finch (Berkeley: University of California Press, 1993), 43–101, here vv. 197–9 and 219–20; *Sir Gawain and the Green Knight, Pearl, and Sir Orfeo*, trans. J.R.R. Tolkien (Boston: Houghton Mifflin, 1975).

18. For a detailed discussion of the Pearl Maiden's attire see A. Schotter, "The Poetic Function of Alliterative Formulas of Clothing in the Portrait of the Pearl Maiden," *Studia Neophilologica* 51(1979): 189–95.

19. Ibid., 190.

20. L. Hodges analyzes Chaucer's treatment of the Wife in detail in her chapter "The Wife of Bath's Costumes: Reading the Subtexts," in *Chaucer and Costume: The Secular Pilgrims in the General Prologue* (Woodbridge, UK: Brewer, 2000), 161–86.

21. Hodges makes a particularly vivid estimation of the effect it would have had: "The air from the forward movement of dame Alisoun, striding toward the altar rail, would have lifted and fluffed the frills of such coverchiefs and added to the appearance of fullness and weight. In motion, she would have looked like a ship in full sail," *Chaucer and Costume*, 170.

22. C. Dinshaw places the Wife firmly in opposition to the patriarchal discourse of other pilgrims, especially that of the Man of Law's Tale, arguing that the Wife, "makes audible precisely [it] would keep silent," and values the carnal over the spiritual. *Chaucer's Sexual Politics* (Madison: University of Wisconsin Press, 1989), 115.

23. Hodges points to the fact that scarlet hose were typically worn by the nobility but that wealthy merchants who could afford them were not punished for doing so. *Chaucer and Costume*, 172–3.

24. G. Renn provides perhaps the strangest argument, associating scarlet with medieval belief that wearing a sympathetic color could ward off disease and asserting that she is attempting to avoid venereal disease with her hose ("Chaucer's 'Prologue'," *Explicator* 46.3 (1988): 4–7). However, color symbolism is a remarkably fluid matter, and despite much ink having flowed over her scarlet hose, the prudent interpretation must focus on the dye rather than more tenuous assertions based solely on color associations.

25. In previous periods, the term scarlet referred not to a color but to a fabric, wool of the finest quality often dyed with the most precious dye available, kermes. Eventually, the association of the fine woolen with the color would become so pervasive that the color term would replace the fabric term, as is the case here.

26. A. Denny-Brown, *Fashioning Change: The Trope of Clothing in High- and Late-Medieval England* (Columbus: Ohio State UP, 2012), 128.

27. Hodges, *Chaucer and Costume*, 163.

28. C. Carlson, "Chaucer's Griselde, Her Smock, and the Fashioning of a Character," in *Styling Texts: Dress and Fashion in Literature*, eds C. Kuhn and C. Carlson (Youngstown, NY: Cambria, 2007), 35.

29. In the first *laisse* of the Anglo-Norman *Romance of Horn*, we identify the hero as the lord of a group of counts' sons primarily due to the superior quality of his attire relative to that of his companions: "All of them were sons of good counts, and all acknowledged Horn, the young man, as their lord. Each one wore a crimson or indigo *bliaut*, but Horn was clad in an Alexandrian brocade," Thomas. *The Romance of Horn*, ed. M. Pope (Oxford: Anglo-Norman Text Society, 1955), vv. 10–13.

30. Chrétien de Troyes, *Le Chevalier de la charrette (Lancelot)*, ed. J. Frappier (Paris: Champion, 1962), vv. 5498–6056. For a thorough discussion of this scene, see M. Bruckner, *Shaping Romance: Interpretation, Truth, and Closure in Twelfth-Century French Fictions* (Philadelphia: University of Pennsylvania Press, 1993), 61–77. Frequent, too, are passages featuring two close friends who meet each other in battle without recognition until after inflicting grievous harm to one another.

31. Béroul, *Le Roman de Tristan*, ed. and trans. N. Lacy (New York: Garland, 1989) vv. 3288–4218. See M. Wright, "Dress For Success: Béroul's *Tristan* and the Restoration of Status through Clothes," *Arthuriana* 18.2 (2008): 3–16, for a more detailed discussion of the function of clothing in this work.

32. See V. Hotchkiss, *Clothes Make the Man: Female Cross Dressing in Medieval Europe* (New York: Garland, 1996).

33. E.J. Burns, "Robes, Armor, and Skin," in *Courtly Love Undressed* (Philadelphia: University of Pennsylvania Press, 2002), 121–48.

34. *Aucassin et Nicolette, Chantefable du XIIIe siècle*, ed. M. Roques (Paris: Champion, 1977).

35. *Thrymskvida*, or *Thrym's Poem*, in *Edda: Die Lieder des Codex regius nebst verwandten Denkmälern*, eds G. Neckel and H. Kuhn (Heidelberg: Winter, 1962).

36. Chrétien de Troyes, *Le Chevalier au Lion* (Yvain), ed. M. Roques (Paris: Champion, 1960), vv. 1150–65.

37. Chrétien de Troyes, *Le Roman de Perceval, ou Le Conte du Graal*, ed. W. Roach (Geneva: Droz, 1959), Of course, as N. Lacy points out, his development has not prepared him for his most important task—asking the right question about the Grail when he sees it at the Fisher King's castle; see *The Craft of Chrétien de Troyes: An Essay on Narrative Art* (Leiden: Brill, 1980), 16–17. And, when we see Perceval for the last time in the unfinished romance, he removes his armor and fine courtly trappings in favor of a hermit's homespun to atone for his failing (Wright, *Weaving Narrative*, 145–6).

38. Marie de France, *Milun*, in *Les Lais de Marie de France*, ed. J. Lods (Paris: Champion, 1959), 126–42. Marie also employs this trope in *Fresne* when the mother of a lost twin recognizes the silk cloth her daughter has in her possession many years later (44–60). Similar tropes appear in *The Mabinogion*, trans. G. Jones and T. Jones (London: Everyman, 1991).

39. In Marie's *Guigemar*, the hero ties his lady's belt so that only he can untie it, and his lady knots the tail of his chemise similarly.

40. In the *Poetic Edda*, Freyia has a feather cloak that allows her to fly.

41. For example, a clothing item that only fits a virgin functions as a chastity test; see *Du mantel mautaillié*, ed. A. Conte (Modena: Mucchi, 2013).

42. Chrétien, *Yvain*, v. 2806 and v. 4316.

43. Without his clothes, Marie de France's Bisclavret cannot recover his human form; see also *Melion* in *The Lays of Desiré, Gaelent, and Melion*, ed. E. Grimes (Geneva: Slatkine, 1976), and *Guillaume de Palerne, roman du XIIIe siècle*, ed. A. Micha (Geneva: Droz, 1990).

44. *Beowulf and the Fight at Finnsburg*, ed. F. Klaeber (Boston: Heath, 1950), lines 670a–84a.

45. E. Howard, "The Clothes Make the Man: Transgressive Disrobing and Disarming in *Beowulf*," in *Styling Texts: Dress and Fashion in Literature*, eds C. Kuhn and C. Carlson (Youngstown, NY: Cambria, 2007), 13–32.

46. Dante Alighieri, *The Divine Comedy of Dante Alighieri*, ed. and trans. R. Durling and R. Martinez (New York: Oxford University Press, 1996–2013).

47. M. Feltham and J. Miller, "Original Skin: Nudity and Obscenity in Dante's *Inferno*," in *Dante and the Unorthodox: The Aesthetics of Transgression*, ed. J. Miller (Waterloo, ON: Wilfrid Laurier UP, 2005), 182–206; A. Hollander, "The Dress of Thought: Clothing and Nudity in Homer, Virgil, Dante, and Ariosto," in eds C. Giorcelli and P. Rabinowitz, *Exchanging Clothes: Habits of Being 2* (Minneapolis: U of Minnesota P, 2012), 40–57.

48. The importance of clothing gifts is clear from Stanza 41 of the *Hávamál*, or *Sayings of the High One*, in the *Poetic Edda*: "With gifts of weapons and raiment friends should gladden one another, for they are most visible; mutual givers and receivers are friends the longest, if the friendship is fated to succeed."

49. The Griselda story appears in Book X, Tale 10 of Boccaccio, *The Decameron*, trans. M. Musa and P. Bondanella (New York: Norton, 1982), 672–81; Petrarch, *Sen* XVII 3 in *Letters of Old Age "Rerum Senilium Libri" I–XVIII*, trans. A. Bernardo, S. Levin, and R. Bernardo (Baltimore: Johns Hopkins University Press, 1992), II, 655–68; Philippe de Mézières, *Le Livre de la vertu du sacrement de mariage*, ed. J. Williamson (Washington: Catholic University of America Press, 1993), 359–77; Chaucer, "The Clerk's Tale," in *The Riverside Chaucer*, VI, 149–53; Christine de Pizan, *La Cité des Dames*, trans. T. Moreau and É. Hicks (Paris: Stock, 2000), 196–201.

50. R. Krueger, "Uncovering Griselda: Christine de Pizan, 'une seule chemise,' and the Clerical Tradition: Boccaccio, Petrarch, Philippe de Mézières and the Ménagier de Paris," in *Medieval Fabrications: Dress, Textiles, Clothwork, and Other Cultural Imaginings*, ed. E.J. Burns (New York: Palgrave, 2004), 71–88.

51. Krueger, "Uncovering Griselda," 76; Carlson, "Chaucer's Griselde," 37.

52. See M. Wright, "'De Fil d'or et de Soie': Making Textiles in Twelfth-Century French Romance," in *Medieval Clothing and Textiles 2* (2006): 61–72. Chrétien provides a counter-example of financially secure cloth-making women in the *tisseuses* in *Yvain*; see E.J. Burns, "Women Silk Workers from King Arthur's France to King Roger's Palermo," in *Sea of Silk: A Textile Geography of Women's Work in Medieval French Literature* (Philadelphia: University of Pennsylvania Press, 2009), 37–69.

53. Chaucer, *General Prologue*, I, vv. 447–8.

54. See chapters 49 and 55 in the *Laxdœla Saga*, ed. Einar Óláfur Sveinsson (Reykjavik: Íslenzka Fornritafélag, 1954), and numerous passages throughout the *Poetic Edda*.

55. D'Ettore, "Clothing and Conflict in the Sagas," 5–7; some of these items are designed to heighten the mood of conflict, but others have a protective purpose.

56. *Philomena*, v. 869ff.

57. *Emaré*, in *The Middle English Breton Lays*, eds A. Laskaya and E. Salisbury (Kalamazoo, MI: Medieval Institute Publications, 1995), 153–82.

58. Amanda Hopkins, "Veiling the Text: The True Role of the Cloth in *Emaré*," in *Medieval Insular Romance: Translation and Innovation*, eds J. Weiss et al. (Cambridge: Brewer, 2000), 81.

59. Ibid., 81–2.

60. Jean Renart, *Le Roman de la Rose, ou de Guillaume de Dole*, ed. F. Lecoy (Paris: Champion, 1962), vv. 8–11 and 14: "car aussi com l'en met la graine / es dras por avoir los et pris, / einsi a il chans et sons mis / en cestui romans de la rose . . . et brodez, par lieus, de biaus vers."

61. In *Cligés*, Alexandre arrives at Arthur's court and shows respect to his new lord by removing his mantle (vv. 314–17); this undressing act opens a narrative thread that includes Alexandre receiving two sartorial gifts: the first, a gift of armor from Arthur (vv. 1123–35), and the second a chemise from Guenevere into which the queen herself has sewn a hair from the lady Alexandre loves but is too shy to approach (vv. 1144–62). This last gift allows the two young people to express their love and eventually marry, thus closing the narrative thread opened by Alexandre's initial undressing act; Chrétien de Troyes, *Cligés*, ed. A. Micha (Paris: Champion, 1982).

62. See D'Ettore, "Clothing and Conflict," 9–10, for a discussion of this episode in light of clothing as a portend of conflict in the saga convention.

63. Ibid., 14.

64. Despite the later composition, the events depicted hearken back to a much earlier period, depicting figures and themes from pre-Christian Germanic heroic tradition and mythology dating to the fifth or sixth century.

65. *Das Nibelungenlied*, stanzas 679–80, trans. A.T. Hatto in *The Nibelungenlied* (London, Penguin, 1969), 92.

66. *Das Nibelungenlied*, stanzas 903–4.

67. Ibid., stanza 976.

68. *Das Nibelungenlied*, stanza 1022, Hatto, 135.

69. *Das Nibelungenlied*, stanza 1026.

70. J. Bumke, *Courtly Culture: literature and society in the high Middle Ages* (Berkeley: University of California Press, 1991), 422. S. Samples argues that Siegfried's "actions in the service of Gunther have marked him as a destabilizing force in the Burgundian kingdom": "The German Heroic Narratives," in *German Literature of the High Middle Ages*, ed. W. Hasty (Woodbridge: Camden House, 2006), 168.

71. Bumke, *Courtly Culture*, 422.

72. Chrétien de Troyes, *Erec et Enide*, ed. and trans. C. Carroll (New York: Garland, 1987).

73. For a detailed discussion of clothing in this romance, see S. Sturm-Maddox and D. Maddox, "Description in Medieval Narrative: Vestimentary Coherence in Chrétien's *Erec et Enide*," *Medioevo Romanzo* 9.1 (1984): 51–64.

74. After his marriage, Erec refuses to participate in tournaments or fulfill his knightly duties, preferring to remain in the company of his wife.

75. *Ystorya Gereint uab Erbin*, ed. R. Thomson (Dublin: Dublin Institute for Advanced Studies, 1997), and "Gereint Son of Erbin," in *The Mabinogion*, trans. Jones and Jones, 189–225.

76. *Erec von Hartmann von Aue*, ed. A. Leitzman (Tübingen: Niemeyer, 1985), and *Erec*, in *The Complete Works of Hartmann von Aue*, trans. K. Vivian (University Park: Pennsylvania State University Press, 2001), 51–163.

77. *Erex saga*, in *Norse Romance: Volume II, Knights of the Round Table*, ed. and trans. M. Kalinke (Woodbridge: Brewer, 1999), pp. 217–65.

78. The Old French term *bliaut* means a luxurious court dress usually made of silk and highly ornamented, typically with orphrey and jewels.

79. *Erex saga*, 258, 259.

80. S.-G. Heller, "Fictions of Consumption: The Nascent Fashion System in *Partonopeus de Blois*," *Australian Journal of French Studies* 46.3 (2009): 191–205.

BIBLIOGRAPHY

Primary Sources

(Alphabetized by medieval author's name if known, then editors/translators; if none listed, then by title).

Aelred of Rievaulx, and John Ayton and Alexandra Barratt (eds) (1984), *Aelred of Rievaulx's De Institutione Inclusarum: Two English Versions*. Early English Text Society o.s. 287, London: Oxford University Press.

Aldebrant (Aldebrandino da Siena), and Louis Landouzy and Roger Pépin (eds) (1978), *Le Régime du corps*, Geneva: Slatkine.

Aldhelm, and Michael Lapidge and Michael Herren (eds and trans.) (1979), *The Prose Works*, Ipswich and Cambridge, D.S. Brewer.

Andrew, Malcolm, Ronald Waldron, and Clifford Peterson (eds), and Casey Finch (trans.) (1993), *The Complete Works of the Pearl Poet*, Berkeley: University of California Press.

Augustine of Hippo, and Roland J. Teske (trans.) (1991), *Saint Augustine on Genesis: Two Books on Genesis Against the Manichees and On the Literal Interpretations of Genesis*, Washington, DC: Catholic University of America Press.

Barrett, W.P. (trans.) (1932), *The Trial of Jeanne d'Arc*. New York: Gotham House Inc.

Béroul, and Norris J. Lacy (ed. and trans.) (1989), *Le Roman de Tristan*, New York: Garland.

Boccaccio, Giovanni, and Mark Musa and Peter Bondanella (trans.) (1982), *The Decameron*, New York, Norton.

Boniface, Saint (Bonifatius), and Michael Tangl (ed.) (1916), *S. Bonifatii et Lulli Epistolae*. Monumenta Germaniae Historica, Epistolae 4, Epistolae Selectae, 1, Berlin: Weidmannschen Verlagsbuchhandlung.

Bhreathnach, Máire (ed. and trans.) (1984), "A New Edition of *Tachmarc Becfhola*," *Ériu* 35: 59–91.

Busby, Keith (ed.) (1983), *Le Roman des eles and the Anonymous Ordene de Chevalerie*, Philadelphia: J. Benjamins.

Challoner, Richard (ed. and trans.) (1963), *The Holy Bible, Douay Version: Translated from the Latin Vulgate (Douay, A.D. 1609, Rheims, A.D. 1582)*, 5th impr, London: Catholic Truth Society.

Champion, Pierre (ed. and trans.) (1920–1), *Procès de condamnation de Jeanne d'Arc*, 2 vols., Paris: Champion.

Chaucer, Geoffrey, and L.D. Benson (ed.) (1987), *The Riverside Chaucer*, 3rd ed., Oxford: University Press.

Chrétien de Troyes, and C. de Boer, ed. (1909), *Philomena: Conte raconté d'après Ovide*, Paris: Paul Geuthner.

—, and Alexandre Micha, ed. (1957), *Cligès*. Paris: Champion.

—, and William Roach, ed. (1959), *Le Roman de Perceval ou le Conte du Graal,* Paris: Champion.

—, and Mario Roques, ed. (1960), *Le Chevalier au Lion*, Paris: Champion.

—, and J. Frappier, ed. (1962), *Le Chevalier de la Charretle (Lancelot)*, Paris: Champion.

—, and Mario Roques, ed. (1976), *Erec et Enide*, Paris: Champion.

—, and William W. Kibler, ed. (1981), *Lancelot ou le chevalier de la charrete*, New York: Garland Press.

—, and Carleton W. Carroll, ed. and trans. (1987), *Erec et Enide*, New York: Garland.

Christine de Pisan, and Renate Blumenfeld-Kosinski, trans., and Kevin Brownlee, ed. (1997), *Book of the City of Ladies*, New York: W.W. Norton.

—, and Thérèse Moreau and Éric Hicks, trans. (2000), *La Cité des Dames*, Paris: Stock.

Conte, Alberto, ed. (2013), *Du mantel mautaillié*, Modena: Mucchi.

Dante Alighieri, and Robert M. Durling and Ronald L. Martinez, ed. and trans. (1996–2013), *The Divine Comedy of Dante Alighieri*, New York: Oxford University Press.

Davis, Norman, ed. (2004), *Paston Letters and Papers of the Fifteenth Century, Part 1*. Early English Text Society S.S.20, Oxford: Oxford University Press.

Davidson, Clifford (1999), "Nudity, the Body and Early English Drama," *The Journal of English and Germanic Philology* 98.4: 499–522.

Dennis, Andrew, Peter Foote, and Richard Perkins, eds and trans. (1980), *Laws of Early Iceland: Grágás, the Codex Regius of Grágás, with material from other manuscripts*, 5 vols., Winnipeg, Canada: University of Manitoba Press.

Doss-Quinby, Eglal, Joan Trasker Grimbert, Wendy Pfeffer, and Elizabeth Aubrey, eds and trans. (2001), *Songs of the Women Trouveres*, New Haven: Yale University Press.

Durand, Guillaume, and A. Davril and Timothy M. Thibodeau, eds (1995–2000), *Guillelmi Duranti Rationale Divinorum Officiorum*, 3 vols., Turnholt: Brepols.

—, and Timothy M. Thibodeau, trans. (2010), *William Durand on the Clergy and Their Vestments: A New Translation of Books 2–3 of the Rationale divinorum officiorum*, Chicago: University of Scranton Press.

Einhard, and Lewis Thorpe, ed. and trans. (1969), "The Life of Charlemagne," in *Two Lives of Charlemagne*, New York: Penguin Books, 49–90.

Eyrbyggarnas Saga. Isländska sagor 1. Hjalmar Alving, ed. (1935), Stockholm: Bonnier; reprint Avesta: Gidlunds, 1979.

Frappier, Jean, ed. (1964), *La Mort Le Roi Artu*, Paris: Champion.

Given-Wilson, C., gen. ed. (2005), *The Parliament Rolls of Medieval England, 1275–1504*, 16 vols., Woodbridge: Boydell.

Gower, John, and E.W. Stockton, ed. and trans. (1962), *The Major Latin Works of John Gower*, Seattle, WA: University of Washington Press.

—, and William Burton Wilson, trans., Nancy Wilson Van Baak, ed. (1992), *Mirour de l'Omme/ The Mirror of Mankind, John Gower*, East Lansing: Colleagues Press.

Green, Monica H., ed. and trans. (2001), *The Trotula: An English Translation of the Medieval Compendium of Women's Medicine*, Philadelphia: University of Pennsylvania Press.

Grimes, Evie Margaret, ed. (1976), *The Lays of Desiré, Gaelent, and Melion*, Geneva: Slatkine.

Guillaume de Lorris et Jean de Meun, and Félix Lecoy, ed. (1965–6, 1970), *Le Roman de la Rose*, 3 vols., Paris: Champion.

—, and Charles Dahlberg, trans. (1971), *The Romance of the Rose*, Princeton, New Jersey: Princeton University Press.

—, and Armand Strubel, ed. and trans. (1992), *Le Roman de la Rose*, Paris: Librairie générale française.

Hartmann von Aue, and Albert Leitzman, ed. (1985), *Erec von Hartmann von Aue*, Tübingen: Niemeyer.

—, and Kim Vivien, trans. (2001), *The Complete Works of Hartmann von Aue*, University Park: Pennsylvania State University Press.

Hatto, A.T., trans. (1969), *The Nibelungenlied*, London: Penguin.

Heldris de Cornuaille, and Lewis Thorpe, ed. (1972), *Le Roman de Silence: A Thirteenth-Century Arthurian Verse Romance by Heldris de Cornuaille*, Cambridge: W. Heffer and Sons.

Hildegard of Bingen, and Hugh Feiss and Christopher P. Evans, eds and trans. (2010), *Two Hagiographies: Vita sancti Rupperti confessoris; Vita sancti Dysbodi episcopi*, Leuven: Peeters.

Hughes, P.L., and J.F. Larkin, eds (1969), *Tudor Royal Proclamations*, 3 vols., New Haven: Yale University Press.

Ibn Butlan, and Luisa Cogliati Arano, ed. and trans. (1976), *The Medieval Health Handbook: Tacuinum Sanitatis*, New York: George Braziller.

Ibn Fadlan, Ahmad, and Marius Canard and André Miquel, eds and trans. (1989), *Voyage chez les Bulgares de la Volga*, Paris: Sindbad.

Jean le Marchant, and Pierre Kunstman, ed. (1973), *Miracles de Notre-Dame de Chartres*, Ottawa: Université d'Ottawa.

John Cassian, and Philip Schaff, ed. (2007), "The Twelve books of John Cassian. Institutes of the Coenobia and the Remedies for the Eight Principal Faults," in *Nicene and Post-Nicene Fathers: Second Series,* Vol. 9, New York: Cosimo.

John of Reading, and James Tait, ed. (1914), *Chronica Johannis de Reading et Anonymi Cantuariensis 1346–1367,* Manchester: Manchester University Press.

Jones, Gwyn (1986), *The Norse Atlantic Saga: Being the Norse Voyages of Discovery and Settlement to Iceland, Greenland, and North America*, Oxford: Oxford University Press.

Jones, Gwyn, and Thomas Jones, trans. (1991), *The Mabinogion*, London: Everyman.

Kalinke, Marianne E., ed. (1999), *Norse Romance: Volume II, Knights of the Round Table*, Woodbridge, UK: Brewer.

Kempe, Margery, and S.B. Meech and H.E. Allen, eds (1940; reprint 1963), *The Book of Margery Kempe*. Early English Text Series o.s. 212, London: Oxford University Press.

Klaeber, F., ed. (1950), *Beowulf and the Fight at Finnsburg*, Boston: Heath.

Larrington, Carolyne, trans. (1996), *The Poetic Edda*, Oxford: Oxford University Press.

Laskaya, Anne, and Eve Salisbury, eds (1995), *The Middle English Breton Lays*, Kalamazoo, MI: Medieval Institute Publications, 1995.

Leander of Seville, and Paul Migne, ed. (1878), "De institutione virginum," *Patrologia Latina* 72: 873–94.

—, and A.C. Vega, ed. (1948), *El "De institutione virginum" de San Leandro de Seville*, Madrid: Escorial.

—, and Claude W. Barrow, trans. (1969), *Iberian Fathers I: Martin of Braga, Paschasius of Dumium, Leander of Seville*, Washington DC: Catholic University of America Press.

Lumiansky, R.M., and David Mills, eds (1974), *The Chester Mystery Cycle*, London: Oxford University Press for the Early English Text Society.

Magnússon, Magnús, and Hermann Pálsson, eds and trans. (1969), *Laxdæla Saga*, Baltimore: Penguin Books.

Marie de France, and Jeanne Lods, ed. (1959), *Les Lais de Marie de France*, Paris: Champion.

—, and K. Warnke, ed., and L. Harf-Lancner, trans. (1990), *Lais de Marie de France*. Paris: Librairie générale française.

Ménard, Philippe, ed. (1970), "Le 'Dit de Mercier'," in *Mélanges de Langue et de Littérature du Moyen Age et de la Renaissance Offerts à Jean Frappier*. Publications romanes et françaises 112, Geneva: Droz, 797–810.

Mézières, Philippe de, and Joan B. Williamson, ed. (1993), *Le Livre de la vertu du sacrement de marriage*, Washington: Catholic University of America Press.

Meyer, Paul, ed. and trans. (1891), *L'histoire de Guillaume le Maréchal, comte de Striguil et de Pembroke, régent d'Angleterre de 1216 à 1219: poème français*, Paris: Librairie Renouard, H. Laurens, successeur.

Micha, Alexandre, ed. (1978–83), *Lancelot: Roman en prose du XIIIe siècle.* 9 vols., Geneva: Droz.

—, ed. (1990), *Guillaume de Palerne, roman du XIIIe siècle*, Geneva: Droz.

Mirkus, Johannes, and T. Erbe, ed. (1905; reprint 1987), *Mirk's Festial: A Collection of Homilies by Johannes Mirkus (John Mirk)*, Early English Text Society e.s. 96. London: Kegan Paul, Trench, and Trübner.

Neckel, Gustav, and Hans Kuhn, eds (Winter 1962), *Edda: Die Lieder des Codex regius nebst verwandten Denkmälern*, Heidelberg, Germany.

Notker the Stammerer, and Lewis Thorpe, ed. and trans. (1969), "Charlemagne," in *Two Lives of Charlemagne*, New York: Penguin Books, 93–172.

Ordericus Vitalis, and Marjorie Chibnall, ed. and trans. (1973), *The Ecclesiastical History of Orderic Vitalis*, Vol. 4, Oxford: Clarendon Press.

Pálsson, Hermann, and Paul Edwards, trans. (1972), *The Book of the Settlements, Landnámabók*, Winnipeg: University of Manitoba Icelandic Studies 1.

Pauphilet, Alfred, ed. (1923), *La Queste del Saint Graal*, Paris: Champion.

Petrarch, Francesco, and Aldo S. Bernardo, Saul Levin, and Rita A. Bernardo, trans. (1992), *Letters of Old Age "Rerum Senilium Libri" I–XVIII*, Baltimore: Johns Hopkins University Press.

Renart, Jean, and Lucien Foulet, ed. (1925), *Galeran de Bretagne*, Paris: Champion.

—, and Félix Lecoy, ed. (1962), *Le Roman de la Rose ou de Guillaume de Dole*, Paris: Champion.

Robert de Blois, and Paul Barrette, ed. (1968), *Robert de Blois's Floris et Lyriope*, Berkeley: University of California Press.

Roques, Mario, ed. (1977), *Aucassin et Nicolette, Chantefable du XIIIe siècle*, Paris: Champion.

Smaragdus of Saint-Mihiel, and David Barry OSB, trans. (2007), *Commentary on the Rule of Saint Benedict*, Cistercian Studies Series, no. 212, Kalamazoo: Cistercian Publications.

Smaragdus, Sancti Michaelis, and Alfredus Spannagel and Pius Engelbert, eds (1974), *Smaragdi Abbatis Expositio In Regulam S. Benedicti*, Siegburg: F. Schmitt Success.

Statutes of the Realm: Printed by Command of His Majesty King George the Third . . . from Original Records and Authentic Manuscripts (1963), London: Dawsons.

Stevens, Martin, and A.C. Cawley, eds (1994), *The Towneley Plays*, Early English Text Society 13–14, Oxford: Oxford University Press,.

Sveinsson, Einar Óláfur, ed. (1954), *Laxdœla Saga*, Reykjavik: Íslenzka Fornritafélag.

Talbot, C.H., ed. and trans. (1959), *The Life of Christina of Markyate, a Twelfth Century Recluse*, Oxford: Clarendon.

Thomas, and Mildred K. Pope, ed. (1955), *The Romance of Horn*, Oxford: Anglo-Norman Text Society.

Thomson, Robert L., ed. (1997), *Ystorya Gereint uab Erbin*, Dublin: Dublin Institute for Advanced Studies.

Þorgilsson, Ari, and Halldór Hermannsson, ed. and trans. (1930), *The Book of the Icelanders (Íslendingabók)*, Ithaca, NY: Cornell University Library.

Tolkien, J.R.R., trans. (1975), *Sir Gawain and the Green Knight, Pearl, and Sir Orfeo*, Boston: Houghton Mifflin.

Walter of Henley, and Oschinsky, Dorothea, ed. (1971), *Walter of Henley and Other Treatises on Estate Management and Accounting*, Oxford: Clarendon Press.

Weber, Robert, et al., eds (1994), *Biblia Sacra iuxta vulgatum versionem*, 4th ed., Stuttgart: Deutsche Bibelgesellschaft.

Wheatley, Henry B., William Edward Mead, John S. Stuart-Glennie, and D.W. Nash, eds (1899; reprinted as 2 vols. 1987), *Merlin; or, the Early History of King Arthur: A Prose Romance (About 1450–1460 A.D.)*, London: Early English Text Society.

Secondary Sources

Abulafia, David (1994), "The Role of Trade in Muslim-Christian Contact during the Middle Ages," in Dionisius Agius and Richard Hitchcock (eds), *The Arab Influence in Medieval Europe*, Reading: Ithaca Press, 1–24.

Alexander, Jonathan J.G. (1992), *Medieval Illuminators and their Methods of Work*, New Haven: Yale University Press.

Alexander, Jonathan and Paul Binski, eds (1987), *Age of Chivalry: Art in Plantagenet England 1200–1400*, London: Royal Academy of Arts.

Alexandre-Bidon, Danièle and Marie-Thérèse Lorcin (2003), *Le Quotidien aux temps des fabliaux*, Paris: Picard.

Anderlini, Tina (2015), "The Shirt Attributed to St Louis," *Medieval Clothing and Textiles* 11: 49–78.

Andersen, Erik, Jytte Milland, and Eva Myhre (1989), *Uldsejl i 1000 år*. Roskilde: Vikingeskibshallen.

Andersen, Erik and Anna Nørgård (2009), *Et uldsejl til Oselven: Arbejdsrapport om fremstillingen af et uldsejl til en traditionel vestnorsk båd*, Roskilde: Vikingeskibsmuseet.

Anderson, Gary A. (2001), "The Garments of Skin in Apocryphal Narrative and Biblical Commentary," in James L. Kugel (ed.), *Studies in Ancient Midrash*, Cambridge: Harvard University Press, 101–43.

Andersson, Eva (1996), *Textilproduktion i arkeologiska kontext, en metodstudie av yngre järnåldersboplatser i Skåne*, Institute of Archaeology Report series, no. 58, Lund: Arkeologiska institutionen och Historiska museet.

— (1999), *The Common Thread. Textile Production during the Late Iron Age – Viking Age*. Institute of Archaeology, Report Series 67, Lund: University of Lund, Institute of Archeology.

— (2000), "Textilproduktion i Löddeköpinge endast för husbehov?" in F. Svanberg and B. Söderberg (eds), *Porten till Skåne, Löddeköpinge under järnålder och medeltid*, Arkeologiska undersökningar 32, Lund: Riksantikvarieämbetet, 158–87.

— (2003a), "Textile production in Scandinavia," in *Textilien aus Archäologie und Geschichte, festschrift Klaus Tidow*, L. Bender Jørgensen, J. Banck-Burgess, and A. Rast-Eicher (eds), Neumünster: Wacholtz, 46–62.

— (2003b), *Tools for Textile Production – from Birka and Hedeby*, Birka Studies 8, Stockholm: Birka Project for Riksantikvarieämbetet.

— (2007), "Textile Tools and Production in the Viking Age," in C. Gillis and M. Nosch (eds), *Ancient Textiles: production, craft, and society: proceedings of the First International Conference on Ancient Textiles, held at Lund, Sweden and Copenhagen, Denmark, on March 19–23, 2003*, Oxford: Oxbow Books: 17–25.

— (2011), 'The organization of textile production in Birka and Hedeby," in S. Sigmundsson (ed.), *Viking Settlements and Viking Society, Papers from the Proceedings of the Sixteenth Viking Congress*, Reykjavik: University of Iceland Press, 1–17.

Andersson, Eva, Linda Mårtensson, Marie-Louise Nosch, and Lorenz Rahmstorf (2008), *New Research on Bronze Age Textile Production*, Bulletin of the Institute of Classical Studies 51, London.

Andersson Strand, Eva, and Ulla Mannering (2011), "Textile production in the late Roman Iron Age – a case study of textile production in Vorbasse, Denmark," in L. Boye, P. Ethelberg, L. Heidemann Lutz, P. Kruse, and Anne B. Sørensen (eds), *Arkæologi I Slesvig Archäologie in Schleswig 61st International Sachsen symposium publication 2010 Haderslev, Danmark*, Neumünster: Wachholtz, 77–84.

Archer, Janice (1995), "Working Women in Thirteenth-Century Paris," PhD Thesis, University of Arizona.

Arcini, Caroline (2005), "The Vikings Bare their Filed Teeth," *American Journal of Physical Anthropology* 128.4: 727–33.

Arnold, Janet (1993), "The jupon or coat-armour of the Black Prince in Canterbury cathedral," *Journal of the Church Monuments Society* 8: 12–24.

Asenjo-González, Maria, ed. (2013), *Urban Elites and Aristocratic Behaviour in the Spanish Kingdoms at the End of the Middle Ages*, Studies in European Urban History (1100–1800) 27, Turnhout: Brépols Publishers.

Ash, Karina Marie (2013), *Conflicting Femininities in Medieval German Literature*, Aldershot and Burlington: Ashgate.

Aspelund, Karl (2011), *Who Controls Culture?: Power, Craft and Gender in the Creation of Icelandic Women's National Dress*, PhD thesis, Boston University.

Aventin, Mercè (2003), "Le legge suntuarie in spagna: stato della questione," in Muzzarelli and Campanini (eds), *Disciplinare il lusso*, 109–20.

Baker, Patricia L. (1995), *Islamic Textiles*, London: British Museum Press.

Baldwin, Francis Elizabeth (1926), *Sumptuary Legislation and Personal Regulation in England*, Baltimore, MD: Johns Hopkins University Press.

Ball, Jennifer L. (2005), *Byzantine Dress: Representations of Secular Dress in Eighth- to Twelfth-Century Painting*, New York: Palgrave Macmillan.

Barthes, Roland (1967), *Système de la mode*, Paris: Seuil.

Batey, Colleen (1988), "A Viking Age Bell from Freswick Links," *Medieval Archaeology* 32: 213–16.

Behre, K.-E. (1984), "Pflanzliche Nahrung in Haithabu," in Herbert Jankuhn and Henning Hellmuth Andersen (eds), *Archäologische und naturwissenschaftliche Untersuchungen an ländlichen und frühstädtischen Siedlungen im deutschen Küstengebiet von 5. Jahrhundert v. Chr. bis zum 11. Jahrhundert n. Chr.* Weinheim: Acta Humaniora, 208–15.

Bek-Pedersen, Karen (2008), "Are the Spinning Nornir Just a Yarn?" *Viking and Medieval Scandinavia* 3. 1: 1–10.

— (2009), "Weaving Swords and Rolling Heads: a Peculiar Space in Old Norse Tradition," *Viking and Medieval Scandinavia* 5: 23–39.

Bell, Adrian R., Chris Brooks and Paul R. Dryburgh (2007), *The English Wool Market c. 1230–1327*, Cambridge: Cambridge University Press.

Bender Jørgensen, Lise (1986), *Forhistoriske textiler i Skandinavien [=Prehistoric Scandinavian Textiles]*. Nordiske Fortidsminder serie B 9, Copenhagen: Det Kongelige Nordiske oldskriftselskab.

— (1992), *North European Textiles Until AD 1000*, Aarhus C, Denmark: Aarhus University Press.

— (2003), "Scandinavia, AD 400–1000," in David Jenkins (ed.), *The Cambridge History of Western Textiles*, 1, Cambridge: Cambridge University Press, 132–8.

— (2012), "The introduction of sails to Scandinavia: Raw materials, labour and land," in *N-TAG TEN: Proceedings of the 10th Nordic TAG conference at Stiklestad, Norway 2009*, Oxford: Archeopress, 173–82.

Bennett, Judith M. and Ruth Mazo Karras, eds (2013), *The Oxford Handbook of Women and Gender in Medieval Europe,* Oxford: Oxford University Press.

Berchow, Jan, Susan Marti, et al., eds (2005), *Krone und Schleier: Kunst aus Mittelalterlichen Frauenklöstern,* Munich: Hirmer Verlag.

Berger, John (1972), *Ways of Seeing,* London: British Broadcasting Corporation.

Berlo, Janet C. (1992), "Beyond Bricolage: Women and Aesthetic Strategies in Latin American Textiles," *Res: Anthropology and Aesthetics* 22: 115–34.

Bevington, David M. (1975), *Medieval Drama,* Boston: Houghton Mifflin.

Blanc, Odile (1997), *Parades et parures: L'invention du corps de mode à la fin du Moyen Age,* Paris: Gallimard.

— (2002), "From Battlefield to Court: The Invention of Fashion in the Fourteenth Century," in Désirée G. Koslin and Janet E. Snyder (eds), *Encountering Medieval Textiles and Dress: Objects, Texts, Images,* New York: Palgrave Macmillan, 157–72.

— (2007), "L'orthopédie des apparences ou la mode comme invention du corps," in Agostino Paravicini Bagliani (ed.), *Le Corps et sa parure/The Body and its Adornment, Micrologus* 15, Florence: Sismel, Edizioni del Galluzzo, 107–19.

Blockmans, Wim, et al., eds (2000), *Marie: l'héritage de Bourgogne* Bruges: Somogy Editions d'art.

Boehm, Barbara Drake and Jiří Fajt, eds (2005), *Prague: The Crown of Bohemia 1347–1437,* New York: The Metropolitan Museum of Art.

Bolens, Guillemette (2012), *The Style of Gestures: Embodiment and Cognition in Literary Narrative,* Baltimore: Johns Hopkins University Press.

Bonfante, Larissa (1975), *Etruscan Dress,* Baltimore: Johns Hopkins University Press.

Boockmann, Hartmut (1995), "Gelöstes Haar und Seidene Schleier: Zwei Äbtissinen im Dialog," in Rainer Beck (ed.), *Streifzüge durch das Mittelalter: Ein historisches Lesebuch,* Munich: Beck.

Bornstein, Kate (1998), *My Gender Workbook,* New York: Routledge.

Botterweck, G. Johannes and Helmer Ringgren, eds, John T. Willis, trans. (1977–), *Theological Dictionary of the Old Testament.* 15+ vols., Stuttgart: William B. Eerdman.

Breward, Christopher (1995), *The Culture of Fashion: A New History of Fashionable Dress,* Manchester: Manchester University Press.

Brown, Alfred L. (1989), *The Governance of Late Medieval England, 1272–1461,* Stanford: Stanford University Press.

Bruckner, Matilda Tomaryn (1993), *Shaping Romance: Interpretation, Truth, and Closure in Twelfth-Century French Fictions,* Philadelphia: University of Pennsylvania Press.

Brundage, James (1987), "Sumptuary Laws and Prostitution in Medieval Italy," *Journal of Medieval History* 13, no. 4: 343–55.

Bulst, Neithard (1993), "Kleidung als sozialer Konfliktstoff: Probleme kleidergesetzlicher Normierung im sozialen Gefüge," *Saeculum: Jahrbuch für Universalgeschichte* 44: 32–46.

— (2003), "La legislazione suntuaria in francia (secoli XIII–XVIII)," in Muzzarelli and Campanini (eds), *Disciplinare il lusso,* 121–36.

Bumke, Joachim (1991), *Courtly Culture: Literature and Society in the High Middle Ages,* Berkeley: University of California Press.

Burns, E. Jane (1993), *Bodytalk: When Women Speak in Old French Literature,* Philadelphia: University of Pennsylvania Press.

— (1994), "Ladies Don't Wear Braies: Underwear and Outerwear in the French *Prose Lancelot,*" in William W. Kibler (ed.), *The Lancelot-Grail Cycle,* Austin: University of Texas Press, 152–74.

— (2002), *Courtly Love Undressed: Reading Through Clothes in Medieval French Culture.* Philadelphia: University of Pennsylvania Press.

— (2006), "Saracen Silk and the Virgin's 'Chemise': Cultural Crossing in Cloth," *Speculum* 81.2: 365–97.

— (2009), *Sea of Silk: A Textile Geography of Women's Work in Medieval French Literature,* Philadelphia: University of Pennsylvania Press.

— (2013), "Shaping Saladin," in Daniel O'Sullivan and Laurie Shepherd (eds), *Shaping Courtliness in Medieval France*, Cambridge, England: D.S. Brewer, 241–53.

Brazil, Sarah (2015), *Covering and Discovering the Body in Medieval Theology, Drama and Literature,* Doctoral thesis, University of Geneva.

— (2017), *The Corporeality of Clothing in Medieval Literature.* Early Drama, Art, and Music. Kalamazoo: Medieval Institute Publications, forthcoming.

Brink, Stefan and Neil S. Price (2008), *The Viking World*, London: Routledge.

Brydon, Anne and S.A. Niessen (1998), *Consuming Fashion: Adorning the Transnational Body,* Oxford, UK: Berg.

Bulst, Neithard (1988), "Zum Problem städtischer und territorialer Luxusgesetzgebung in Deutschland (13. bis Mitte 16. Jahrhundert)," in A. Gouron and A. Rigaudière (eds), *Renaissance du pouvoir législatif et genèse de l'état*, 29–57. Montpellier: Publications de Ia Société d'Histoire du Droit et des Institutions des Anciens Pays de Droit Écrit, 1988, 29–57.

— (1993), "Les ordonnances somptuaires en Allemagne: expression de l'ordre urbain (XIVe–XVIe siècle," in *Comptes rendus des séances de l'année*. Paris: Académie des Inscriptions et Belles-Lettres, 1993, 771–84.

Buren, Anne H. van and Roger Wieck (2011), *Illuminating Fashion: Dress in Medieval France and the Netherlands, 1325–1515*, New York: The Morgan Library and Museum.

Butler, Judith (1990), *Gender Trouble: Feminism and the Subversion of Identity*, New York: Routledge.

— (1993), *Bodies That Matter: On the Discursive Limits of "Sex,"* New York: Routledge.

Bynum, Caroline Walker (1997), "Presidential Address: Wonder," *American Historical Review* 102.1: 1–26.

— (2011), *Christian Materiality: An Essay on Religion in Late Medieval Europe*, New York: Zone Books.

Byock, Jesse L. (1993), *Medieval Iceland: Society, Sagas, and Power*, Enfield Lock: Hisarlik Press.

Calligaro, Thomas and Patrick Périn (2009), "D'Or et des grenats," *Histoire et images médiévales* 25: 24–5.

Camille, Michael (1998), *The Medieval Art of Love: Objects and Subjects of Desire*, New York: Harry N. Abrams.

— (2001), "'For Our Devotion and Pleasure': The Sexual Objects of Jean, Duc de Berry," *Art History* 24.2: 1–69.

Cannon, Aubrey (1998), "The Cultural and Historical Contexts of Fashion," in A. Brydon and S. A. Niessen (eds), *Consuming Fashion: Adorning the Transnational Body*, Oxford, UK: Berg, 23–38.

Cardon, Dominique (1998), *La Draperie Au Moyen Age: Essor d'une grande industrie européenne*, Paris: CNRS.

— (2007), *Natural Dyes: Sources, Tradition, Technology and Science*, Caroline Higgitt, (trans.), London: Archetype.

Carlin, Martha (2007), "Shops and shopping in the early thirteenth century," in Lawrin Armstrong, Ivana Elbl, and Martin M. Elbl (eds), *Money, Markets and Trade in Late Medieval Europe: essays in honour of John H.A. Munro*. Leiden: Brill, 491–537.

Carlson, Cindy (2007), "Chaucer's Griselde, Her Smock, and the Fashioning of A Character," in Cynthia Kuhn and Cindy Carlson (eds), *Styling Texts: Dress and Fashion in Literature*, Youngstown, NY: Cambria, 33–48.

Carruthers, Mary (2013), *The Experience of Beauty in the Middle Ages*, Oxford: Oxford University Press.

Carus-Wilson, E.M (1962–3), "The Medieval trade of the ports of the Wash," *Medieval Archaeology* 6–7.

Carus-Wilson, E.M. and Olive Coleman (1963), *England's Export Trade 1275–1547*, Oxford: Clarendon Press.

Caviness, Madeline H. (2001), *Visualizing Women in the Middle Ages: Sight, Spectacle, and Scopic Economy*, Philadelphia: University of Philadelphia Press.

Charlier, Philippe, et al. (2013), "The embalmed heart of Richard the Lionheart (1199 AD): a biological and anthropological analysis," in *Scientific Reports*, Nature Publishing Group, February 28. http://www.nature.com/srep/2013/130228/srep01296/full/srep01296.html [accessed April 21, 2015].

Chaudhuri, K.N. (1990), *Asia before Europe: Economy and Civilisation of the Indian Ocean from the Rise of Islam to 1750*, Cambridge: Cambridge University Press.

Clarke, Helen (1984), *The Archaeology of Medieval England*, London: British Museum Publications.

Clegg Hyer, Maren (2012), "Recycle, reduce, reuse: imagined and re-imagined textiles in Anglo-Saxon England," *Medieval Clothing and Textiles* 8: 49–62.

Colby, Alice M. (1965), *The Portrait in Twelfth-Century French Literature*, Geneva: Droz.

Coss, Peter R. (1995), "Knights, Esquires and the Origins of Social Gradation in England, *Transactions of the Royal Historical Society*, 6th ser., 5: 155–78.

Coss, Peter R. (2003), *The Origins of the English Gentry*, Cambridge: Cambridge University Press.

Coss, Peter and Maurice Keen, eds (2002), *Heraldry, Pageantry and Social Display in Medieval England*. Woodbridge: Boydell.

Crane, Susan (2002), *The Performance of Self: Ritual, Clothing, and Identity During the Hundred Years War*, Philadelphia: University of Pennsylvania Press.

Crawford, Barbara (1987), *Scandinavian Scotland*. Scotland in the Early Middle Ages 2, Leicester: Leicester University Press.

Crawford, Joanna (2004), "Clothing Distributions and Social Relations c. 1350–1500," in Richardson, *Clothing Culture*, 153–64.

Cressy, David (1999), *Birth, Marriage and Death: Ritual, religion and the life-cycle in Tudor and Stuart England*, Oxford: Oxford University Press.

Crowfoot, Elisabeth, Frances Pritchard, and Kay Staniland (1992), *Textiles and Clothing c. 1150–c. 1450*. Medieval Finds from Excavations in London 4, London: HMSO.

Damsholt, Nanna (1984), "The Role of Icelandic Women in the Sagas and in the Production of Homespun Cloth," *Scandinavian Journal of History* 9.2–3: 75–90.

Davis, Fred (1994), *Fashion, Culture, and Identity*, Chicago: University of Chicago Press.

Delort, Robert (1993), "Notes sur les livrées en milieu de cour au XIVe siècle," in Philippe Contamine, Thierry Dutour, and Bertrand Schnerb (eds), *Commerce, finances et société (XIe–XVIe siècles): Recueil de travaux d'histoire médiévale offert à M. le professeur Henri Dubois*, Paris: Presses de l'Université de Paris-Sorbonne, 361–8.

Delphy, Christine (1993), "Rethinking Sex and Gender," *Women's Studies International Forum* 16 (1): 1–9.

De Marchi, Andrea (2005), *Autour de Lorenzo Veneziano: Fragments de polyptyques vénitiens du XIVe siècle*, Tours: Musée des beaux-arts: Silvano.

Denny-Brown, Andrea (2004), "Rips and Slits: The Torn Garment and the Medieval Self," in Catherine Richardson (ed.), *Clothing Culture, 1350–1650*, Aldershot and Burlington: Ashgate, 223–37.

— (2012), *Fashioning Change: The Trope of Clothing in High- and Late-Medieval England*, Columbus: The Ohio State University Press.

Deshman, Robert (1995), *The Benedictional of St. Aethelwold*, Princeton: Princeton University Press.

Dinshaw, Carolyn (1989), *Chaucer's Sexual Politics*, Madison: University of Wisconsin Press.

Dodds, Jerelyn. ed. (1992), *Al-Andalus: The Art of Islamic Spain*, New York: The Metropolitan Museum of Art.

Dommasnes, Liv Helga (1982), "Late Iron Age in Western Norway. Female Roles and Ranks as Deduced from an Analysis of Burial Customs," *Norwegian Archaeological Review* 15.1–2: 70–84.

Douglas, Mary (1984), *Purity and Danger: An Analysis of the Concepts of Pollution and Taboo*, London: Routledge.

Duffy, Eamon (1992), *The Stripping of the Altars: Traditional Religions in England 1400–1580*, New Haven: Yale University Press.

Dumolyn, Jan (2013), "Later Medieval and Early Modern Urban Elites: Social Categories and Social Dynamics," in Asenjo-González, *Urban Elites*, 3–18.

Easton, Martha (2012), "Uncovering the Meanings of Nudity in the Belles Heures of Jean, Duke of Berry," in Sherry C.M. Lindquist (ed.), *The Meanings of Nudity in Medieval Art*, Farnham: Ashgate, 149–82.

Edler de Roover, Florence (1950), "Lucchese Silks," *Ciba Review* 80: 2902–30.

Edmondson, J.C. and Alison Keith, eds (2008), *Roman Dress and the Fabrics of Roman Culture*, Toronto: University of Toronto Press.

Effros, Bonnie (2002), "Appearance and Ideology: Creating Distinctions between Clerics and Lay Persons in Early Medieval Gaul," in Koslin and Snyder, *Encountering Medieval Textiles*, 7–24.

— (2004), "Dressing conservatively: women's brooches as markers of ethnic identity?" in Leslie Brubaker and Julia M.H. Smith (eds), *Gender in the Early Medieval World: East and West 300–900*, Cambridge: Cambridge University Press, 165–84.

Eicher, Joanne B. and Mary E. Roach-Higgins (1992), "Definition and classification of dress: Implications for analysis of gender roles," in Ruth Barnes and Joanne B. Eicher (eds), *Dress and Gender: Making and Meaning*, New York: Berg, 8–28.

Einarsson, Bjarni F. (1994), *The Settlement of Iceland: A Critical Approach: Granastaðir and the Ecological Heritage*, Gothenburg: Gothenburg University, Dept. of Archaeology.

El-Cheikh, Nadia Maria (2004), *Byzantium Viewed by the Arabs*, Cambridge, MA: Harvard University Press.

Eldjárn, Kristján P. (1956), *Kuml og haugfè; ur heidnum sid á Íslandi*, Reykjavík: Bókaútgáfan Nordri.

Entwistle, Joanne (2000), *The Fashioned Body: Fashion, Dress and Modern Social Theory*, Cambridge: Polity Press.

d'Ettore, Kate (2009), "Clothing and Conflict in the Icelandic Family Sagas: Literary Convention and Discourse of Power," in *Medieval Clothing and Textiles* 5: 1–14.

Evans, Helen C., ed. (2004), *Byzantium: Faith and Power (1261–1557)*, New York: The Metropolitan Museum of Art.

Farmer, Sharon (2006), "*Biffes, Tiretaines*, and *Aumonières*: The Role of Paris in the International Textile Markets of the Thirteenth and Fourteenth Centuries," *Medieval Clothing and Textiles* 2: 72–89.

Fell, Christine, Cecily Clark, and Elizabeth Williams (1984), *Women in Anglo-Saxon England*, London: British Museum.

Feltham, Mark, and James Miller (2005), "Original Skin: Nudity and Obscenity in Dante's Inferno," in James Miller (ed.), *Dante and the Unorthodox: The Aesthetics of Transgression*, Waterloo, ON: Wilfrid Laurier University Press, 182–206.

Finke, Laurie A., and Martin B. Shichtman (2010), *Cinematic Illuminations: The Middle Ages on Film,* Baltimore: Johns Hopkins University Press.

Fissell, Mary Elizabeth (2004), *Vernacular Bodies: The Politics of Reproduction in Early Modern Britain*, Oxford: Oxford University Press.

Fitzhugh, William W., and Elisabeth I. Ward (2000), *Vikings: The North Atlantic Saga*, Washington: Smithsonian Institution Press.

Fleming, Robin (2007), "Acquiring, flaunting and destroying silk in late Anglo-Saxon England," *Early Medieval Europe* 15.2: 127–58.

Forbes R.J. (1971), *Studies in Ancient Technology* 8, Leiden: Brill, 56.

Franklin, Caryn et al. (2012), *Fashion: The Ultimate Book of Costume and Style*, London and New York: Dorling Kindersley.

Frick, Carole Collier (2005), *Dressing Renaissance Florence: Families, Fortunes, and Fine Clothing*, Baltimore: Johns Hopkins University Press.

Friedman, John Block (2005), "The Iconography of Dagged Clothing and Its Reception by Moralist Writers," in *Medieval Clothing and Textiles* 9: 121–38.

— (2010), *Breughel's Heavy Dancers: Transgressive Clothing, Class and Culture in the Late Middle Ages*, Syracuse: Syracuse University Press.

Garber, Marjorie (1992), *Vested Interests: Crossdressing and Cultural Anxiety,* New York: Routledge.

Garnier, François (1982), *Le Langage de l'image au Moyen Âge,* II: *Grammaire des gestes*, Paris: Le Léopard d'Or.

Garver, Valerie (2009), *Women and Aristocratic Culture in the Carolingian World*, Ithaca: Cornell University Press.

Geary, Patrick J. (2002), *The Myth of Nations: The Medieval Origins of Europe*, Princeton, NJ: Princeton University Press.

Geijer, Agnes (1938), *Die Textilfunde aus den Gräbern*. Doctoral thesis, Universitet Uppsala, Birka 3, Uppsala: Almqvist and Wiksell.

— (1979), *A History of Textile Art*, London: Pasold.

Geijer, Agnes, Anne Marie Franzén, and Margareta Nockert (1994), *Drottning Margaretas gyllene kjortel i Uppsala domkyrka/The Golden Gown of Queen Margareta in Uppsala Cathedral*, Stockholm: Kungl. Vitterhets historie och antikvitets akademien.

Gell, Alfred (1990), *Art and Agency: An Anthropological Theory*, Oxford: Clarendon Press.

Gelsinger, Bruce E. (1981), *Icelandic Enterprise: Commerce and Economy in the Middle Ages*, Columbia, SC: University of South Carolina Press.

Gérard-Marchant, Laurence (1995), "Compter et nommer l'étoffe À Florence Au Trecento (1343)," *Médiévales* 29 (automne): 87–104.

Gies, Frances, and Joseph Gies (1994), *Cathedral, Forge, and Waterwheel: Technology and Invention in the Middle Ages*, New York: HarperCollins.

Gilchrist, Roberta (2013), *Medieval Life: Archaeology and the Life Cours*, Woodbridge: Boydell.

González Arce, José Damián (1998), *Apariencia y poder: La legislación suntuaria castellana en los siglos XIII–XV*. Jaén: Universidad de Jaén.

Gordon, Stewart, ed. (2001), *Robes of Honor: The Medieval World of Investiture*, New York: Palgrave.

Gosden, Chris, and Chantal Knowles (2001), *Collecting Colonialism: Material Culture and Colonial Change*, Oxford: Berg.

Graham-Campbell, James (1980), *Viking Artefacts: A Select Catalogue*. London: British Museum Publications.

— (1994), *Cultural Atlas of the Viking World*, Oxford: Andromeda Oxford.

Grant, Annie (1988), "Animal resources," in Grenville Astill and Annie Grant (eds), *The Countryside of Medieval England*, Oxford: Blackwell, 149–87.

Green, Monica H. (2010), "Introduction," in Linda Kalof (ed.), *A Cultural History of the Human Body in the Medieval Age*, Oxford and New York: Berg.

Grew, Francis, Margrethe de Neergaard, and Susan Mitford (2006), *Shoes and Pattens*, 2nd ed., Medieval Finds From Excavations in London 2, Woodbridge: Boydell Press.

Guðjónsson, Elsa E. (1962), *Forn röggvarvefnaður*, Reykjavík: Árbók hins Íslenzka Fornleifafélags.

Guerrero-Navarrete, Yolanda (2013), "Gentlemen-Merchant in Fifteenth-Century Urban Castile: Forms of Life and Social Aspiration," in Asenjo-González, *Urban Elites*, 49–60.

Haas-Gebhard, Brigitte and Britt Nowak-Böck (2012), "The Unterhaching Grave Finds: Richly Dressed Burials from Sixth-Century Bavaria," *Medieval Clothing and Textiles* 8: 1–23.

Hafter, Daryl M., ed. (1995), *European Women and Preindustrial Craft*, Bloomington: Indiana University Press.

Hägg, Inga (1974), *Kvinnodräkten i Birka: livplaggens rekonstruktion på grundval av det arkeologiska materialet* Uppsala: Institute of North European Archeology.

— (1983), "Birkas orientaliska praktplagg," *Fornvännen* 78 (1983): 204–23.

— (1984a), *Die Textilfunde aus dem Hafen von Haithabu*, Mit Beiträgen von G. Grenander Nyberg, Neumünster: Wachholtz.

— (1984b), *Textilfunde aus der Siedlung und aus den Gräbern von Haithabu. Beschreibung und Gliederung*, Berichte über die Ausgrabungen in Haithabu, 29, Neumünster: Wachholtz.

Hansen, Karen Tranberg (2004), "The World in Dress: Anthropological Perspective on Clothing, Fashion, and Culture," *Annual Review of Anthropology* 33: 369–92.

Hansson, Anne-Marie and James Holms Dickson (1997), "Plant Remains in Sediment from the Björkö Strait Outside the Black Earth at the Viking Age Town of Birka, Eastern Central Sweden," in Urve Miller, Helen Clarke, Ann-Marie Hansson, Birgitta M. Johansson (eds), *Environment and Vikings with Special Reference to Birka*, PACT 52 = Birka Studies 4, Rixensart: PACT, 205–16.

Happé, Peter (1975), *English Mystery Plays: a selection*, Harmondsworth: Penguin.

Harmand, Adrien (1929), *Jeanne d'Arc, ses costumes, son armure: Essai de reconstitution*, Paris: Librairie E. Leroux.

Harris, Jennifer (1998), "'Estroit Vestu Et Menu Cosu': Evidence for the Construction of Twelfth-Century Dress," in Gale R. Owen-Crocker and Timothy Graham (eds), *Medieval Art: Recent Perspectives: A Memorial Tribute to C.R. Dodwell*, Manchester: Manchester University Press, 89–103.

Harte, Negley (1976), "State Control of Dress and Social Change in Pre-Industrial England," in D.C. Coleman, F.J. Fisher, and A.H. John (eds), *Trade, Government and Economy in Pre-Industrial England*, London: Weidenfeld and Nicolson, 132–65.

Hayeur Smith, Michèle (2003), "Dressing the Dead: Gender, Identity and Adornment in Viking-Age Iceland," in Shannon Lewis-Simpson (ed.), *Vinland Revisited: the Norse World at the Turn of the First Millennium*, St. John's, NL: Historic Sites Association of Newfoundland and Labrador, 227–40.

— (2004), *Draupnir's Sweat and Mardöll's Tears: An Archaeology of Jewellery, Gender and Identity in Viking Age Iceland*. Oxford, England: John and Erica Hedges.

— (2012), "Some in Rags, Some in Jags and Some in Silken Gowns: Textiles from Iceland's Early Modern Period," *International Journal of Historic Archaeology* 16.3: 509–28.

— (2013a), "Thorir's Bargain, Gender, Vaðmál and the Law," *World Archaeology* 45.5: 730–46.

— (2013b), "Viking Age Textiles in Iceland," paper presented at Félag fornleifafræðinga, Papers presented in honor of Kristján Eldjárn, December 6, Þjóðminjasafn Íslands, Reykjavík.

— (2014), "Dress, Cloth and the Farmer's Wife: Textile from Ø172, Tatsipataakilleq, Greenland with Comparative Data from Iceland," *Journal of the North Atlantic* 6 (sp. 6): 64–81.

— (2015), "Weaving Wealth: Cloth and Trade in Viking Age and Medieval Iceland," in A. Ling Huang and Carsten Jahnke (eds), *Textiles and the Medieval Economy, Production, Trade and Consumption of Textiles, 8th–16th Centuries.* Oxford, Oxbow Books, 23–40.

— (forthcoming), "Rumpelstiltskin's Feat: Cloth and Hanseatic Trade with Iceland," in *Hanseatic Trade in the North Atlantic*, conference held May 29 –1 June 1, 2013 in Avaldnes, Norway.

Hayward, Maria (2009), *Rich Apparel: Clothing and the Law in Henry VIII's England*, Burlington, VT: Ashgate.

Helgason, Agnar, et al. (2000), "mtDNA and the Origin of the Icelanders: Deciphering Signals of Recent Population History," *American Journal of Human Genetics* 66.3 999–1016.

Heller, Sarah-Grace (2004a), "Anxiety, Hierarchy, and Appearance in Thirteenth-Century Sumptuary Laws and the *Romance of the Rose*," *French Historical Studies* 27.2: 311–48.

— (2004b), "Limiting Yardage and Changes of Clothes: Sumptuary Legislation in Thirteenth-Century France, Languedoc, and Italy," in E. Jane Burns (ed.), *Medieval Fabrications: Dress, Textiles, Clothwork, and Other Cultural Imaginings*, New York: Palgrave MacMillan, 121–36.

— (2007), *Fashion in Medieval France*, Woodbridge: Boydell and Brewer.

— (2009a), "Fictions of Consumption: The Nascent Fashion System in *Partonopeus de Blois*," *Australian Journal of French Studies* 46.3: 191–205.

— (2009b), "Obscured Lands and Obscured Hands: Fairy Embroidery and Ambiguous Vocabulary of Medieval Textile Decoration," *Medieval Clothing and Textiles* 5: 15–35.

— (2015), "Angevin-Sicilian Sumptuary Statutes of the 1290s: Fashion in the Thirteenth-century Mediterranean," *Medieval Clothing and Textiles* 11: 79–97.

Henry, Philippa (2005), "Who produced Textiles? Changing Gender Roles," in Frances Pritchard and J.P. Wild (eds), *Northern Archaeological Textiles. NESAT 7*, Oxford: Oxbow, 51–7.

Herlihy, David (1990), *Opera muliebria: women and work in medieval Europe*, Philadelphia: Temple University Press.

Herlihy, David and Anthony Molho (1995), *Women, Family, and Society in Medieval Europe: historical essays, 1978–1991*, Providence, RI: Berghahn Books.

Hermanns-Auðardóttir, Margrét (1989), *Islands tidiga bosättning: studier med utgångspunkt i merovingertida-vikingatida gårdslämningar i Herjólfsdalur, Vestmannaeyjar, Island*, Umeå: Umeå Universitet Arkeologiska institutionen.

Hill, David and Robert Cowie, eds (2001), *Wics: the Early Medieval Trading Centres of Northern Europe*, Sheffield Archaeological Monographs 1, Sheffield: Sheffield Academic Press.

Hjálmarsson, Jón R. (1993), *History of Iceland: From the Settlement to the Present Day*, Reykjavík: Iceland Review.

Hodges, Laura (2000), *Chaucer and Costume: The Secular Pilgrims in the General Prologue*, Woodbridge, UK: Brewer.

Hodne, Lasse (2012), *The Virginity of the Virgin: A Study in Marian Iconography*, Rome: Scienze E Lettere.

Hoeniger, Cathleen (2006), "The Illuminated *Tacuinum sanitatis* Manuscripts from Northern Italy c. 1380–1400: Sources, Patrons, and the Creation of a New Pictorial Genre," in Jean

A. Givens, Karen M. Reeds, Alain Touwaide (eds), *Visualizing Medieval Medicine and Natural History, 1200–1550*, Aldershot and Burlington: Ashgate, 51–81.

Hoffmann, Marta (1964), *The Warp-weighted Loom: Studies in the History and Technology of an Ancient Implement*, Studia Norvegica 14, Oslo: Universitetsforlaget.

Hollander, Anne (1995), *Sex and Suits: The Evolution of Modern Dress*, New York: Kodansha International.

— (2002), *Fabric of Vision: Dress and Drapery in Painting*, London/New Haven: National Gallery Company/Yale University Press.

— (2012), "The Dress of Thought: Clothing and Nudity in Homer, Virgil, Dante, and Ariosto," in Cristina Giorcelli and Paula Rabinowitz (eds), *Exchanging Clothes: Habits of Being 2*, Minneapolis: University of Minnesota Press, 40–57.

Holmes, Urban T., Jr. (1952), *Daily Living in the Twelfth Century. Based on the Observations of Alexander Neckham in London and Paris*, Madison, WI: University of Wisconsin Press.

Hopkins, Amanda (2000), "Veiling the Text: The True Role of the Cloth in *Emaré*," in Judith Weiss, Jennifer Fellows, and Morgan Dickson (eds), *Medieval Insular Romance: Translation and Innovation*, Cambridge: Brewer, 71–83.

Hotchkiss, Valerie R. (1996), *Clothes Make the Man: Female Cross Dressing in Medieval Europe*, New York: Garland.

Howard, Elizabeth (2007), "The Clothes Make the Man: Transgressive Disrobing and Disarming in *Beowulf*," in Cynthia Kuhn and Cindy Carlson (eds), *Styling Texts: Dress and Fashion in Literature*, Youngstown, NY: Cambria, 13–32.

Howell, Martha C. (2010), *Commerce Before Capitalism in Europe, 1300–1600*, Cambridge University Press.

Huang, Angela Ling and Carsten Jahnke (2015), *Textiles and the Medieval Economy: Production, Trade and Consumption of Textiles, 8th–16th Centuries*, Oxford: Oxbow.

Hughes, Diane Owen (1983), "Sumptuary Law and Social Relations in Renaissance Italy," in John Bossy (ed.), *Disputes and Settlements: Law and Human Relations in the West*, Cambridge: Cambridge University Press, 69–100.

— (1986), "Distinguishing Signs: Ear-Rings, Jews and Franciscan Rhetoric in the Italian Renaissance City," *Past & Present* 112 (August): 3–59.

— (1992–4), "Regulating Women's Fashion," in Christiane Klapisch-Zuber (ed.), *Silences of the Middle Age*, Vol. 2 of *A History of Women in the West*, Georges Duby and Michelle Perrot (eds), Cambridge, MA: Belknap Press, 136–58.

Hunt, Alan (1996), *Governance of the Consuming Passions: A History of Sumptuary Law*, New York: St. Martin's Press.

Hunt, Tony (1991), *Teaching and Learning Latin in the Thirteenth Century*, 3 vols., Cambridge: D.S. Brewer.

Isaacs, Harold R. (1975), "Basic Group Identity: The Idols of the Tribe," in Nathan Glazer, Daniel P. Moynihan, and Corinne Saposs Schelling (eds), *Ethnicity: Theory, and Experience*, Cambridge: Harvard University Press, 29–52.

Jacobs, Jane (1995), *Cities and the Wealth of Nations: Principles of Economic Life*, New York: Vintage.

Jacoby, David (1997), *Trade, Commodities and Shipping in the Medieval Mediterranean*, Aldershot: Variorum.

Jaeger, C. Stephen (1985), *The Origins of Courtliness: Civilizing Trends and the Formation of Courtly Ideals, 939–1210*, Philadelphia: University of Pennsylvania Press.

Jager, Erik (1993), *The Tempter's Voice: Language and the Fall in Medieval Literature*, Ithaca, NY: Cornell University Press.

Jahnke, Carsten (2009), "Some aspects of Medieval Cloth Trade in the Baltic Sea Area," in Vestergård Pedersen and Nosch (eds), *The Medieval Broadcloth*, Vol. 6, 74–89.

Jansson, Ingmar (1985), *Ovala spännbucklor: en studie av vikingatida standardsmycken med utgangspunkt fran Björköfynden/Oval brooches: a study of Viking period standard jewellery based on the finds from Björkö Sweden*, Uppsala: University of Uppsala Institutionen for arkeologi.

Jesch, Judith (1991), *Women in the Viking Age*, Woodbridge: Boydell Press, 1991.

Jochens, Jenny (1995), *Women in Old Norse Society*, Ithaca: Cornell University Press.

Jones, Tom Devonshire and Peter and Linda Murray (2013), *The Oxford Dictionary of Christian Art and Architecture,* 2nd ed., Oxford: Oxford University Press.

Justice, Alan D. (1979), "Trade Symbolism in the York Cycle," *Theatre Journal* 31.1 (March): 47–58.

Kaiser, Susan B. (1998), *The Social Psychology of Clothing: Symbolic Appearances in Context*, 2nd ed., revised. New York: Fairchild Publications.

Kelly, Douglas (1992), *The Art of Medieval French Romance*, Madison, WI: University of Wisconsin Press.

Kershaw, Ian (1973), *Bolton Priory: The Economy of a Northern Monastery, 1286–1325*, Oxford: Oxford University Press.

Killerby, Catherine Kovesi (2002), *Sumptuary Law in Italy 1200–1500*, Oxford: Oxford University Press.

Kinoshita, Sharon (2004), "Almería Silk and the French Feudal Imaginary: Toward a 'Material' History of the Medieval Mediterranean," in E.J. Burns (ed.), *Medieval Fabrications: Dress, Textiles, Cloth Work, and Other Cultural Imaginings*, New York: Palgrave, 165–76.

Kirjavainen, Heini (2009), "A Finnish Archaeological Perspective on Medieval Broadcloth," in Vestergård Pedersen and Nosch (eds), *The Medieval Broadcloth*, Vol. 6, 90–8.

Koslin, Désirée (2002), "Value-added Stuffs and Shifts in Meaning: An Overview and Case Study of Medieval Textile Paradigms," in Koslin and Snyder (eds), *Encountering Medieval Textiles and Dress,* New York: Palgrave MacMillan, 233–49.

Koslin, Désirée, and Janet Snyder, eds (2002), *Encountering Medieval Textiles and Dress: Objects, Texts, Images*, New York: Palgrave MacMillan.

Krueger, Robert L. (2004), "Uncovering Griselda: Christine de Pizan, 'une seule chemise,' and the Clerical Tradition: Boccaccio, Petrarch, Philippe de Mézières and the *Ménagier de Paris*," in Burns, *Medieval Fabrication*, 71–88.

Lachaud, Frédérique (1996), "Liveries of Robes in England, c. 1200–c. 1330," *The English Historical Review* 111.441, 279–98.

Lacy, Norris J. (1980), *The Craft of Chrétien de Troyes: An Essay on Narrative Art*, Leiden: Brill.

Ladd, Roger A. (2010), "The London Mercer's Company, London Textual Culture, and John Gower's *Mirour de l'Omme*," *Medieval Clothing and Textiles* 6: 127–50.

Laforce, F. Marc. (1978), "Woolsorters' disease in England," *Bulletin of the New York Academy of Medicine*, Vol. 54.10: 957. Accessed 1 February 2010 from http://www.ncbi.nlm.nih.gov/pmc/articles/PMC1807561/pdf/bullnyacadmed00135-0058.pdf.

Lallouette, Anne-Laure (2006), "Bains et soins du corps dans les textes médicaux (XIIe–XIVe)," in Sophie Albert (ed.), *Laver, monder, blanchir: Discours et usages de la toilette dans l'occident médiéval,* Paris: Presses de l'Université Paris-Sorbonne, 33–49.

Lambden, Stephen N. (1992), "From Fig Leaves to Fingernails: Some Notes on the Garments of Adam and Eve in the Hebrew Bible and Select Early Postbiblical Jewish Writings," in Paul Morris and Deborah Sawyer (eds), *A Walk in the Garden: Biblical, Iconographical and*

Literary Images of Eden, Journal for the Study of the Old Testament, Supplement Series 136: 74–90.

Lansing, Carol (2008), *Passion and Order: Restraint of Grief in the Medieval Italian Communes*, Ithaca: Cornell University Press.

Larsson, Annika (2008), "Viking Age Textiles," in Stefan Brink and Neil Price (eds), *The Viking World*, New York: Routledge, 181–5.

Lebecq, Stéfane (1997), "Routes of change: Production and distribution in the West (5th–8th century)," in L. Webster and M. Brown (eds), *The Transformation of the Roman World AD 400–900*, Berkeley: University of California Press, 67–78.

LeGoff, Jacques (1988), *Medieval Civilization 400–1500*, trans. Julia Barrow, Oxford: Basil Blackwell.

Lévi-Provençal, Evariste (1953), *Histoire de l'Espagne musulmane*, Vol. 3: *Le Siécle du Califat de Cordoue*, Leiden: Brill.

Lewis, Christopher P., and A.T. Thacker, eds (2003), *A History of the County of Chester*, Vol. V, Part 1: The City of Chester: General History and Topography, London: Boydell and Brewer.

Leyser, Conrad (2011), "From Maternal Kin to Jesus as Mother," in Conrad Leyer and Lesley Smith (eds), *Motherhood, Religion and Society in Medieval Europe, 400–1400*. Aldershot and Burlington: Ashgate, 21–40.

Lipovetsky, Gilles (1987), *L'Empire de l'éphémère: La mode et son destin dans les sociétés modernes*, Paris: Gallimard.

— (2004), *The Empire of Fashion: Dressing Modern Democracy*, trans. Catherine Porter, Princeton: Princeton University Press.

Lloyd, T. (1978), "Husbandry practices and disease in medieval sheep flocks," *Veterinary History* 10: 3–13.

Lopez, Robert S. (1945), "Silk Industry in the Byzantine Empire," *Speculum* 20.1: 1–42.

— (1971), *The Commercial Revolution of the Middle Ages, 950–1350*, Englewood Cliffs, NJ: Prentice-Hall.

Lorenzo, Amalia Descalzo (2010), "Les vêtements royaux du monastère Santa Maria la Real de Huelgas," in Rainer C. Schwinges and Regula Schorta (eds), *Fashion and Clothing in Late Medieval Europe*, Riggisberg and Basel: Abegg-Stiftung, 97–106.

Lucas, Gavin (2009), "The Tensions of Modernity: Skálholt during the 17th and 18th centuries," *Archaeologies of the Early Modern North Atlantic, Journal of the North Atlantic* 2, special Vol. 1: 75–88.

Madden, Thomas F. (2012), *Venice: A New History*, New York: Viking.

Marks, Richard and Paul Williamson, eds (2003), *Gothic: Art for England 1400–1547*, London: V&A Publications.

Marshall, Claire (2000), "The Politics of Self-Mutilation: Forms of Female Devotion in the Late Middle Ages," in Darryll Grantley and Nina Taunton (eds), *The Body in Late Medieval and Early Modern Culture*, Aldershot and Burlington: Ashgate.

Mårtensson, Linda, M.-L. Nosch, and Eva B. Andersson Strand (2009), "Shape of Things: Understanding a Loom Weight," *Oxford Journal of Archaeology* 28:4: 373–98.

Marti, Susan, ed. (2005), *Krone und Schleier: Kunst aus Mittelalterlichen Frauenklöstern*, Bonn: Ruhrlandmuseum.

Marti, Susan, et al. eds (2008), *Splendour of the Burgundian Court: Charles the Bold 1422–1477*, Berne: Mercatorfonds.

Martin, Hervé (2001), *Mentalités médiévales II: Représentations collectives du XIe au XVe siècle*, Coll. Nouvelle Clio: l'histoire et ses problèmes, Paris: PUF.

Mastykova, Anna, Christian Pilet, and Alexandre Egorkov (2005), "Les perles multicolores d'origine méditerranéenne provenant de la nécropole mérovingienne de Saint-Martin de Fontenay (Calvados)," *Bulletin Archéologique de Provence* supp. 3: 299–311.

Mazzaoui, Maureen Fennell (1981), *The Italian Cotton Industry in the Later Middle Ages 1100–1600*, Cambridge: Cambridge University Press.

McGovern, Thomas (1980), "Cows, Harp Seals, and Churchbells: Adaptation and Extinction in Norse Greenland." *Human Ecology* 8.3 (1980): 245–275.

— (2000), "The Demise of Norse Greenland," in William W. Fitzhugh and Elizabeth I. Ward (eds), *Vikings, The North Atlantic Saga*, Washington: Smithsonian Institution Press, 327–39.

McNamara, Jo Ann (1996), *Sisters in Arms: Catholic Nuns Through Two Millennia*, Cambridge, MA: Harvard University Press.

McNamara, Jo Ann and John E. Halborg, eds and trans. (1992), *Sainted Women of the Dark Ages*, Durham: Duke University Press.

Mellinkoff, Ruth (1993), *Outcasts: Signs of Otherness in the Northern European Art of the Middle Ages*, 2 vols., Berkeley: University of California Press.

Mérindol, Christian de (1989), "Signes de hiérarchie sociale à la fin du Moyen Âge d'après les vêtements: méthodes et recherches," in *Le Vêtement*, Paris: Léopard d'Or, 181–224.

Merrick, P. (1997), "The administration of the ulnage and subsidy on woollen cloth between 1394 and 1485, with a case study in Hampshire," MPhil thesis, University of Southampton.

Meulengracht Sørensen, Preben (1983), *The Unmanly Man: Concepts of Sexual Defamation in Early Northern Society*, Odense: Odense University Press.

Miller, Christopher L., and George R. Hamell (1986), "A New Perspective on Indian-White Contact: Cultural Symbols, and Colonial Trade," *The Journal of American History* 73.2: 311–28.

Miller, Daniel (2000), *Stuff*, Cambridge: Polity.

— (2005), "Introduction," in Susanne Küchler and Daniel Miller (eds), *Clothing as Material Culture*, Oxford: Berg Publishing, 1–19.

Miller, Maureen C. (2014), *Clothing the Clergy: Virtue and Power in Medieval Europe, c. 800–1200*. Ithaca, NY: Cornell University Press.

Millet, Bella and Jocelyn Wogan-Browne, eds and trans. (1990), *Medieval English Prose for Women: From the Katherine Group and* Ancrene Wisse, Oxford: Clarendon Press.

Minar, C. Jill (2001), "Motor Skills and the Learning Process: The Conservation of Cordage Final Twist Direction in Communities of Practice," *Journal of Anthropological Research, Learning, and Craft Production* 57.4: 381–405.

Molà, Luca (2003), "Leggi suntuarie in Veneto," in Muzzarelli and Campanini (eds), *Disciplinare il lusso*, 47–58.

Monnas, Lisa (2008), *Merchants, Princes and Painters: Silk Fabrics in Italian and Northern Paintings 1300–1550*, New Haven: Yale University Press.

Moore, R.I. (2007), *The Formation of a Persecuting Society: Power and Deviance in Western Europe, 950–1250*, 2nd ed., Malden MA: Blackwell Publishing.

Munro, John H. (2003), "Medieval woolen textiles, textile technology and industrial organisation, c. 800–1500," in David Jenkins (ed.), *The Cambridge History of Western Textiles* Cambridge: Cambridge University Press, Vol. 1, 181–227.

— (2009), "Three Centuries of Luxury Textile Consumption in the Low Countries and England, 1330–1570: Trends and Comparisons of Real Values of Woollen Broadcloths (Then and Now)," in Vestergård Pedersen and Nosch (eds), *The Medieval Broadcloth*, 1–73.

Muthesius, Anna (1982), "The silk fragment from 5 Coppergate," in A. MacGregor (ed.), *Anglo-Scandinavian finds from Lloyds Bank, Pavement and other sites*, The Archaeology of

York, 17.3, London: Published for the York Archaeological Trust by the Council for British Archaeology, 132–6.

Muzzarelli, Maria Giuseppina (2009), "Reconciling the Privilege of a Few with the Common Good: Sumptuary Laws in Medieval and Early Modern Europe," *Journal of Medieval and Early Modern Studies* 39, no. 3 (2009): 597–617.

Muzzarelli, Maria Giuseppina and Antonella Campanini, eds (2003), *Disciplinare il lusso: La legislazione suntuaria in Italia e in Europa tra medioevo ed età moderna*, Rome: Carocci.

— "Una società nello specchio della legislazione suntuaria: Il caso dell'Emilia-Romagna."

Netherton, Robin (2008), "The View from Herjolfnes: Greenland's Translation of the European Fitted Fashion," *Medieval Clothing and Textiles* 4: 143–71.

Newbold, Ron F. (2005), "Attire in Ammianus and Gregory of Tours," *Studia Humaniora Tartuensia* 6.A.4: 1–14.

Newett, Mary Margaret (1907), "The Sumptuary Laws of Venice in the Fourteenth and Fiffteenth Centuries," in T.F. Tout and James Tait (eds), *Historical Essays by Members of the Owens College, Manchester*, Manchester: University of Manchester Press, 245–78.

Newman, Barbara (1995), *From Virile Woman to Womanchrist: Studies in Medieval Religion and Literature*, Philadelphia: University of Pennsylvania Press.

Newton, Stella Mary (1980; reprint, 1990), *Fashion in the Age of the Black Prince: A Study of the Years 1340–1365*, Woodbridge, Boydell.

Nicholson, Karen (2015), "The Effect of Spindle Whorl Design on Wool Thread Production: A Practical Experiment Based on Examples from Eighth-Century Denmark," *Medieval Clothing and Textiles* 11: 29–48.

Nielsen, Leif-Christian (1990), *Trelleborg*, Aarbøger: København.

Nilson, Ben (1998), *Cathedral Shrines of Medieval England*, Woodbridge: Boydell Press.

Nockert, Margareta (1989), "Vid Sidenvägens ände. Textilier från Palmyra till Birka," in Pontus Hellström, Margareta Nockert, and Suzanne Unge (eds), *Palmyra. Öknens drottning*, Stockholm: Medelhavsmuseet, 77–105.

Nockert, Margareta and Dag Fredriksson (1985), *Bockstensmannen och hans dräkt*, Varberg: Stiftelsen Hallands länsmuseer, Halmstad och Varberg.

Noweir, Madbuli H. et al. (1975), "Dust Exposure in manual flax processing in Egypt," *British Journal of Industrial Medicine* 32: 147–54 (accessed January 28, 2010 from http://www.ncbi.nlm.nih.gov/pmc/articles/PMC1008040/pdf/brjindmedooo86-0055.pdf).

Oldland, John (2013), "Cistercian Clothing and Its Production at Beaulieu Abbey, 1269–70," *Medieval Clothing and Textiles* 9: 73–96.

Oliver, Judith H. (2007), *Singing with Angels: Liturgy, Music, and Art in the Gradual of Gisela von Kerssenbrock*, Leiden: Brepols.

Ormrod, W. Mark (2005), "Introduction, Parliament of 1363," in *Edward III, 1351–1377*, ed. W.M. Ormrod, Vol. 5 of *The Parliament Rolls of Medieval England, 1275–1504*, 16 vols., ed. C. Given-Wilson, Woodbridge, Boydell Press, 155–7.

Østergård, Else (1998), "The Textiles – a Preliminary Report," in *Man, Culture and Environment in Ancient Greenland: Report on a Research Programme*, Jette Arneborg and Hans Christian Gulløv (eds), Copenhagen: The Danish National Museum and Danish Polar Centre, 55–65.

— (2003), *Som syet til jorden: tekstilfund fra det norrøne Grønland*, Aarhus: Aarhus universitatsforlag.

— (2004), *Woven into the Earth: Textiles from Norse Greenland*, Aarhus: Aarhus University Press.

— (2005), "The Greenlandic Vaðmál," in *Northern Archaeological Textiles: NESAT VII, textile symposium in Edinburgh, 5th–7th May 1999*, Frances Pritchard and Peter Wilds (eds), 80–3.

Owen, Olwyn and Magnar Dalland (1999), *Scar: A Viking Boat Burial on Sanday, Orkney*, East Linton: Tuckwell Press in association with Historic Scotland.

Owen-Crocker, Gale R. (2004), *Dress in Anglo-Saxon England*, revised and enlarged edition, Manchester: Manchester University Press; Woodbridge: Boydell and Brewer.

Owen-Crocker, Gale R., Elizabeth Coatsworth and Maria Hayward, eds (2012), *Encyclopedia of Medieval Dress and Textiles of the British Isles c. 450–1450*, Leiden: Brill.

Owst, G. R. (1933; reprint 1961), *Literature and Pulpit in Medieval England,* Cambridge: Cambridge University Press; Oxford: Basil Blackwell.

Øye, Ingvild (1988), *Textile Equipment and its Working Environment, Bryggen in Bergen c. 1150–1500*, The Bryggen Papers, Main Series 2, Bergen: Norwegian University Press.

Page, Agnès (1993), *Vêtir le Prince: Tissus et couleurs à la cour de Savoie (1427–1447)*, Lausanne: Université de Lausanne.

Parani, Maria G. (2003), *Reconstructing the Reality of Images: Byzantine Material Culture and Religious Iconography 11th–15th Centuries*, Leiden: Brill.

Pastoureau, Michel, ed. (1989), *Le Vêtement: Histoire, archéologie et symboliques vestimentaires au Moyen Âge*, Cahiers du Léopard d'Or 1, Paris: Léopard d'Or.

Pastoureau, Michel (2001), *Blue: the history of a color*, Markus Cruse (trans.), Princeton, NJ: Princeton University Press.

Paterson, Caroline (1997), "The Viking Age Trefoil Mounts from Jarlshof: a Reappraisal in the Light of Two New Discoveries," *Proceedings of the Society of Antiquaries of Scotland* 127: 649–57.

Pedersen, Anne, Stig Welinder, and Mats Widgren, eds (1998), *Jordbrukets första femtusen år, 4000 f. Kr.–1000 e. Kr*, Stockholm: NOK-LTs förlag.

Périn, Patrick, et al. (2009), "Enquête sur les Mérovingiens," *Histoire et images médiévales* 25: 14–27.

Perkinson, Stephen (2012), "Likeness," in *Studies in Iconography* 33: 14–28.

Phillips, Kim M (2007), "Masculinities and the Medieval English Sumptuary Laws," *Gender & History* 19, no. 1 (2007): 22–42.

Piponnier, Françoise (1989), "Une révolution dans le costume masculin au XIVe siècle," in Pastoureau (ed.), *Le Vêtement,* 225–42.

Piponnier, Françoise and Perrine Mane (1995), *Se vêtir Au Moyen Âge*, Paris: Adam Biro.

Platelle, Henri (1975), "Le problème du scandale: Les nouvelles modes masculines aux XIe et XIIe siècles," *Revue belge de philologie et d'histoire* 53, no. fasc. 4: 1071–96.

Poirion, Daniel and Claude Thomasset, eds (1995), *L'art de vivre au Moyen Âge: Codex vindobonensis series nova 2644, conservé à la Bibliothèque nationale d'Autriche.* Paris: Editions du Félin.

Polhemus, Ted, and Lynn Procter (1978), *Fashion & Anti-Fashion: Anthropology of Clothing and Adornment*, London: Thames & Hudson.

Post, Paul (1910), "Die französisch-niederländische Männertracht einschliesslich der Ritterrüstung im Zeitalter der Spätgotik, 1350–1475. Ein Rekonstruktionsversuch auf Gründ der zeitgenössichen Darstellungen," Halle a. d. Saale, Dissertation.

Þorláksson, Helgi (1981), "Arbeidskvinnens, särlig veverskens, økonomiske stilling på Island i middelalder," in Hedda Gunneng, and Birgit Strand (eds), *Kvinnans ekonomiska ställning under nordisk medeltid,* Gothenberg: Strand, 50–65.

— (1991), *Vaðmál og verðlag: vaðmál í utanlandsviðskiptum og búskap Íslendinga á 13. og 14. öld*, Reykjavik, Háskóli Íslands.

— (1999), *Sjórán og siglingar: ensk-íslensk samskipti 1580–1630*, Reykjavík: Mál og menning.

Power, Eileen (1942), *The Wool Trade in English Medieval History, Being the Ford Lectures*, Oxford: Oxford University Press.

Price, Neil S. (2002), *The Viking Way: religion and war in late Iron Age Scandinavia*, Uppsala: Dept. of Archaeology and Ancient History.

Price, T. Douglas and Hildur Gestsdottir (2006), "The First Settlers of Iceland: an isotopic approach to colonization," *Antiquity* 80: 130–44.

Pritchard, Frances (2003), "The uses of textiles, c. 1000–1500," in D. Jenkins (ed.), *The Cambridge History of Western Textiles*, 2 vols., Cambridge: Cambridge University Press, Vol. 1, 355–77.

Pulliam, Heather (2012), "Color," *Studies in Iconography* 33: 3–14.

Quicherat, Jules (1875), *Histoire du costume en France depuis le temps les plus reculés jusqu'à la fin du XVIIIe siècle*, Paris: Hachette.

Rainey, Ronald E. (1985), "Sumptuary Legislation in Renaissance Florence," Ph.D. dissertation, Columbia University.

Reid, Patricia Margaret (2003), "Embodied Identity as Process: Performativity through Footwear in Mid-Medieval (AD 800–1200) Northern Europe," D.Phil. dissertation, Institute of Archaeology, University College, London.

Renn, George A. (1988), "Chaucer's 'Prologue'." *Explicator* 46.3: 4–7.

Reuling, Hanneke (2006), *After Eden: Church Fathers and Rabbis on Genesis 3:16–21*. Leiden: Brill.

Reyerson, Kathryn (1992), "Medieval Silks in Montpellier: The Silk Market c. 1250–1350," *Journal of Economic History* 11: 117–40.

Richard, Jules Marie (1887; 2010/2013), *Mahaut, comtesse d'Artois et de Bourgogne, 1302–1329. Une petite-nièce de Saint-Louis : étude sur la vie privée, les arts et l'industrie, en Artois et à Paris au commencement du XIVe siècle*, Paris: Champion; Cressé: Editions des Régionalismes.

Richardson, Catherine (2004), *Clothing Culture, 1350–1650*, Aldershot: Ashgate.

Ricks, Steven D. (2000), "The Garment of Adam in Jewish, Muslim, and Christian Tradition," in *Judaism and Islam: Boundaries, Communication and Interaction. Essays in Honor of William M. Brinner*, Leiden: Brill, 203–25.

Rigby, S.H. (1995), *English Society in the Later Middle Ages: Class, Status and Gender*, London: Macmillan Press.

— (1999), "Approaches to Pre-Industrial Social Structure," in J.H. Denton (ed.), *Orders and Hierarchies in Late Medieval and Renaissance Europe*. Toronto: University of Toronto Press, 6–25.

Riley, Denise (1988), *Am I that Name? Feminism and the Category of "Women" in History*, Minneapolis: University of Minnesota Press.

Riley, H.T., ed. (1868), *Memorials of London and London Life: In the 13th, 14th, and 15th Centuries. Being a Series of Extracts, Local, Social, and Political, from the Early Archives of the City of London, A.D. 1276–1419*, London: Longmans, Green and Co., 1868, in British History Online, http://www.british-history.ac.uk/report.aspx?compid=57692 [accessed August 26, 2014].

Riu, Manuel (1983), "The Woollen Industry in Catalonia in the Later Middle Ages," in N. Harte and K. G. Ponting (eds), *Cloth and Clothing in Medieval Europe: Essays in Memory of Prof. E. M. Carus-Wilson*, Pasold Studies in Textile History 2, London: Heinemann Educational, 205–29.

Roach-Higgins, Mary Ellen, and Joanne B. Eicher (1992), "Dress and Identity," *Clothing and Textiles Research Journal* 10: 1–8.

Róbertsdóttir, Hrefna (2008), *Wool and Society: Manufacturing Policy, Economic Thought and Local Production in 18th-Century Iceland*, Göteborg: Makadam.

Roover, Raymond de. (1969), "The Commercial Revolution of the Thirteenth Century," originally published in *Bulletin of the Business Historical Society*, 1942, reprinted in A. Molho (ed.), *Social and Economic Foundations of the Italian Renaissance*, New York: Wiley.

Rowe, Nina, guest ed. (2012), *Studies in Iconography: Medieval Art History Today – Critical Terms* 33.

Rubin, Miri (2009), *Mother of God: A History of the Virgin Mary*, London: Allen Lane.

Ryder, M.L. (1981), "British Medieval sheep and their wool types," in D.W. Crossley (ed.), *Medieval Industry*, Council for British Archeology, Research Report 40, London: 16–27.

Samples, Susann (2006), "The German Heroic Narratives," in Will Hasty (ed.), *German Literature of the High Middle Ages*, Woodbridge: Camden House, 161–83.

Sand, Alexa (2005), "Vision, Devotion and Difficulty in the Psalter-Hours of 'Yolande of Soissons'," *Art Bulletin* 87.1: 6–23.

Schmitt, Jean-Claude (1990), *La Raison de gestes dans l'Occident médiéval*, Paris: Gallimard.

Schotter, Anne Howland (1979), "The Poetic Function of Alliterative Formulas of Clothing in the Portrait of the Pearl Maiden," *Studia Neophilologica* 51: 189–95.

Schulze, Mechthilde (1976), "Einflusse byzantinischer Prunkgewander auf die frankische Frauentracht," *Archeologhische Korrespondanzblatt* 6.2: 149–161.

Seiler-Baldinger, Anne-Marie (1994), *Textiles: a classification of techniques*, Bathurst: Crawford House.

Serjeant, R.B. (1972), *Islamic Textiles, Material for a History Up to the Mongol Conquest*, Beirut: Librairie du Liban.

Shahar, Shulamith (2003), *Fourth Estate: A History of Women in the Middle Ages*, London: Routledge.

Sherman, Heidi M. (2004), "From Flax to Linen in the Medieval Rus Lands," *Medieval Clothing and Textiles* 4: 1–20.

Silverman, Eric Kline (2013), *A Cultural History of Jewish Dress*, London: Bloomsbury.

Smith, Katherine Allen (2011), *War and the Making of Medieval Monastic Culture*, Woodbridge: Boydell.

Smith, Kathryn (2003), *Art, Identity and Devotion in Fourteenth-Century England: Three Women and Their Books of Hours*, Toronto, University of Toronto Press.

Snyder, Janet (2002), "From Content to Form: Court Clothing in Mid-Twelfth-Century Northern French Sculpture," in Koslin and Snyder, (eds) *Encountering Medieval Textiles and Dress*, 85–102.

Solberg, Bergljot (1985), "Social Status in the Merovingian and Viking Periods in Norway from Archaeological and Historical Sources," *Norwegian Archaeological Review* 18.1–2: 61–76.

Sponsler, Claire (1992), "Narrating the Social Order: Medieval Clothing Laws," *CLIO* 21: 265–83.

— (1997), *Drama and Resistance: Bodies, Goods, and Theatricality in Late Medieval England*, Minneapolis: University of Minnesota Press.

Spufford, Peter (2003), *Power and Profit: The Merchant in Medieval Europe*, New York: Thames & Hudson.

Steele, Valerie (1996), *Fetish: Fashion, Sex and Power*, New York, Oxford University Press.

Strutt, Joseph (1842; 1970), *A Complete View of the Dress and Habits of the People of England*, 2 vols., London; reprint The Tabard Press.

Stuard, Susan Mosher (2006), *Gilding the Market: Luxury and Fashion in Fourteenth-Century Italy*, Philadelphia: University of Pennsylvania Press.

Sturm-Maddox, Sara, and Donald Maddox (1984), "Description in Medieval Narrative: Vestimentary Coherence in Chrétien's *Erec et Enide*," *Medioevo Romanzo* 9.1: 51–64.

Sutton, Anne (1995), "The *Tumbling Bear* and Its Patrons: A Venue for the London Puy and Mercery," in Julia Boffey and Pamela King (eds), *London and Europe in the Later Middle Ages*, London: Centre for Medieval and Renaissance studies of Queen Mary and Westfield College, 85–110.

Svanberg, Fredrik, Bengt Söderberg, Eva Andersson, and Torbjörn Brorsson (2000), *Porten till Skåne: Löddeköpinge under järnålder och medeltid*, Lund: Riksantikvarieämbetet, Avdelningen för arkeologiska undersökningar.

Swann, Jan (2010), "English and European Shoes from 1200 to 1520," in Rainer C. Schwinges (ed.), *Fashion and Clothing in Late Medieval Europe – Mode und Kleidung im Europa des späten Mittelalters*, Riggisberg: Abeg-Stiftung.

Strömberg, Elisabeth, Agnes Geijer, M. Hald, and Marta Hoffmann (1967; reprint 1979), *Nordisk textilteknisk terminologi*, Lyon: CIETA; Oslo: Tanum.

Sylvester, Louise, Mark C. Chambers, and Gale R. Owen-Crocker, eds (2014), *Dress and Textiles in Medieval Britain: A Multilingual Sourcebook*, Woodbridge, Boydell.

Tajfel, Henri, and John Turner (1979), "An Integrative Theory of Intergroup Conflict," in William G. Austin and Stephen Worchel (eds), *The Social Psychology of Intergroup Relations*, Monterey CA: Brooks/Cole Publishing Co, 33–47.

(Anon.) (1963), "(A) Thirteenth-Century Castilian Sumptuary Law," *The Business History Review* 37, no. 1/2: 98–100.

Toaff, Ariel (2003), "La prammatica degli ebrei e per gli ebrei," in Muzzarelli and Campanini (eds), *Disciplinare il lusso*, 91–108.

Turner, Terence (1993), "The Social Skin," in C.B. Burroughs and J. D. Ehrenreich (eds), *Reading the Social Body*, Iowa City: University of Iowa Press, 15–39.

Vale, Malcolm (2000), *The Princely Court: Medieval Courts and Culture in North-West Europe 1270–1380*, Oxford: Oxford University Press.

Vecellio, Cesare (1590; reprint 1977), *Vecellio's Renaissance Costume Book/De gli Habiti antichi et moderni de Diversi Parte del Mundo*, New York: Dover Publications.

Vésteinsson, Orri (2007), "The North Expansion Across the North Atlantic," in J. Graham-Campbell and M. Valor (eds), *The Archaeology of Medieval Europe*, Aarhus: Aarhus University Press, Vol. 1, 52–7.

Vestergård Pedersen, Kathrine, and Marie-Louise Nosch (2009), *The Medieval Broadcloth: Changing Trends in Fashions, Manufacturing and Consumption*, Oxford: Oxbow Books.

Vincent, Susan J. (2003), *Dressing the Elite: Clothes in Early Modern England*, Oxford: Berg Publishing.

Waller, Gary (2011), *The Virgin Mary in Late Medieval and Early Modern English Literature and Popular Culture*, Cambridge: Cambridge University Press.

Walton, Penelope (1989), *Textiles, Cordage and Raw Fibre from 16–22 Coppergate*, The Archaeology of York 17.5, London: Published for the York Archaeological Trust by the Council for British Archaeology.

— (1991), "Textiles," in J. Blair and N. Ramsay (eds), *English Medieval Industries: craftsmen, techniques, products*, London and Rio Grande: Hambledon, 319–54.

— (1997), *Textile Production at 16–22 Coppergate,* The Archeology of York, Vol. 17, fasc. 11, York: Council for British Archeology.

— (2003), "The Anglo-Saxons and Vikings in Britain, AD 450–1050," in David Jenkins. (ed.), *The Cambridge History of Western Textiles*, Cambridge: Cambridge University Press, Vol. 1, 124–32.

— (2007), *Cloth and Clothing in Early Anglo-Saxon England, AD 450–700*, York: Council for British Archaeology.

— (2013), *Tyttels Halh: The Anglo-Saxon Cemetery at Tittleshall, Norfolk: the archeology of the Bacton to King's Lynn Gas Pipeline*, East Anglian Archeology 150, Vol. 2, Norwich: East Anglian Archaeology.

Wardwell, Ann E. (1998–9), "Panni Tartarici: Eastern Islamic Silks woven with gold and silver," in *Islamic Art* 3 (1998–9): 95–173.

Warner, Marina (1982), *Joan of Arc: The Image of Female Heroism*, New York: Vintage Books.

— (1999), *Alone of All Her Sex: The Myth and the Cult of the Virgin Mary*, New York: Knopf.

Waugh, Christina Frieder (1999), "'Well-Cut through the Body': Fitted Clothing in Twelfth-Century Europe," *Dress* 26: 3–16.

Weiner, Annette B. and Jane Schneider (1989), *Cloth and Human Experience*, Washington: Smithsonian Institution Press.

Welander, R.D.E., Colleen Batey, T.G. Cowie, et al. (1987), "A Viking Burial from Kneep, Uig, Isle of Lewis," *Proceedings of the Society of Antiquaries of Scotland* 117: 149–74.

Welch, Evelyn (2009), *Shopping in the Renaissance: Consumer Cultures in Italy 1400–1600*, New Haven, CT: Yale University Press.

Wenzel, Siegfried (2005), *Latin Sermon Collections from Later Medieval England*, Cambridge: Cambridge University Press.

White, Lynn Jr. (1978), *Medieval Religion and Technology: Collected Essays*, Berkeley and Los Angeles: University of California Press.

Whitfield, Niamh (2006), "Dress and Accessories in the Early Irish Tale 'The Wooing of Becfhola'," *Medieval Clothing and Textiles* 2: 1–34.

Wild, John Peter (1970), *Textile Manufacture in the Northern Roman Provinces*, Cambridge: Cambridge University Press.

Wilson, David M. and Ole Klindt-Jensen (1966), *Viking Art*, London: Allen & Unwin.

Wilson, Katharina M. and Nadia Margolis, eds (2004), *Women in the Middle Ages: An Encyclopedia*, 2 vols., Westport, CT: Greenwood Press.

Wilson, Laurel Ann (2011), "'De Novo Modo': The Birth of Fashion in the Middle Ages," Ph.D. diss., Fordham University.

— (forthcoming), "Common Threads: A New Look At Medieval European Sumptuary Laws," *The Medieval Globe* 2.1.

Wincott Heckett, Elizabeth (2002), "The Margaret Fitzgerald Tomb Effigy: A Late Medieval Headdress and Gown in St. Canice's Cathedral, Kilkenny," in Désirée Koslin and Janet Snyder (eds), *Encountering Medieval Textiles and Dress*, New York: Palgrave MacMillan, 209–31.

Wincott Heckett, Elizabeth (2003), *Viking Headcoverings from Dublin*, National Museum of Ireland, Medieval Dublin Excavations 1962–81, Ser. B, Vol, 6, Dublin: Royal Irish Academy.

Winston-Allen, Anne (1997), *Stories of the Rose: The Making of the Rosary in the Middle Ages*, Pennsylvania: Pennsylvania State University Press.

Witkowski, Joseph A. and Charles Lawrence Parish (2002), "The story of anthrax from Antiquity to present: a biological weapon of nature and humans," *Clinics in Dermatology*, Vol. 20.4: 336–42.

Wobst, Hans Martin (2002), "Stylistic Behavior and Information Exchange," *Anthropological Papers, University of Michigan, Museum of Anthropology* 61: 317–42.

Wolf, Kristen (2006), "The Color Blue in Old Norse—Icelandic Literature," *Scripta Islandica: Isländska Sällskapets Årsbok* 57: 55–78.

Wolter, Gundula (1988), *Die Verpackung des Männlichen Geschlechtes: Eine Illustrierte Kulturgeschichte der Hose*, Marburg: Jonas.

— (1994), *Hosen, weiblich: Kulturgeschichte der Frauenhose*, Marburg: Jonas, 1994.

— (2002), *Teufelshörner und Lustäpfel: Modekritik in Wort und Bild 1150–1620*, Marburg: Jonas.

Woolf, Rosemary (1968), *The English Religious Lyric in the Middle Ages*, Oxford: Clarendon Press.

Woolgar, C.M. (2006), *The Senses in Late Medieval England*, New Haven: Yale University Press.

Wright, Monica (2006), "'De Fil d'Or et de Soie': Making Textiles in Twelfth-Century French Romance," *Medieval Clothing and Textiles* 2: 61–72.

— (2008), "Dress For Success: Béroul's *Tristan* and the Restoration of Status through Clothes," *Arthuriana* 18.2: 3–16.

— (2010), *Weaving Narrative: Clothing in Twelfth-Century French Romance*, University Park, PA: Penn State University Press.

Zanchi, Anna (2008), "'Melius Abundare Quam Deficere': Scarlet Clothing in *Laxdœla Saga* and *Njáls Saga*," *Medieval Clothing and Textiles* 4: 21–37.

NOTES ON CONTRIBUTORS

Eva Andersson Strand is Associate Professor of Textile Archaeology at the University of Copenhagen. Her publications range from Viking Age Scandinavia (*Tools for Textile Production: From Birka and Hedeby*, 2003) to the Aegean and Eastern Mediterranean Bronze Age (*Tools, Textiles and Contexts: Investigating Textile Production in the Aegean and Eastern Mediterranean Bronze Age*, 2015). She currently manages a research program on experimental archaeology in combination with new computer applications, and works on the topic "Traditional Textile Craft, an Intangible Culture Heritage?"

Guillemette Bolens is Professor of medieval English literature and comparative literature at the University of Geneva. She has published on the history of the body and kinesic analysis in literature. Her approach is interdisciplinary, linking the fields of narratology, gesture studies, and embodied cognition. She is the author of *La Logique du corps articulaire* (2000/2007); *The Style of Gestures: Embodiment and Cognition in Literary Narrative* (2012); and *L'Humour et le savoir des corps: Don Quichotte, Tristram Shandy et le rire du lecteur* (2016).

Sarah Brazil is a lecturer in medieval English literature at the University of Geneva, where she received her doctorate in 2015. She is currently preparing a monograph entitled *The Corporeality of Clothing in Medieval Literature* (forthcoming in 2017) for the series Early Drama, Art, and Music in conjunction with Medieval Institute Publications (Kalamazoo), ARC Medieval Press, and Amsterdam University Press.

E. Jane Burns, recently retired as the Druscilla French Distinguished Professor of Women's and Gender Studies at the University of North Carolina, Chapel Hill, is the author of numerous publications on gender and clothing, including *Bodytalk: When Women Speak in Old French Literature* (1993); *Courtly Love Undressed: Reading Through Clothes in Medieval French Culture* (2002); and *Sea of Silk: A Textile Geography of Women's Work in Medieval French Literature* (2009). She also edited *Medieval Fabrications: Dress, Textiles, Clothwork and Other Cultural Imaginings* (2004).

Elizabeth Coatsworth held the title of Honorary Research Fellow at the Manchester Institute for Research and Innovation in Art and Design (MIRIAD) at Manchester Metropolitan University. Her research focuses on material culture of the early medieval period, and textiles over a longer period. Her publications include the *Corpus of Anglo-Saxon Stone Sculpture*, Vol. 8, *Western Yorkshire*; *The Art of the Anglo-Saxon Goldsmith*; *Medieval Textiles of the British Isles AD 450–1100: An Annotated Bibliography*; and *The Encyclopedia of Medieval Dress and Textiles of the British Isles c. 450–1450*.

Andrea Denny-Brown is Associate Professor of English at the University of California, Riverside. She is the author of *Fashioning Change: The Trope of Clothing in High- and Late-Medieval England* (2012), and the co-editor of *Lydgate Matters: Poetry and Material*

Culture in the Fifteenth Century (2008) and *The Arma Christi in Medieval and Early Modern Material Culture* (2014). She is currently writing a book about poetic ornament in fifteenth-century literature and culture.

Sarah-Grace Heller is Associate Professor of medieval French at the Ohio State University. She is the author of *Fashion in Medieval France* (2007), and articles on a range of topics including fashion, embroidery, sumptuary laws, semiotics, and representations of the crusades in the contexts of French, Occitan, and Mediterranean medieval literature and material culture. She is currently working on an illustrated history evaluating the presence of fashion in European society c. 450–1300.

Désirée Koslin teaches at the Fashion Institute of Technology, New York. An art historian with a focus on dress and textiles in the medieval period, she includes global perspectives in her work, particularly the interaction between cultures across Asia. Her publications include "Under the Influence: Copying the Revelaciones of St. Birgitta of Sweden," in *Tributes to Jonathan J.G. Alexander: The Making and Meaning of Illuminated Medieval and Renaissance Manuscripts, Art and Architecture* (2006), and *Encountering Medieval Textiles and Dress: Objects, Texts, Images* (2002).

Gale R. Owen-Crocker is Professor Emerita, the University of Manchester, having previously been Professor of Anglo-Saxon Culture and Director of the Manchester Centre for Anglo-Saxon Studies. Her books include *Dress in Anglo-Saxon England*; *The Bayeux Tapestry: Collected Papers*; and *An Encyclopedia of Dress and Textiles of the British Isles, c. 450–1450*. She directed the production of a database of dress/textile terms in all languages of the British Isles (http://lexisproject.arts.manchester.ac.uk/) and is co-founder and co-editor of the journal *Medieval Clothing and Textiles*.

Michèle Hayeur Smith is a research associate at Brown University's Haffenreffer Museum of Anthropology in Providence, Rhode Island. An anthropological archeologist, she examines gender, textiles, dress, adornment, and material culture through fieldwork in Iceland and North America. Her doctoral research focused on projection of social and cultural identity in jewelry and dress from Viking Age Icelandic burials. She has held two grants from the National Science Foundation (NSF) to study textiles, gender, and labor in the Norse colonies of the North Atlantic.

Laurel Ann Wilson received her PhD from Fordham University with her dissertation, "'De Novo Modo': The Birth of Fashion in the Middle Ages" (2011). She continues to research and publish on late medieval fashion and status questions. Her article "Common Threads: A Reappraisal of Medieval Sumptuary Law" appeared in the *The Medieval Globe* (2016) in a special issue entitled "Legal Worlds and Legal Encounters."

Monica L. Wright is the Joseph P. Montiel Associate Professor of French at the University of Louisiana at Lafayette. Her first book, *Weaving Narrative: Clothing in Twelfth-Century Romance* (2010) explores the relationship between sartorial signifiers and narrative structure in medieval French literature. Her current book project examines carnivalesque elements shared by the French Middle Ages and Louisiana folk traditions, analyzing medieval French literature in light of specific cultural and literary strategies practiced in modern Louisiana.

INDEX